BRIAN KELLY

Cricket in the Second World War

Other books by John Broom

Reported Missing in the Great War: 100 Years of Searching for the Truth
(Pen & Sword Military, 2020)

Faithful in Adversity: The Royal Army Medical Corps in the Second World War
(Pen & Sword Military, 2019)

Opposition to the Second World War: Conscience, Resistance &
Service in Britain 1933–45
(Pen & Sword Military, 2018)

A History of Cigarette and Trade Cards: The Magic Inside the Packet
(Pen & Sword History, 2018)

Fight the Good Fight: Voices of Faith from the Second World War
(Pen & Sword Military, 2016)

Fight the Good Fight: Voices of Faith from the First World War
(Pen & Sword Military, 2015)

Cricket in the Second World War

The Grim Test

John Broom

First published in Great Britain in 2021 by
Pen & Sword History
An imprint of
Pen & Sword Books Ltd
Yorkshire – Philadelphia

ISBN 978 1 52678 017 1

Typeset by Mac Style
Printed and bound by CPI Group (UK) Ltd,
Croydon, CR0 4YY

Pen & Sword Books Limited incorporates the imprints of Atlas,
Archaeology, Aviation, Discovery, Family History, Fiction, History,
Maritime, Military, Military Classics, Politics, Select, Transport,
True Crime, Air World, Frontline Publishing, Leo Cooper, Remember
When, Seaforth Publishing, The Praetorian Press, Wharncliffe
Local History, Wharncliffe Transport, Wharncliffe True Crime
and White Owl.

For a complete list of Pen & Sword titles please contact

PEN & SWORD BOOKS LIMITED
47 Church Street, Barnsley, South Yorkshire, S70 2AS, England
E-mail: enquiries@pen-and-sword.co.uk
Website: www.pen-and-sword.co.uk

Or

PEN AND SWORD BOOKS
1950 Lawrence Rd, Havertown, PA 19083, USA
E-mail: Uspen-and-sword@casematepublishers.com
Website: www.penandswordbooks.com

To my late parents, who inculcated a great love of the game of cricket, during visits to Hull CC's Circle Ground, trips to the Scarborough Cricket Festival and a special day out at Headingley in 1981 for a certain famous Test match. The soundtrack to my childhood seemed to be *Test Match Special* wireless coverage.

And to my wife and children, who I hope never live through times such as those covered in this book.

Contents

Acknowledgements

During the research for this project I was overwhelmed by the knowledege, generosity and sagacity of so many followers of the great game of cricket. I wish to acknowledge the contributions of the following people to the bringing to fruition of this book: Dave Allen, David Battersby, Stephen Chalke, Martin Chandler, Brian Cowley, Peter Crabtree, Allan Draycott, Martin Fiennes, Rob Franks, David Frith, Cheryl Grice, Peter Griffiths, Mike Hall, Andrew Hignell, David Jeater, Tim Jones, Steve LeMottee, Stephen Musk, Rafelle Nicholson, Jonathan Northall, Andrew Radd, John Raw, Chris Ridler, Mike Shaw, Roy Telfer, Harry Watton, Martin Williamson, James Wilson, Jack Winn, Ross Woollard.

Also to my editor Linne Matthews and the staff at Pen & Sword books for their assiduousness in assuring the timely presentation and appearance of this book.

Every reasonable effort has been made to seek copyright permissions for the images included and acknowledgements have been made where these have been known. Should I have inadvertently overlooked any copyright holders I should be happy to correct this omission in any future editions of the book.

Foreword

Anybody who lived through the Second World War, adults and children alike, now seems to belong to a separate species, largely free of the pettiness and anger and, to use one of the modern expressions, the sad and grim 'wokeness' which burden us in this twenty-first century. Trepidation stemming from this Covid-19 pandemic has almost replicated the deep-rooted fear that afflicted us between 1939 and 1945. Many have been praying day and night for an end to this plague, just as people did in the early 1940s, when those on the battlefront and those left behind, and boys like me, all prayed nightly (and intensely) for a merciful end to that terrible war. Diversions were scarce: a couple of wireless stations, newspapers, no television, and occasional cricket matches (some at our local park in Rayners Lane). Guided by my mother, I prayed as I knelt by my bed: 'Please, God, thank the Russians for helping us. And keep Daddy safe, and Uncle Bill too.'

When peace was finally delivered, cricketers and everybody else celebrated exuberantly. Countless cricketers had been in the thick of combat. Some had been prisoners of war, often enduring wicked ill-treatment, particularly in the Far East. Losses were numerous among the ranks of those who had played the summer game. These men's names stand out every time I come across them, none more so than three who were linked eternally in a mesmerising and unique entry on the Test match scorecard for the Ashes thriller at Melbourne in February 1937: R.G. Gregory c Verity b Farnes 80. It was the dark fate of all three to be killed during the war that was looming.

I happen to be quite superstitious. A fortnight after that tragic scoreline, I was born. And it seems I was destined to acquire young RAAF navigator Ross Gregory's wartime diary at auction, with some school trophies and his cricket sweaters. The animated diary became a platform for a book which I completed in 2003. The great and glamorous Keith Miller, whose blunt utterance about 'pressure' and Messerschmitts lives on for most cricket lovers, supplied me with an amazing quote concerning young Ross, whom he had known well: 'I would love to have been like him!' This from a player who was idolised for his own wonderfully flamboyant cricket at Lord's during the war and well beyond.

I read many cricket books each year. This one from John Broom is in a special category. One important area of fundamental reasoning is that the game of cricket (and let it not be forgotten that it is essentially just a game, notwithstanding its utilisation as a tool for profit) is often taken much too seriously, particularly in this modern grim period, the Age of Greed. The pursuit of money obsesses most of the people who run the game. The worship of pounds, dollars, rupees and rands influences every administrative decision. It causes those who recall earlier times and attitudes to lament the course that cricket has followed, with due acknowledgement of the fact that the game has always been changing, mirroring society, now needing bundles of cash to keep going.

The author writes of Lord's during wartime, with MCC ordering 2,000 sandbags as defence against bomb blasts. What an odd sight that presented. Today those sandbags would surely have been adorned with commercial logos.

Somehow *The Cricketer* magazine was kept going through the perils of the war years, Home Gordon being quoted here for his perhaps predictable remark: 'England has now started the grim Test match with Germany.' What no one knew then was that the war slowly took on the menacing feel of a timeless Test match, way beyond the famous unfinished affair at Cape Town in March 1939 which was called off after ten days. A few months later the West Indies team that had toured England hurried back across the Atlantic in fear of German U-boats.

The war at sea can easily be forgotten: but not in this book. And there is no more heart-rending example of sacrifice than the story of Peter McRae. When I first read it some years ago, sleep was a long time coming that night.

Not the least fascinating story concerns D.R. Jardine: Australians would perhaps have been surprised to read of his war service. And I wish I'd known that Arthur McIntyre, Surrey and one-time England wicketkeeper and coach, had fought in the traumatic Anzio chapter. No wonder he was so short-tempered when we (Surrey 2nd XI) failed to keep one side of the ball polished. He was not some grumpy old coach. He was a war veteran, and therefore fully entitled to heap scorn on us raw and ignorant amateurs.

Cricket-writer Alex Bannister was also at Anzio. Late in life he told me of the horror of seeing his best mate shot through the head in the trench beside him. Surviving warriors were blood brothers for life – as witness Alex's later success in obtaining scoops for his newspaper from Alec Bedser, who had been at Dunkirk. I had the pleasure of tape-recording Sir Alec's war memories for the Imperial War Museum's sound archive. Bob Cristofani, an old St George (Sydney) club colleague and RAAF pilot, was another to commit to a recording. I also interviewed Queensland's Ernie Toovey (after his ship was sunk he became a 'guest' of the Japanese in Changi). These were men apart. To be in a room full of war veteran cricketers in Sydney in 1994 was easily the most moving experience of all my numerous cricket social occasions: Stan Sismey, Ross Stanford, Reg Ellis, Martin Donnelly, Bob Cristofani, Colin Bremner, Bert Cheetham, and a dozen more. These were the true heroes.

John Broom has done a very fine job of gathering material for this book. His researches have stretched across a wide landscape. If any reader should fail to be moved by the drama and poignancy here, it will not be the author's fault.

David Frith
Guildford, 2021

Preface

Lord's Cricket Ground, London, 28 August 1945. With just eight minutes remaining on the clock beneath Old Father Time, Bob Cristofani bowled out Doug Wright to secure a 45-run victory for a Dominions XI against an England XI. Cristofani, from New South Wales, had flown Bristol Beaufighters for 455 Squadron RAAF during the war whilst Wright, of Kent, who had been named one of *Wisden*'s Five Cricketers of the Year for 1939, had lost his prime playing years serving in the British Army. The bank holiday weekend spectators had been treated to a feast of scintillating cricket as the match had tilted this way, then that; 1,241 runs had been scored, mostly with flamboyance and verve. Wickets had been taken with speed, swing, seam and spin.

On display were players who represented many fine aspects of the British and Commonwealth war effort. Bill Edrich, who had won the Distinguished Flying Cross for his heroism serving with Bomber Command, scored 78 and 31 batting at No. 8 for England. The home side's captain, Walter Hammond, scored 121 and 102, becoming the first player to score two centuries in a first-class match on seven occasions. Hammond had served with the RAF across Africa, organising

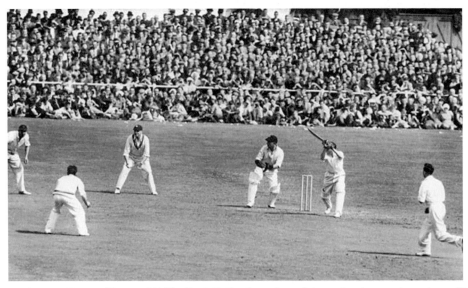

22 August. Victory Test at Old Trafford. D.R. Cristofani of Australia drives a boundary off Doug Wright. (*Australian War Memorial*)

many entertainments to maintain the crucial morale of the fighting men in that pivotal theatre of war.

For the Dominions, Kiwi Martin Donnelly scored a first-innings century. He had risen to the rank of major serving as a tank commander in North Africa and Italy. Australian flyer Keith Miller, an RAAF fighter pilot, scored a quite brilliant 185. His fellow Aussie, Graham Williams, had been languishing five months previously in a German prisoner-of-war camp, having sacrificed four years to the desolation of incarceration. The Dominions' captain, 43-year-old West Indian Learie Constantine, had been repeatedly overlooked for the leadership of his own Test team due to the colour of his skin. During the war he had experienced the best of British spirit,

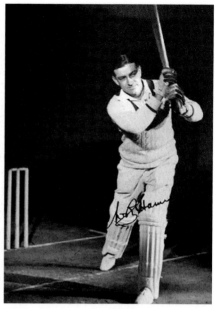

Walter Hammond poses for the camera, 3 May 1940. (*Courtesy Andy Collier*)

acclaimed as a folk hero in the Lancashire and Yorkshire leagues where he had plied his cricketing trade, and the worst, having been refused entry to a London hotel on a racist pretext. Now, in his final first-class match, he had the honour of leading a team out at Lord's in front of thousands of appreciative spectators.

The crowd contained many who had kept the game alive in Britain during the previous five summers. Keen club cricketers who had managed to organise

Learie Constantine.

Sir Pelham Warner in the pavilion at Lord's, 1940.

and complete matches between air-raid sirens and raids. Players of greater renown who had raised over £60,000 for the Red Cross and countless monies for local wartime charities. And sitting in the famous old pavilion, looking out on the action, Sir Pelham Warner, acting secretary of Marylebone Cricket Club (MCC), whose tireless efforts to liaise with the coalition government on behalf of the game had given cricket a secure and respected status in wartime Britain.

The celebratory mood masked years of dislocation, devastation, and despair. Thoughts turned to those who would never again experience the joy of cricketing combat, having paid the ultimate price for the victory of right over might. Nine of them had played for their countries at Test level. Dozens of others had played first-class cricket for their county, state, province, or university. At club level, teams mourned the loss of those with whom they had shared afternoons of common cricketing endeavour.

In the pages that follow, the story of the game during those turbulent years will be told. I hope that the reader will turn the final page with a fresh appreciation of the cricketers who endured the Grim Test of 1939 to 1945.

Chapter 1

1939: Carry On as Usual

'Like peeping through the wrong end of a telescope at a very small but happy world.'

R.C. Robertson-Glasgow

By 1939, English cricket was facing a polarisation of fortunes between the county and international game. Surrey, traditionally one of the strongest counties, was unable to produce a balanced budget whilst others faced the potential of insolvency in the medium term. Gloucestershire, complete with England captain Walter Hammond, and Lancashire, county champions in 1934, drifted into financial difficulties. Sussex lost £1,863 in 1939, as their attractive late-season fixture against the West Indies was cancelled. Even Yorkshire, the pre-eminent county of the decade who enjoyed widespread support throughout the three ridings, only managed to turn a small profit. However, this would have been larger had the county not donated half the proceeds of their match against Surrey at Headingley to the Civil Defence Service. Derbyshire's AGM minutes noted the slump in gate receipts caused by the wet summer whilst Walter Robins, secretary of Middlesex, constantly fretted about the terms of the lease for his county's playing facilities at Lord's. Some counties were fortunate in having wealthy benefactors. For a decade, Sir Julien Cahn had donated an annual £20,000 to Nottinghamshire.

Corrective action, such as reduction in the number of first-class counties, was frequently discussed but repeatedly the metaphorical can was kicked down the road. Events far beyond the control of the game's guardians at MCC would provide for a period of retrenchment and reconstruction, but the process would be painful. Six summers without regular fixtures or any competitive cricket were around the corner. Familiar faces on the playing field and on the groundstaff would disappear on military or civilian duty, some tragically never to serve the counties and their members again. Grounds falling into an increasing state of disrepair would suffer egregious damage from German bombs, thus giving an impetus to renovation and reconstruction.

R.C. Robertson-Glasgow, reflecting on the 1939 season and looking forward to 1940 in *Wisden Cricketers' Almanack*, wrote, 'Three-day cricket, in peace, was scarcely maintaining the public interest except in matches between the few best, or the locally rivalrous teams, and how many will [now] pay even sixpence to watch cricket for three days between scratch or constantly varying elevens?' The writer, who frequently suffered from bouts of intense gloom, should have been pleasantly surprised by the extent to which the public were willing to pay their sixpences and shillings to watch such arbitrary wartime elevens, albeit most usually in one-day format.

Whilst the county game teetered on the edge of the need for remedial reformation, Test matches remained well supported. For example, over 100,000 supporters had watched the four days of action in the 1938 England *v* Australia Test match at The Oval. As well as bodies passing through Test match turnstiles, the game was reaching into the 10 million households that held a radio licence. E.W. Swanton had been dispatched to provide live broadcasts of England's encounters with South Africa in 1938–39 and the BBC, in a pre-war forerunner of *Test Match Special*, provided ball-by-ball commentary of the 1939 West Indies Test series. Some live television coverage was also available to the small number of homes who had invested in John Logie Baird's wondrous invention.

The 1940 *Wisden Cricketers' Almanack* devoted 105 closely typed pages to public school cricket but failed to give even a paragraph of coverage to the strong leagues across the North and Midlands. A couple of state schools had managed to elbow their way into some coverage amongst the ranks of their fee-paying cousins. Just as the county and international games were becoming increasingly bifurcated, so the country at large seemed ill at ease with itself. Historian Richard Overy has dubbed the interwar period The Morbid Age. Mass unemployment in Britain's industrial areas, the abdication of King Edward VIII in 1936, and the growing insecurity over international tensions left a pervading sense of foreboding.

Cricket was a game still organised along class lines, with a distinction between the Gentleman amateur and Player professional. Usually these two groups would use separate changing rooms of distinctly differing quality and comfort, and sometimes enter the field of play by different gates. With few exceptions, a county captain had to be an amateur. The 1930s had seen some switching between the classes, with grammar school educated Walter Hammond being offered a sinecure at a Gloucestershire firm in order that he may captain the county, and thence England. His teammate Charlie Barnett had made the opposite move, from amateur to professional, in 1929. Others, such as Maurice Turnbull at Glamorgan and Bob Wyatt at Warwickshire, were given remunerated posts within their county clubs to retain their amateur status and therefore the club captaincy.

English cricket had taken the decision to copy its Australian and South African counterparts and experiment with the 8-ball over for 1939 and 1940 in order to reduce the time spent changing ends and thus increase the amount of play during the day. As the MCC tour of South Africa commenced in early November 1938, events that would lead inexorably to war progressed. Sir Samuel Hoare told the Cabinet that the Home Office was preparing an

Air Raid Precaution bill. Meanwhile, terrible violence was being inflicted on German Jews during Kristallnacht. Ken Farnes, the Essex and England bowler, wrote to a friend, 'A Napoleonic character, Herr Hitler. What will happen now?' A few months later his fellow future victim of Hitler's aggrandisement, Hedley Verity, struck a more belligerent tone when talking to his sister, Grace: 'This is no chuffing garden party. This fellow Hitler means it if we don't stop him. We have got to stop him.' Their England skipper, Walter Hammond, further escalated the phonological forcefulness with his reaction to news of a possible Nazi-Soviet pact: 'Oh Christ. Now the cat's among the fucking pigeons.' By early August 1939, as German-Polish relations deteriorated, Learie Constantine's more muted assessment was, 'There is such terrible news from Poland. The war is now inevitable. We go out to play the final Test tomorrow.'

Hedley Verity.

* * *

Aside from the Test and county games, cricket was played by hundreds of thousands of people in varying contexts. Many employers – including factories, mines, banks and public sector – ran teams, and in many cases provided ground facilities and playing equipment as part of welfare provision for their workers. Intensively competitive league cricket was hugely well supported and several clubs competed to a high standard across Yorkshire, Lancashire, Durham, Birmingham, Staffordshire and South Wales. Their southern counterparts, 1,150 of them operating under the aegis of the Club Cricket Conference by 1939, displayed less competitive zeal, organising instead friendly fixtures that could frequently experience laxity of starting times and tea intervals. It was considered in the south that non-competitive fixtures encouraged adventure and spice whilst league and cup competitions crushed sporting spirit. Many southern friendly only clubs tended to be socially exclusive and organising league and cup competitions would have compelled a greater degree of player selection on merit rather than social class. Jack Williams, in his *Cricket and England: A Cultural and Social History of the Interwar Years*, identified the attitude of MCC to the higher levels of league cricket as 'one of grand indifference'. There was sparse or no coverage in publications such as *Wisden Cricketers' Almanack* or *The Cricketer*.

However, such matches were avidly reported on in the regional press, and somewhere approaching 400,000 adult males played cricket on a weekly basis in England and Wales in the 1930s.

There was also a thriving women's cricket scene in the UK and abroad. Almost 900 women's cricket teams functioned during the interwar period, far more than the 150 teams that played association football. Two separate governing bodies, the Women's Cricket Association (WCA) and English Women's Cricket Federation (EWCF), codified and organised the game. In addition, many workplace-based teams existed as employers sought to encourage healthy lifestyles and camaraderie amongst the females in their workforces.

The EWCF aimed to provide cricket for working-class women in Yorkshire and Lancashire, growing substantially from 1931 to 1938. Play was based on that of the popular men's leagues that flourished in the Midlands and North of England. Matches were played over limited overs and were fast paced and competitive, with trophies and cups to win. In addition, female players achieving a five-wicket haul or a half-century could expect a collection from spectators. The WCA was dominated by women belonging to upper socio-economic backgrounds. Formed in 1926, a constitution had been agreed by 1931, with Mrs Patrick Heron-Maxwell CBE, its first chairman, hosting matches at her home at Great Comp, Kent. The WCA's aims were to encourage the founding of cricket clubs throughout the country, and to provide facilities, by means of touring teams and one-day matches, for women and girls who previously had little opportunity for playing the game after leaving school and college. By 1938, the WCA had 210 affiliated clubs, a quadrupling since 1927. These were heavily concentrated in the south-east of England, with the exception of the cricketing powerhouses of Yorkshire and Lancashire. By 1937, there were nineteen Women's County Associations, and regular inter-county matches. The women's game under the auspices of the WCA remained resolutely amateur, with matches non-competitive, with no trophies or points on offer.

Marjorie Pollard, a tall, bespectacled advocate of the women's game who acted as press representative of the WCA, launched *Women's Cricket* magazine in 1930. It was published monthly during the England summer cricket season and subscribers were spread as far as America, Australia, Canada, France, Holland, India, Kenya, New Zealand, Shanghai,

Marjorie Pollard.

South Africa and Argentina. A Test tour of Australia and New Zealand had taken place during the winter of 1934/35.

Cricket was not just important as an end in itself, but as a means to maintaining and improving the physical health of the nation. The King George Jubilee Trust had been established in March 1935, and Lord Portal, its vice-chairman, was shortly to write that 'large numbers of boys and girls who are approaching the age of full citizenship are ill-equipped for the responsibilities which face them – and this at a time when it is clear that the manhood and womanhood of this nation may yet be tested as never before'. The Central Council of Recreative Physical Training (CCRPT), the brainchild of PE teacher Phyllis Colson, was set up on 4 July 1935. It was a mixture of governing body representatives and other interested parties. Such was the concern about the fitness of the nation that fourteen of the original thirty-four members of the council were from the medical profession.

The government was anxious not to appear to be echoing Nazi ideals of a physically superior master warrior race, but did establish a Fitness Council to run a National Fitness Campaign. Its chairman was Lord Aberdare, formerly C.N. Bruce, who had excelled at tennis and racquets while also representing Oxford University and Middlesex at cricket. The campaign had some limited successes, including poster, leaflet and film campaigns with the slogans 'Fitness Wins' and 'Get Fit, Keep Fit', but it never managed to establish the proposed National College of Physical Training in Surrey.

Amidst growing concern about the physical fitness of the British population to withstand a war on the fighting and home fronts, the Physical Training and Recreation Act of 1937 established the Women's Team Games Board, allowing women's sporting organisations to request grants for equipment and land. The WCA took advantage of this opportunity and by the end of the interwar period, relations between women's cricket organisations in different countries were strong enough to lead to the formation of an international women's cricket council.

* * *

Professional cricketers were not expansively remunerated for their endeavours. Even Herbert Sutcliffe, veteran of fifty-four Test matches with a batting average of over 60, earned about £600 in 1939, an amount that placed him in the lower reaches of a middle-class income. This sum was supplemented by the profits from the prudent professional's two sporting goods shops in Leeds and Wakefield. This enabled Sutcliffe, a solidly respectable member of the Congregational Church, to seek social elevation for his family, sending his eldest son Billy to the fee-paying Rydal School in North Wales.

The selection of the West Indies team that toured England in 1939 indicated continuing racial prejudice in the game. The Cambridge-educated Rolph Grant had been appointed captain in succession to his brother, Jackie, at a point at which both Learie Constantine and George Headley had far superior claims to be considered for the post. During the tour, Constantine, despite the generally cordial welcome extended by England's cricket community, often ran up against deeply ingrained prejudices in hotels and restaurants: 'The old bugaboos of black men preying upon white women and being morally devious played into people's fears. We were fine so long as we restricted ourselves to playing sport.' The team's manager, Jack Kidney, was informed that in order for his players to use a public swimming baths in Plymouth, a separate appointment would need to be made and the water drained and replaced afterwards. The mercurial Leslie Hylton rightly objected to a spectator in the Oval pavilion repeatedly making ape gestures as the players entered and left the field of play.

Elsewhere, domestic cricket was in a strong state in the Test-playing countries Australia, New Zealand, India, South Africa and the Caribbean colonies. The British Empire had implanted the game in Nigeria, Kenya, Ghana and Ceylon, whilst outposts of people with recent British ancestry maintained league and cup competitions in America, Canada and Argentina, amongst other places.

* * *

The 1939 English season was overshadowed and ultimately prematurely curtailed by the war. MCC ordered 2,000 sandbags for the protection of Lord's Cricket Ground. Rupert Howard, secretary of Lancashire CCC, received instructions on preparing Old Trafford for war. Air-raid shelters needed to be built, first-aid and gas training had to be provided and the ground had to be ready to be requisitioned at short notice. During the Lord's Test, England captain Walter Hammond appealed through a megaphone for people to volunteer for National Service in preparation for the looming war with Germany. Hoardings around the ground challenged the spectators: 'National Service – are YOU playing?' As a schoolboy, Hammond had been called to his headmaster's study to receive the news that his father had been killed on the Western Front. This memory did not dull the enthusiasm with which he supported the nation's call to arms to meet the foe once more. On the outbreak of war, Hammond immediately joined up, receiving a commission as a pilot officer in the RAFVR.

When Essex visited Bramall Lane on 19 August for a match against Yorkshire, the team was greeted with barbed wire tied around the gate, with the sound of the nearby factories in the steel city pounding out the weapons of war. Around the country, trenches were dug, air-raid shelters prepared, and 40 million British men, women and children each received a gas mask.

Amidst this war preparation, MCC, on the same day *The Times* carried a story about plans to evacuate British children to the countryside, decided to announce the sixteen names who would tour India over the winter of 1939/40. It was an odd mix of players, with only Jim Langridge and Stan Nichols survivors from the previous winter's tour of South Africa. The selection of several part-time amateurs, under the captaincy of 40-year-old Jack Holmes, suggested that the tour was more a diplomatic mission than one designed to strain the competitive cricketing sinews.

The third match of the England *v* West Indies series at The Oval, played on 19, 21 and 22 August, would prove to be the final page written in domestic Test match history for seven years. Barrage balloons loomed up behind the pavilion and spectators entering via the Harleyford Road passed by an anti-aircraft gun mounted on a tractor. Hutton and Hammond, the greatest pre-war and post-war England batsmen, signed off with centuries. Both would return to the post-war fray, but for all too many players on display over those three days, the curtain would fall on their Test career. Tyrell Johnson, West Indies' tall and slender left-hand opening bowler, took a first-ball wicket, that of Walter Keeton, in what would turn out to be his only Test appearance, and the last of his eighteen first-class matches. The 37-year-old Learie Constantine dazzled with five for 75 and a blistering 79, in addition to electric fielding in the covers. Kenneth 'Bam Bam' Weekes, one of only two Test cricketers to be born in the USA, would exit the Test arena with a mightily impressive batting average of 57.66, but a figure that would be the result of a mere two appearances. Of the English players, Stan Nichols, Walter Keeton, Norman Oldfield, Arthur Wood, Tom Goddard and Reg Perks bowed out of Test cricket.

The West Indies were due to travel down to Hove for a three-day match against Sussex, beginning on 26 August. Events conspired against them. Already Gerald Hough, secretary of Kent CCC, had questioned whether the tourists' match at Canterbury starting on 30 August was appropriate under the circumstances. A discussion was held by squad members as to the best course of action. Learie Constantine, Manny Martindale and Bertie Clarke, all of whom would spend the war in England, voted to stay on but the majority decided to cancel the Sussex and Kent fixtures, as well as a limited-overs match against a Billy Butlin XI at Skegness, and return home at the earliest opportunity. On 26 August, most of the touring party left Greenock docks on the SS *Montrose*, bound for the New World. The team were between a rock and a hard place. Their prolonged presence in England would have drawn opprobrium for the continuation of frivolous festival fixtures. Their departure, nevertheless, was greeted with accusations of 'a cowardly and unsporting thing' by Sussex CCC aficionado Lætitia Stapleton, and with a rueful glance at his bank balance by the county's 1939 beneficiary, Jim Parks. Parks could have hoped to receive a collection of £50 during the match.

The Sussex servant, who in 1937 had become the only player to achieve a double of 3,000 runs and 100 wickets, was saved from a catastrophic collapse of his benefit prospects by the decision of Yorkshire to complete their programme for the season. This was not a lightly taken resolution, as the prospect of war weighed heavily on many white rose shoulders. The back of the scorecard of their recent match against Essex at Bramall Lane bore witness to the impending challenge. The front of the scorecard recorded an unremarkable but retrospectively poignant dismissal: 'K. Farnes b Verity 0'. The pre-eminent English spin bowler of the 1930s, Hedley Verity had already borrowed several books on military strategy from his future Green Howards commanding officer, Arnold Shaw. In addition, the match was now superfluous to deciding the outcome of the championship, as Yorkshire had wrapped up yet another title in their match against Hampshire. However, in the words of Yorkshire skipper Brian Sellers, 'We are public entertainers and until we have instructions to the contrary we will carry on as usual.'

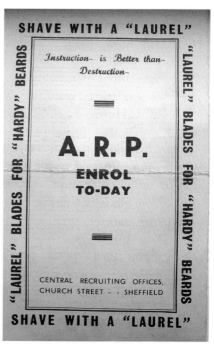

An appeal for ARP volunteers on the reverse of the Yorkshire *v* Essex fixture at Sheffield, 19–22 August 1939.

Meanwhile, Surrey's home fixture against Lancashire was switched to Old Trafford as The Oval had been requisitioned by the military. Other county fixtures were either completed within two days or cancelled due to

The Oval, complete with cages ready to receive Axis prisoners of war.

the international situation. That left 1 September 1939, the day the Wehrmacht pounced on Poland, with just one remaining ground in England with first-class cricket on offer. As the spectators at Hove watched the final rites of the season being played out, many had parked their cars on the boundary, and listened to wirelesses in the vain hope of a glimmer of light in the political gloom. Brian Sellers had received the instruction not to carry on as usual from his county committee that morning, but saw fit, after consulting with his players, to disregard it.

Yorkshire's final seven first-innings wickets fell for 62 runs on a drying pitch, giving them a slender first-innings lead of 5 runs. Hedley Verity, in

Dorothy and Len Hutton.

his denouement in major cricket, dismissed Sussex for 33, the peerless master achieving figures of seven for 9. Yorkshire quickly knocked off the 30 runs required for victory, as the crowd sang patriotic songs from the stands. Saying farewells that in some cases were permanent, the Tykes boarded their coach and started their long journey back up north, via Sussex villages ready for war. Windows were boarded up, and Len Hutton recalled hundreds of cars passing by with suitcases and even bits of furniture strapped to their roofs.

They reached Leicester, where the Yorkshire team enjoyed a final dinner together, evidently keen to mark the occasion in style with champagne and oysters. Bowes and Verity sat up into the small hours discussing their futures. Mrs Bowes was due to give birth to their second child in October and both players initially registered for ARP duties. Eventually both men received commissions in infantry regiments. War would not be kind to the Bowes and Verity families. Meanwhile, Len Hutton married Dorothy Dennis and accepted an appointment as an Army physical training instructor (PTI). Down on

Jim Parks.

the south coast, a thoughtful Jim Parks reflected on the sportsmanship of the Yorkshiremen in having played his benefit match despite the circumstances. He walked home with his young son Jim junior, the future Sussex and England wicketkeeper, £800 to the better.

* * *

As the players of Yorkshire and Sussex faded from the field to a trepidatious future, Jack Parsons, recently installed as vicar of Liskeard, preached to his congregation on Sunday, 3 September. Parsons had played both as a professional and an amateur for Warwickshire from 1910 to 1934. Considered by many to be one of the finest batsmen never to receive an England call-up, Parsons had enjoyed a rich and varied career as a labourer, engineer, private soldier, army officer, sportsman and parson. He was keenly aware of what war meant for the world, proclaiming:

> Once again … we are plunged into the ghastly horrors of war. To those of us, of the 1914 war generation, the thought of having to go through all that futile business of killing and being killed is … a terrible indictment of our present-day so-called civilisation. And what of those millions of dead in the last war – of what avail has been their sacrifice?

Parsons realised that the current war would be all-encompassing, saying, 'This war will not only be a question of professional soldiers, sailors and airmen fighting, it unfortunately means everybody. Civilians – men, women and children – will be drawn into this cauldron of destruction.'

The Reverend Parsons' prophesies proved correct. The game he loved also faced an uncertain future. He would have listened to King George VI's Christmas broadcast with keen interest. The Empire's monarch urged his people, standing at the anxious gate of a passing year, to 'Go out into the darkness and put your hand into the Hand of God'. Through endeavour, through faith and through perseverance, cricket would endure the following summer.

Chapter 2

1940: We Serve the Side

'One felt that somehow it would take more than totalitarian war to put an end to cricket.'

H.S. Altham

Sir Home Gordon, writing in *The Cricketer* in September 1939, declared that 'England has now started the grim Test Match with Germany.' During the winter, cricket's administrators had the advantage of watching how the Football Association responded to the challenge of organising a national sport in wartime. League activity was suspended but friendly matches were soon organised in most areas. A regionally based league was organised but this eventually petered away as players were absorbed into the military. Nevertheless, the continuation of sport, albeit in a much-altered format, was widely agreed to be important for morale. A 1940 Mass-Observation survey stated: 'Sports like football have an absolutely major effect on the morale of people.' Failure to continue with sport would represent a moral capitulation to the enemy.

All British cricketers were subject to the same terms of National Service as the rest of society. There was no pressure on voluntarism as in the previous war, thus charges of scrimshanking could not be levelled against those playing the game in England as war erupted elsewhere. Cricket was also in the unique position of being the game of empire. India, Australia, New Zealand and various Caribbean colonies had automatically entered the war alongside the mother country; South Africa, after the confirmation of a general election, also came on board. Thus, a game that could unite these nations in sporting comradeship was only to be encouraged.

As the Phoney War stretched out through the winter of 1939/40, the English game peered through a glass darkly as to

Sir Home Gordon.

what the coming season would bring. Sir Stanley Jackson, presiding over the Yorkshire CCC AGM in January, struck a defiant note. Cricket would be played in the summer, 'behind the lines in France, on village greens and some club grounds at home. ... We shall have need of cricket, all the same, to exercise the muscles and rest the minds of soldiers and workers with its health-giving comradeship.' Jackson thought that grassroots cricket would form the backbone of the game, as planning for first-class matches would strike the wrong tone. Time and travel resources spent on organising top-class cricket would be 'altogether indefensible in time of war'.

Cricket should not be speeded up to cramp it into a short timeframe, but:

> Let us rather think of long summer afternoons, with figures in white flannels dotted over the green grass, while the score mounts slowly and the sun seems to stand still overhead, and hope that after the war enough sanity will be left in England to enjoy these pleasures once again.

For Pelham Warner, writing in *The Cricketer Spring Annual* of 1940, whatever cricket might be played was of minor importance:

> Everything must give place to the prosecution of [the] war to a successful end, for we are fighting not only for a way of life but for our very existence against a ruthless, bullying, cruel and efficient enemy. Nothing else matters.

Cricket historian Harry Altham wrote in the 1940 *Wisden* of a gloomy visit to Lord's on a dark December day:

> There were sandbags everywhere, and the Long Room was stripped and bare [yet] the turf was a wondrous green, Old Father Time on the Grand Stand was gazing serenely at the nearest balloon, and one felt that somehow it would take more than totalitarian war to put an end to cricket.

He diverged from Warner on cricket's place in wartime society:

> When the game can be played without interfering with the national effort it can only be good for morale. ... MCC have already arranged one or two big charity matches at Lord's with a couple of minor matches and undertaken a long programme against the schools.

F.A.J. Godfrey's poem 'The Prospect' summed up the feelings of most players, from the eminent to the modest, that all were to serve 'the side':

> What will the season bring (we ask)-
> What does it hold in store?
> Does it veil success that defies a guess,
> And a thousand runs or more?
> Has it marked us out for the mighty shout

That the heroes knew of yore?
What does the season hold for us—
What does the curtain hide?
Does it matter a lot, if we shine or not,
So long as we serve the side?
So long as we play in a good, clean way,
With the knowledge that we have tried.

Despite these noble sentiments, some have argued that the cricket authorities dithered during the early part of 1940. Cricket historian Eric Midwinter maintained that they should have been on the front foot, creating a new regional county competition. This had been the suggestion of Lancashire's secretary, Rupert Howard, who had written a five-page letter to MCC suggesting such a scheme, which would also include the minor counties. Howard argued that 'no one wishes to see a blank summer'. For Midwinter, months that could have been used to create new structures were spent expressing noble sentiments but failing to innovate. Sussex, Essex and Middlesex mooted the idea of a south-east series of two-day matches at weekends, including Sunday play, realising that players would not be able to be released from civil and military duties for three consecutive days.

Midwinter's argument has some merit, as rigid thinking meant that the three-day game was considered to be the purest form of cricket, and the only true training ground for Test players. However entertaining it might be, the shorter game could never be 'proper' cricket to its administrators, and therefore not the basis of officially endorsed competition. So no attempt was made to set up a regional competition of one or two-day matches based on the existing county structure, nor competitions involving services teams. In retrospect, however, it would have been nigh-on impossible to proceed with such a competition, given the requisitioning and damage to many county grounds, the prolonged unavailability of many star players, and limitations on travel for leisure purposes.

The improvised friendly match was to be the principal wartime cricketing fare. An Army cricket selection panel was formed by Pelham Warner, who invited Brian Sellers, Gubby Allen, Tom Pearce and Maurice Turnbull to support him in drawing up a potential summer fixture list for services teams. At the Army's disposal were many grounds of first-class standard: the Officers' Club at Aldershot, the United Services at Portsmouth, and garrison facilities at Woolwich, Tidworth, Colchester and Catterick. All three branches of the armed forces had welfare officers who were attached to each army command and each air and naval base, and voluntary organisations were drafted in to aid the local organisation of entertainment and recreation. Sport became an entrenched feature of military life in the war years, being played at unit, regimental, brigade and divisional level, as well as inter-service large-scale charity matches.

By April 1940, as thoughts turned to the imminent arrival of the cricket season, *The Times* was devoting a mere three columns to the sport instead of the usual twenty. The popular press followed suit, with the *Daily Herald* reducing coverage from twenty-five columns to five. The Club Cricket Conference, representing over a thousand clubs across the south of England, held its AGM in London on 30 March. Stanley Christopherson, MCC President, stated that the Adjutant General had expressed a wish that as much cricket as circumstances would allow should be played in the summer. The conference's president, F.E. Whitehead, spoke stirringly:

> As black shadows lengthened over Europe during the closing days of last August, there must have been many who wondered … when next we should be able to enjoy the fellowship of cricket. As we laid aside our gear our hearts were heavy – and there stirred in us an anger that such things should have to be because of the overwhelming wickedness of a man in whose mind there was no understanding of cricket or of things that the word 'cricket' has come to stand for through the years. …
>
> Cricketers have played their part and will continue to do so until Victory is ours, and what we hope and pray will be a righteous and abiding Peace is established.

Whitehead also articulated the importance of the continuation of the club game for two further reasons: firstly, the practicality that it was difficult to revive a club after dormant seasons; and secondly, 'that it is an important piece of National Service to provide recreation for those who have for a short time a period of relief from War Duties'. *The Cricketer* magazine helpfully allowed clubs based in the Home Counties to list their vacant fixture dates alongside contact details of fixture secretaries. This echoed the foundation of what was then the London and Southern Counties Club Cricket Conference, which had been formed in 1915 as an emergency fixture bureau arranging matches at short notice. It was also agreed that every player taking part in a Club Cricket Conference fixture should donate 1d per match to the Red Cross Fund.

The *Western Gazette* of 5 April carried a letter from the icon of the Edwardian Golden Age, Gilbert Jessop, stating that the forthcoming season in the Dorchester Evening League 'will afford a great chance to the 16s, and may bring some of the sixties out of their shells to keep the cricket flag flying'. Not all clubs were as bullish about their prospects. Market Harborough Town Cricket Club, founded in the 1840s, resolved not to be wound up, but stated that no cricket would be played during the course of the war. This was more down to the significant debt the club found itself in, rather than as a direct consequence of recent events. Bestwood Park Cricket Club in Nottinghamshire was 'making strenuous efforts to keep the flag flying, although it was feared that there would be restrictions in the activities of Nottingham cricket clubs, owing to many younger members joining the armed forces'. Their fixture list was severely curtailed due to transport difficulties and a deficit of £35 due to a drop in paying members. St Boswell's Cricket Club in the Scottish Borders experienced 'some difficulty in raising a team' as 'King Cricket [got] down to real business in May', with only six players 'discernible on the horizon' a few days before their opening fixture.

Preseason optimism abounded in the North East. Many clubs in the Tyneside Senior Cricket League, the Durham Senior League and Northumberland League expected to be able to run second teams. The *Newcastle Journal* helpfully offered to print a list of vacant dates, available teams, and names and addresses of club secretaries in its pages. In order to manage the exigencies of war, the Philadelphia Cricket Club decided to introduce a limited-overs format for the matches, and to dispense with formal player registrations. Umpires would be expected to officiate without remuneration and a new ball would not necessarily be available for every match.

The continuation of the game in the North East was not universally well-received. Following a successful season which had seen them emerge as league winners, the vice-president of Alnwick Cricket Club declined to be re-elected, saying that 'the team might find something more important to help the war effort than play games'. This sentiment caused resentment from the club's chairman, asserting that 'In the Army it was recognised that games played a most important part in making a fit and efficient soldier.'

The annual meeting of the Sevenoaks Vine Cricket Club resolved to 'do its very best to carry on in some measure in the coming season, if only with the younger generation and members not liable for military service. There would be cricket on the Vine as there had been for the last two hundred years.' In the Midlands, the AGM of the Warneford Hospital Cricket Knockout Competition determined to continue to raise funds, with entries promised from Leamington, Lockheed (two entries), Eagle Sports, Butlin's, Kenilworth St John's, Leamington YMCA, Bishop's Itchington and Lighthorne. It was agreed that matches might need to be grouped to reduce travelling. Some support to financially straitened clubs was provided by local authorities. Woodford Council reduced the rental on the South Woodford Ground from £60 to £40, with it being reported that 'Several other councils have treated clubs in similar generous manner'.

* * *

All seventeen first-class counties had suspended the contracts of their professional players. A fortunate few would receive a monthly retainer but most were left to live off the pay from their military or civilian engagements. By March the county clubs were busy trying to arrange friendly matches. Derbyshire and Nottinghamshire agreed to meet at Whitsun and in August, and Leicestershire approached neighbouring counties. Surrey were in a quandary, having lost The Oval, but intended to tour the county and hoped to meet all the services. The club had been reorganised on a wartime footing, with a skeleton administrative staff being retained and a sliding scale of payments to their players, based on their earnings. As with Lancashire, the Surrey Committee had been calling 'since the earliest days of the war to get support for the formation of a Cricket Competition for 1940 but … the project had to be abandoned'. The club's yearbook also stated that coaching for schoolboys would continue at the Sandham and Strudwick Indoor Cricket School.

Essex intended to play club sides throughout the county, and Sussex hoped to continue their weeks at their out grounds. Hampshire's AGM agreed that Stuart Boyes would supervise junior coaching classes and the County Ground would be available for club matches. By December 1940, more than a thousand members had renewed their subscriptions. Several clubs were able to play in the county during the season, despite the area being a target for heavy bombing, with competitions in Southampton, Bournemouth and Winchester. At the Southampton Sports Centre, an Australian XI scored 152 for seven to beat Southampton Touring Club (110). At the County Ground, Arthur Holt and Stan Broomfield shared a century opening partnership for H. Eggerton's XI and Charlie Knott took eight for 40 to beat John Kemp's XI. Luftwaffe bombing damaged the pavilion at Southampton's County Ground. Dean Park in Bournemouth was put to army use, with a captured German bomber being put on display.

Following the fall of France, and with a keenly felt fear of imminent invasion, several zones across southern England were labelled 'defence areas', in which public assemblies for outside entertainment were prohibited. Despite these restrictions, twenty-six matches were held at Lord's during that momentous summer, when the nation's fate hung in the balance. A Lord's XI demolished a Public Schools XI on 15 August, with Essex and England fast bowler Ken Farnes returning match figures of ten for 87. This tall and kindly gentleman's final appearance at Lord's came a week later, for Pelham Warner's XI v West Indies. Farnes' swansong on a cricket field came for the British Empire XI v J.W.A. Stephenson's XI at Cheltenham. He took three wickets, including that of his county captain and, unusually for this modest batsman, top scored with 25 not out. The fast bowler took what

Ken Farnes.

cricketing chances came his way in 1940. Playing for Worksop College Masters *v* Craven Gentleman, he took six for 39. Then off Farnes went to war, never to return. Fellow England fast bowler Gubby Allen, playing for the Eton Ramblers against the Forty Club at Lord's, reduced the opposition from 124 for nought to 169 all out, with figures of nine for 23. He was at the wicket with another former England captain, Lord (formerly Hon. Lionel) Tennyson when the Ramblers hit the winning runs.

Due to a more informal atmosphere during matches at Lord's, many charity matches saw an invasion of small autograph hunters between innings or during an interval. One on occasion Ken Farnes was walking off the field at the close of an innings when a very small child approached him, stopped and looked most intensely at his face. Farnes, somewhat taken aback by this close scrutiny, asked the child if he could do anything for him. 'No,' replied the infant, producing a cigarette card. 'I only wanted to see if you looked like your picture on this card.'

* * *

The Women's Cricket Association committee attempted to gauge how many county associations and clubs were still playing cricket, and an address list was circulated. An anonymous article in *Women's Cricket* magazine had appeared the previous year arguing that 'the team games player learns discipline through

Myrtle Maclagan. (*Women's Cricket Association*)

games so … she will fall into the ways of an organised service all the more easily'. Despite this sentiment many women's clubs had to disband. A cricket week was proposed at Colwall, should sufficient entries be received, although the WCA would not be able to organise any official matches. This had to be postponed, many of the players being 'otherwise engaged', not to be revived until 1945.

However, there was not a total absence of women's cricket. *The Cricketer* reported that 'Leeds possesses a flourishing women's cricket club. One of their members is Leila White, who toured Canada with the English schoolgirls' team last summer.' Historian Rafaelle Nicholson has demonstrated how factories organised cricket teams for women serving in the Civil Defence Service via the Civil Defence Sports Committee. The Factory and Welfare Department of the

An Australian Women's Services Match. (*Australian War Memorial*)

Ministry of Labour was keen to see the leisure time of female munitions workers used productively to promote physical fitness and workplace camaraderie via team sports, including cricket. Evidence was found of Women's Land Army recruits organising sport, including cricket matches, at an informal level.

By 1945, there were 445,000 women serving in the ATS, WAAF and WRNS. From 1942, members had been subject to compulsory physical training, including the playing of team sports. The most common of these were hockey, netball, tennis and cricket. Occasionally, talented women would be selected to play in Officers *v* Sergeants cricket matches. Myrtle Maclagan, a sports officer for thirteen ATS companies at Aldershot in 1940, recalled, 'cricket had many ardent followers of a low standard of play, but we had matches every week-end and nets most evenings.' A match was arranged against the officers of Command HQ, Maclagan scoring a century in a total of 140.

* * *

The enemy had attempted to evaluate the significance of cricket in British cultural life. The German Institute for Foreign Political Research produced a 1940 paper stating that cricket:

best personifies the British Imperial system and the British sense of values. … Cricket is considered a sport that embodies the chivalry of a past era, all the decorum, the inner fulfilment and … the beauty of the English nation. It enhances a thousand other attributes which a wretched foreigner neither understands, possesses or may aspire to.

As well as physical adroitness, attributes of the successful cricketer included 'the strength to suffer boredom, the ability to cultivate a beautiful but idle figure on the green. … In cricket English self-conceit, English pride and English vanity have been raised to a sort of divine service.' With a swipe at the twin pillars of Britain's religious and cricketing cultures, the report asserted that 'cricket is a holy affair and can therefore be played on Sundays on the village green … one must assume that the special qualities of this pious game do not conflict with observation of the Sabbath.'

* * *

Whilst plans were being drawn up for the unknown quantity of the English season, Commonwealth troops summoned to the Allied cause were beginning to make their own playing provisions. February saw the arrival of the first of 76,000 troops from 2 New Zealand Expeditionary Force (NZEF), who would pass through Maadi Camp, 9 miles south of Cairo. Sporting activities soon became a regular feature of camp life. Cricket matches would range from improvised knockabouts using any rudimentary equipment that came to hand, through to organised fixtures in the lush surroundings of Cairo sporting clubs.

Matches between various units of 2 NZEF, including Signals, Engineers, Artillery and Nos. 1, 2 and 4 Companies, were organised. In an area devoid of grass, the action took place in sandy outfields with a hard strip of reddish-brown sand or concrete covered with matting serving as a pitch. Eventually these matches would develop into a formal Inter-Unit Cricket Competition played the following summer. Cricketers were keen to accumulate the various equipment needed, with one battalion shelling out over £100 in matting and other material to create their own pitch. Requests were dispatched to relatives back in New Zealand to send out cricket clothing. The New Zealand War Service Association appealed for donations of cricket gear, 'well aware that cricketers have responded nobly in reply to the appeal for gear for the Forces'.

Meanwhile in Australia, the domestic first-class season proceeded as normal. In March, veteran spinner Clarrie Grimmett took ten wickets

New Zealand soldiers play cricket in Syria, May 1942. (*Alexander Turnbull Library*)

bowling for The Rest *v* New South Wales, completing the highest aggregate of wickets in an Australian first-class season during which there were no overseas touring teams. His compatriots in the 6th Division of the Australian Imperial Forces based in Gaza, Palestine, undertook a twelve-day tour of Egypt featuring six matches. The tourists won their opening match against Willcocks Sports Club at Gezira on 8 May but were defeated in their next fixture against a strong Gezira Sporting Club team, with New Zealand's Denis Blundell taking four for 27. The first inter-Antipodean cricketing contest took place on 15 May between the AIF and a NZEF Base XI at the Maadi Sporting Club. Set amongst lush gardens and also enjoying a golf course and several tennis and squash courts, the Maadi club exuded colonial opulence which could be enjoyed by the town's expatriate and native middle classes. The cricket ground had sightscreens, a seating area and a well-equipped officers' bar inside the pavilion. The pitch was covered by coconut matting.

In 85°F heat with no breeze, many Kiwi soldiers turned up from the local camp to support their team. Egyptian waiters served trays of drinks to thirsty spectators. Both teams were introduced to Major General Bernard Freyberg, commander of the NZEF. Captained by future Governor General of New Zealand Denis Blundell, who had enjoyed some first-class success for Cambridge University and Wellington, the NZEF Base XI won a close encounter. More importantly for morale was the convivial atmosphere in which the match was played, which augured well for future fixity of purpose in the grimmer struggles ahead.

Following on from some mercurial performances in a tour of Egypt in the spring of 1940, on 15 August Perth's *Daily News* reported that twenty-five players had been selected to attend a special AIF cricket training camp in order to identify the best sixteen, who would form a representative team. Senior officers had expressed disappointment with previous results, therefore, 'Strict discipline will be enforced in the camp and the men will be expected to train as hard fitting themselves for the cricket field as they previously trained for soldiering.' Further Antipodean bragging rights were earned by the Kiwis when men from the NZEF Second Echelon played an XI representing the second contingent of the AIF at Aldershot on 24 August. The match was remarkable for the stoicism of both teams in playing through a forty-five-minute air-raid warning.

A week later, the NZEF played Aldershot Command. Their batting was opened by Eric Tindill, a member of the 1937 Test touring side who would go on to play in his country's first two post-war Test matches, as well as to represent the All Blacks at Rugby Union. Tindill scored 70 at a run a minute, but it was not enough to overhaul the total set by a strong Aldershot Command team which included Bryan Valentine, Brian Sellers and Alf Gover. Another large concentration of cricketers was to be found at Catterick Garrison in the North Riding of Yorkshire. A good ground played host to several members of the Yorkshire XI who had joined the Army, among them Hedley Verity, Bill

Bowes and Len Hutton, along with Nottinghamshire's Arthur Carr, Alan Lavers of Essex, and Bill Roberts of Lancashire. Inter-unit and inter-garrison matches were keenly contested and some players also took the opportunity to play in local club fixtures.

* * *

The Club Cricket Conference had advised its members to cease playing once an air-raid warning had been sounded, with all players and spectators taking cover as soon as possible. Throughout the season, this became the usual practice on cricket fields across the land. However, Home Gordon did witness a match 'somewhere in England' that continued not only during an air-raid warning but with an enemy plane flying over the ground with a number of British fighters in pursuit. Two of the home side, which was fielding, left for LDV duty and the opponents provided two substitutes. The game continued without any pause and 328 runs were scored in three and a half hours. None of the few spectators sought shelter. Gordon somewhat prematurely concluded, 'What an illustration of the failure of Blitzkrieg.' L.W. 'Laurie' Hall was playing for Franciscans against NALGO on Hackney Marshes, one of several matches taking place across the broad expanse, when an air-raid warning sounded, followed by 'heavy gunfire.

We waited until the gunfire stopped and then started the game.' Hall scored 26 in an opening stand of 90 with a player named Dalmage. The Franciscans totalled 125 for three then dismissed the NALGO team for 44. Soon afterwards the 1940 cricket season ended. Hall was called up to the RAF and found himself en route for India.

A forces match at Hull's Circle Ground on 25 August raised £50 for a local Comforts Fund. However, reported the *Hull Daily Mail*, the sum would have been greater, but 'very prolonged visits from the enemy ruined the gate'. A match on the same ground on 28 July between Maurice Leyland's XII and H.N.D. Meyer's XII had resulted in a profit of £200 being handed over to the Lady Mayoress of Hull's Red Cross Fund and the Hull Daily Mail Comforts Fund. The city had further cause for pride as Hull CC ran out winners of the Yorkshire League that summer.

Maurice Leyland.

* * *

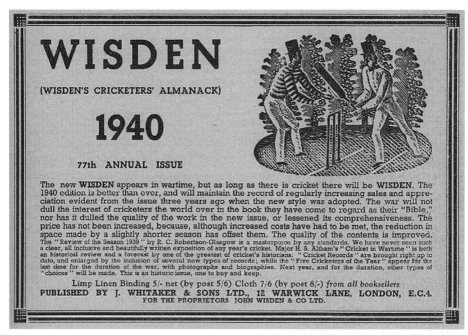

WISDEN

(WISDEN'S CRICKETERS' ALMANACK)

1940

77th ANNUAL ISSUE

The new **WISDEN** appears in wartime, but as long as there is cricket there will be **WISDEN**. The 1940 edition is better than ever, and will maintain the record of regularly increasing sales and appreciation evident from the issue three years ago when the new style was adopted. The war will not dull the interest of cricketers the world over in the book they have come to regard as their "Bible," nor has it dulled the quality of the work in the new issue, or lessened its comprehensiveness. The price has not been increased, because, although increased costs have had to be met, the reduction in space made by a slightly shorter season has offset them. The quality of the contents is improved. The "Review of the Season 1939" by R. C. Robertson-Glasgow is a masterpiece by any standards. We have never seen such a clear, all inclusive and beautifully written exposition of any year's cricket. Major H. S. Altham's "Cricket in Wartime" is both an historical review and a forecast by one of the greatest of cricket's historians. "Cricket Records" are brought right up to date, and enlarged by the inclusion of several new types of records; while the "Five Cricketers of the Year" appear for the last time for the duration of the war, with photographs and biographies. Next year, and for the duration, other types of "choices" will be made. This is an historic issue, one to buy and keep.

Limp Linen Binding 5/- net (by post 5/6) Cloth 7/6 (by post 8/-) *from all booksellers*
PUBLISHED BY J. WHITAKER & SONS LTD., 12 WARWICK LANE, LONDON, E.C.4.
FOR THE PROPRIETORS JOHN WISDEN & CO LTD.

Wisden would not cease production due to war, as this strident message states.

Wisden Cricketers' Almanack had been produced annually since 1864, including in much-reduced format during the previous world war. It had become known as the 'bible of cricket', a term coined by Alec Waugh in a review for the *London Mercury*. In 1940, Haddon Whitaker replaced Wilfred Brookes as editor and endured the most trying years in the publication's history. The publication's offices were bombed and all records lost. Whitaker warned that this would be the last *Almanack* in full format and that future volumes would 'conform with the smaller issues of the Great War' due to dwindling paper supplies and a paucity of major matches to report. However, Whitaker hoped that 'the time will not be far distant when we can recover all our steady bulk'. The volume exuded 871 pages of memories of the final peacetime season, with the Five Cricketers of the Year announced as Bill Edrich, Learie Constantine, Doug Wright, Brian Sellers and Walter Keeton, and 12,500 copies were printed – the highest number that would be issued during the war years.

* * *

The first major engagement of the war, which saw land, sea and air forces in co-operation, was Operation Dynamo, the evacuation of more than 338,000 Allied troops from the beaches of Dunkirk. Many cricketers found themselves swapping the lush greenswards of England for the scarred terrain of northern France and Flanders. Captain J.W.A. Stephenson, who had captained Essex

J.W.A. Stephenson.

in the immediate pre-war summers, rejoined the Army on the outbreak of war and was soon dispatched to France with the British Expeditionary Force. It was disclosed in *The Cricketer Spring Annual* that he had met a lady in a French café, 'and greatly to his surprise found that "she lived for cricket!"' The lady had spent nearly two years in Australia and declared the game to be '*Le plus meilleur jeu du monde*'. The magazine remarked, 'Imagine Don Bradman and lbw being discussed in French. ... As Captain Stephenson remarks, "I could hardly believe myself or her."' In May 1940, Stephenson reported to *The Cricketer* that he had discovered a ground behind the front line which possessed a matting wicket and pavilion, and he was 'looking forward to some cricket'.

Former England captain Douglas Jardine had endured more than his share of verbal assaults during his controversial leadership of the 1932–33 England team that won back the Ashes from Australia. By 1940 he was fending off a more deadly attack, as a company commander with 4th Royal Berkshire Regiment. His unit had been cut to ribbons in a rearguard action at Elverdinghe to the west of the Ypres Canal. More than 400 men had been killed, wounded or were missing, and the unit had lost their commanding officer, Lieutenant Colonel Geoffrey Bull. Jardine had been sent to Belgium to join his platoon, only to find they had been wiped out. Stranded, he commandeered a troop carrier and drove through enemy lines to Boulogne, where he volunteered to help hold Calais. He was eventually evacuated from the beaches of Dunkirk, on board HMS *Verity*. Some confusion exists as to Jardine's experience in Dunkirk, with a more recent history claiming that Jardine had returned to England shortly before the fighting started.

Alec Bedser and his twin brother Eric were amongst the beleaguered and bedraggled troops fleeing towards the French coast. They had made their Surrey debuts in the same match in June 1939. Having both joined the RAF, they were present at Merville airfield on the Franco-Belgian border when the shout went up that 'German bombers are coming over'. They ran with a comrade into a field. 'The German bomber was about 200 feet up and we were at his mercy. We were lucky, the tracer bullets passed between us.'

As they stood on the crowded lanes leading to the Channel port, Alec and Eric were growing increasingly anxious about their chances of making it back to England. An army van then drew to a halt beside them and the driver shouted, 'I can't leave you behind.' It soon transpired that he was a member of Surrey CCC. Having eventually reached the coast, the twins huddled beneath the cliffs to the south of Dunkirk before a rescue boat picked them up and transported them back to England. They were sent to Halton transit camp, which boasted a fine cricket ground. The camp's padre was Group Captain Francis Cocks, who would later serve as the RAF Chaplain-in-Chief. As the remit of most military chaplains across all branches of service extended to organising leisure activities, as well as serving the spiritual needs of their flock, Cocks granted a forty-eight-hour pass for the twins to return home to Woking to collect their cricket kit.

Eric (left) and Alec Bedser.

Ted Garrett, a club cricketer and an Artillery NCO, was ordered to leave behind everything except the clothes he stood in. Garrett objected to entering the rescue boat without his cricket bat. Eventually the bat was forcibly removed from him and thrown into the sea. 'Stupid English' was the comment from the Dutch boat captain. Other cricketers were less fortunate. A.C. Pirie, a well-known member of the Thames Ditton club, was reported missing. Pirie, a driver in the RASC, had been lost in action in the scramble towards Dunkirk. His body was never to be identified and he is one of 4,511 names inscribed on the Dunkirk Memorial to the missing. Jack Haye, who had played for Cornwall in the Minor Counties Championship and captained Penzance CC, was killed in action on 20 May in Belgium. E.W. Lovegrove, who had played for Suffolk in the same competition, fell on 1 June. Captain R.G.W. Melsome, who played for Gloucestershire and The Army, was captured and taken to Oflag VII-C. Gilbert Hodgkinson, who had played a few first-class matches for Derbyshire before the war, was reported to have been wounded in the head and was missing. It was a relief to his family and teammates when it transpired that he had been taken prisoner, returning from the war fit enough to captain his county in the 1946 season.

Men returning from the hell of the beaches were placed on trains and dispersed to rest camps and military hospitals around Britain. Those journeying on the weekend of 1–2 June passed towns and villages where fields speckled with white-flannelled enthusiasts could be seen. Some of the returnees would have had cause to be grateful to Acting Brigadier Raleigh Chichester-Constable. The

Brigadier had captained Yorkshire's Second XI for many years and toured India with MCC in 1926–27. For his efforts during the retreat, he was awarded a bar to the DSO he had won in the previous war, having shown 'marked leadership, great personal energy and a complete disregard for personal safety'. Chichester-Constable had managed to force the enemy back into a marsh, buying precious time for the final withdrawal of troops from Dunkirk.

As Stephenson, Jardine and the Bedser twins struggled to hold off the advance of the German divisions on the ground, Essex batsman Pilot Officer Reginald Taylor became the first professional cricketer to win the DFC for his contribution as an observer with a Lysander squadron in Bomber Command during the evacuation. Serving with 26 Squadron during a reconnaissance sortie on 19 May, Taylor spotted a section of German tanks held up by a broken bridge. The enemy opened fire on Taylor's aircraft and he sustained a wound in his left calf. Despite this he kept his gun in action and when the pilot flew a low-level attack he replied to the enemy's fire. On return to base, Taylor could not be evacuated to a military hospital immediately and it was more than twelve hours before he received specialist medical attention. Despite this extended painful wait, Taylor remained cheerful and was recommended for the DFC. Later in the season Taylor appeared for Sir Pelham Warner's XI *v* a Club Cricket Conference XI at Lord's and received a wonderful ovation as he went in to bat. Perhaps this reception caused a lack of concentration and Taylor was dismissed first ball. He then received another ovation on his way back to the pavilion, perhaps the 'greatest reception ever accorded to man out for a "duck"', Don Bradman's final test innings notwithstanding.

* * *

Thanks in part to the decision of the Central Lancashire League to prohibit the employment of professionals and the discontinuation of the County Championship, Bradford League clubs were able to call on a glittering array of cricketing talent and become the pre-eminent professional league during the Second World War. From 1940 to 1945, more than a hundred first-class players would appear in the league, including thirty-six of previous or future Test status. In 1940, Learie Constantine took seventy-six wickets and smashed 376 runs for Windhill whilst Derbyshire ex-miner George Pope bagged eighty-eight wickets and hit 641 runs for Lidget Green. Constantine said his contract with Windhill was the best he had ever had and he did not disappoint the large crowds who came to watch him play. His tally of wickets included a hat-trick against Spen Victoria as his club swept to a fourth league title in a row. The Trinidadian's best bowling performance was eight for 39, one month after scoring his maiden league century of 105 not out.

England opener Len Hutton returned to his home club, Pudsey St Lawrence, to top the league batting averages for the season, whilst Lancashire's diminutive left-hander Eddie Paynter amassed a colossal 1,040 league runs for Keighley. This sum included a new league record score of 150 not out, achieved on Whit Monday against Lightcliffe. The pre-war custom of collecting talent money for a player scoring a fifty or taking five wickets continued, and Yorkshire batsman Wilf Barber set a splendidly humanitarian example by donating the proceeds of his collection to the Red Cross, a particularly altruistic action as he had been due his county benefit match during the 1940 season. One Saturday, Barber hit a century in thirty-six minutes for Brighouse v Bradford.

Wilf Barber.

Saltaire Cricket Club's Roberts Park Ground, situated in the shadow of the vast mill erected by Victorian industrialist and philanthropist Titus Salt, and bounded on one side by the river Aire and on the other by neatly laid out flower beds, was a picturesque spot to play the competitive cricket that characterised the Bradford League. In 1940, the club's batting averages for all matches were headed by an unlikely name, James Charles Laker. The man who would become the greatest exponent of right-arm off-spin bowling that England ever produced compiled 357 runs in the season, including a century against Bankfoot.

The depth of quality that Bradford League clubs could muster was highlighted on 12 August when a Yorkshire XI took on a League XI including Learie Constantine, 'Manny' Martindale and Eddie Paynter at Bradford Park Avenue in front of 7,000 spectators. The £300 in gate receipts was augmented by a collection of £80 for the Red Cross. Constantine hit 100 in an hour, three times smiting the ball out of the ground. Herbert Sutcliffe treated the Yorkshire pleasure-seekers to a dashing innings of 129, as he and Paul Gibb added 100 in 35 minutes.

The Yorkshire public had enjoyed a previous opportunity of seeing their cricketing heroes in action at Headingley as Herbert Sutcliffe's XI took on Maurice Leyland's XI on 29 June. Len Hutton made 56 for Sutcliffe's XI as a crowd of 6,000 raised over £300 for the Lord Mayor of Leeds's Red Cross Fund. One notable attendee was 83-year-old Bobby Peel, an early member of the immortal line of outstanding left-arm spin bowlers the county produced for over a century.

Yorkshire cricket followers were fortunate to have available a host of competitive leagues where good quality play could be seen on a weekly basis. One such was the Huddersfield and District League. On 25 May 1940, Slaithwaite played Bradley Mills in a remarkable match with some of the finest hitting ever seen, as J.K. Senior and S. Beaumont added 150 runs in thirty minutes, including 136 from 7.2 overs. The league's Sykes Cup Final proved a big attraction at Huddersfield's Fartown Ground, with a crowd of 5,215 generating receipts of £116 as Elland comfortably beat Slaithwaite. The generosity of the West Riding crowd was evident in a collection of £18 11s 0d for W.S. Hammond and F.H. Sykes, who made fifties for the winning side.

Meanwhile in Lancashire, the *Burnley Express* reported in April: 'Cricket bats, balls and other sporting equipment will be pulled from the Burnley Cricket Club's lockers at Turf Moor this afternoon, when it is expected that many cricket enthusiasts will avail themselves of the first opportunity to engage in practice.' The ground was declared to be in excellent condition and, despite the absence of a few players on military service, 'the club feels that there is plenty of talent available to field an exceptionally strong Lancashire league side'. Trials would be offered to youngsters playing in local junior cricket. It was also reported that the Nelson Sunday School League would go ahead in 1940 with ten teams competing for a championship prize of £5 10s. Despite this optimism, the 1940 season got off to an uncertain start. Burnley's opening fixture at Rawtenstall generated gate receipts of only seven guineas whilst Bacup *v* Lowerhouse in the same league realised half that amount. The absence of star bowlers facilitated the breaking of the league record for a first wicket stand, as W. Whitworth and J. Pearson put on 240 together for Ramsbottom *v* Rawtenstall, surpassing a 25-year-old record. Remarkably, Rawtenstall knocked off the runs with five wickets in hand.

The Lancashire League, probably the strongest non-first-class competition in the 1930s, had taken the dramatic step of cancelling all professional contracts during the season. This accounted for the dramatic fall in attendances and gate receipts, with the normally keen encounter between Burnley and Nelson realising just £14 rather than the previous £200. This policy was rescinded for the 1941 season. Some professionals migrated to the Lancashire and Bolton Leagues whilst in the North Staffordshire League the 67-year-old S.F. Barnes, whose first-class debut had been as far back as 1894, continued to play for Stone. The Birmingham League was exceptionally strong in 1940, with former Warwickshire and England skipper Bob Wyatt topping the batting averages

Bob Wyatt.

with 516 runs for Moseley. Eric Hollies broke the league record aggregate for a season with ninety-nine wickets for Old Hill, whilst New Zealander Bill Merritt achieved a phenomenal double of 878 runs and eighty wickets for Dudley.

Occasionally, famous stars would appear in the less prominent leagues. On leave from the Army in June, Bill Bowes played for York against Sheffield United in the Yorkshire League, whilst Herbert Sutcliffe turned out for Pudsey Britannia against Clayton Sports in a Leeds and District League match. Len Hutton's 115 and seven for 16 helped Salts vanquish Sowerby Bridge in the Yorkshire Council in July. The following week he hit 144 in ninety minutes against Scholes. However, the Coventry and District League was suspended in June due to the extra demands on players who were on munitions work in the manufactories of the West Midlands.

* * *

At the start of 1940, England's most renowned cricket writer, Neville Cardus, had walked past Lord's in the foggy winter air, finding the ground 'blind, vacant, lost to the world'. Gloomily, he mused, 'We shall perhaps never see cricket again.' Despite this pessimism the famous and venerable ground was extensively used to host matches of inconsequential importance in terms of the standard of play, but which lifted the spirits of club and service players selected to play in them. Teams from the City Police, St Mary's Hospital, Hampstead CC, the Balloon Barrage and the BBC trod in the renowned footsteps of Pilch, Mynn, Grace, Hobbs and Bradman. Sir Pelham Warner, appointed as temporary secretary of MCC, wrote, 'If Goebbels had been able to broadcast that the war had stopped cricket at Lord's, it would have been valuable propaganda for the Germans.' Therefore, there was no question that the game must go on. Members of the London Fire Service, who had to endure the anxious anticipation of air raids through the summer, managed five matches at Lord's and twenty at other venues.

It had taken two summers during the First World War before the English game felt it appropriate to organise any high-profile charity matches. The Second World War would be different, with an immediate acceptance of the importance to morale of the game continuing in some form. The British Empire XI was established by 19-year-old Desmond Donnelly, with Warner serving as president. Its players appeared as amateurs, and the team managed to play thirty-eight matches in 1940, raising over £1,200 for the Red Cross. Its first match was played against Rosslyn Park with the reward for the winning team being a barrel of beer. Donnelly's vision was to replicate the collective effort the Empire was expending in fighting the war in a cricket team. Comradeship between players from the Dominions and Empire would be fostered. West Indian leg-spinner C.B. 'Bertie' Clarke, who had returned to England to continue his medical studies, was the bowling star of 1940, claiming eighty-three wickets at just over ten apiece during the season. Clarke was remembered by Trevor Bailey, an outstanding schoolboy cricketer of the era and later a major force in the England team, for his 'enthusiasm, ability and unfailing cheerfulness'.

On 1 June, as Operation Dynamo entered its final frantic hours, the British Empire XI beat the London Fire Service by 144 runs. Essex all-rounder Ray Smith, a playing and administrative stalwart over the succeeding six seasons, scored 55 and took three for 42. In a twelve-a-side match against Oxford University the college men rampaged to a total of 491 for three dec, with Nathaniel Fiennes and Ian Phillips adding 295 in just over two hours. Fiennes ended up with 157. Recollecting the

Nathaniel Fiennes batting for Eton against Harrow at Lord's in 1939. (*Courtesy the Fiennes family*)

occasion over eighty years later, having achieved a further century by celebrating his hundredth birthday in September 2020, Fiennes recalled a diet of 'rank long-hops all afternoon – anyone could have made 100'.

Meanwhile, Hitler suggested peace with Britain in mid-July but Home Gordon, who had volunteered as a staff captain in the Local Defence Volunteers, expressed the country's defiance in cricketing terms. The dictator had 'captured the first two wickets with his express grubs … our best bats have still to go in'. An endorsement of E.V. Lucas's classic *The Hambledon Men*, originally published in 1907, stressed that 'In these days of threatened invasion many of us no doubt feel, if possible, an even added interest in our Hambldeon heroes, for they know what it is to live under the threat of a very great military power on the Continent.' A copy of this book would be carried in the pack of the author's father, from El Alamein to Tunis in 1942–43.

Another wartime-specific outfit was the London Counties XI, the brainchild of Charles Jones. Jack Hobbs agreed to serve as president of the side, which comprised mainly of professionals from the Home Counties. According to R.C. Robertson-Glasgow in *Wisden's* notes on the 1940 season, the team 'sparkled with hitters and known fast scorers'. There was concern amongst cricket professionals that their future livelihoods were at risk as a lack of competitive cricket could cause a loss of form. Furthermore, many professional cricketers, due to their social status, were only able to secure positions in the lower echelons of the armed forces, or less remunerative civilian employment. Therefore, the matches that the London Counties XI undertook, mostly against club sides on the capital's outskirts, were played in a competitive manner, 'however weak or strong the opposition'. The gate money from their encounters was shared between wages for the players and war charities.

The inaugural match between the British Empire XI and London Counties XI took place on 13 July at Lord's. Kent's Arthur Fagg, Middlesex's Joe Hulme, and big-hitting Arthur Wellard of Somerset made good contributions for the victorious London side whilst Sergeant Denis Compton failed to shine for the Empire XI, falling for just one run. A crowd of 8,000 raised £120 for the Red Cross. A week later, the great man was more successful, compiling 51 as Eleven of Middlesex drew with Eleven of Lord's. As the summer rose to its height, the English cricket community was becoming increasingly confident that the game could sit comfortably within the execution of total war. As *The Cricketer* put it, 'Obviously the only thing that matters in these days of war is the successful prosecution of it, but a few hours in recreation in the delightful atmosphere of Lord's can do nothing but good to all.'

The two sides met once again on 10 August, in front of 10,326 paying spectators who raised £145 for the Red Cross and Cricketers' Fund Friendly Society. Robert Nelson, captain of Northamptonshire, shone for the Empire XI, whilst the distinguished veteran Frank Woolley, who had made his first-class debut in 1906, received a tremendous reception each time he came on to bowl, claiming two for 23. There were attractive innings from Len Parslow and Denis Compton whilst Woolley managed 38 before being caught and bowled by Compton, who took six for 81 with his left-arm unorthodox spin, as the British Empire XI won by 53 runs. Parslow, a prolific run-scorer in London club cricket, was given the opportunity to play alongside Test and county stars, and finished second in the British Empire XI batting averages behind Bob Nelson. Despite his emergence in wartime cricket, Parslow would only play one first-class match after the war, with little success.

The match received some wireless coverage, with Howard Marshall – pioneer of the art of ball-by-ball commentary – in the chair. Edmund Blunden wrote, 'On the air, Mr Howard Marshall makes every ball bowled, every shifting of a fieldsman so fertile with meaning that any wireless set may make a subtle cricket student of anybody.' Marshall was appointed Director of Public Relations at the Ministry of Food in 1940 and, as a war correspondent, famously broadcast from a Normandy beach immediately after the D-Day landings. He was later to commentate on some of the 1945 'Victory Tests'.

The success of such big matches at Lord's, in financial and cricketing terms, was in no small part due to the willingness of the commanding officers of those cricketers serving in the forces to release them from duty. It had been officially intimated to MCC, according to Warner, that subject to military exigencies cricket was to be encouraged wherever possible. In return, anyone wearing military uniform was admitted to the ground without charge, with officers being granted entry to the pavilion. For the lesser matches, some players appeared on the field in khaki. Matches such as St John's Wood War Reserve Police *v* Hampstead War Reserve Police, Paddington Rescue Services *v* Paddington ARP Services, and 1st Battalion Scots Guards *v* 903 Squadron Balloon Barrage took place on the ground. All members of the military and auxiliary services were welcomed to use the nets, with up to fifty people a time bowling seven or eight to a net. Warner glowed, 'The whole atmosphere was delightful even amidst the stress and strain of modern warfare.'

* * *

Away from the home of cricket, club officials across the land had to grapple with the practical and ethical dilemmas total war presented. Officials at Stirling County Cricket Club had to address the thorny issue of conscientious objection. In the early stages of the war, around 2 per cent of men called up into National Service invoked the conscience clause, registering as objecting to enter the armed forces. Many were forced from their jobs and held up to public approbation and ridicule. Peter Kennedy, a playing member of Stirling, had been told by two members of the ladies' committee who 'looked after the teas' that they would have nothing more to do with the club if a CO who was a member of the county team was allowed to play.

Opinions were divided in the club, with wicketkeeper Willie Clark stating, 'This is a free country and we are all entitled to our opinions. I don't see why anybody should be debarred from playing,' and two military members of the club, Lieutenants J.B. Jones (club captain) and R.M. Dun, a former secretary, believing that to debar anyone because of his views 'would not be a good advertisement for cricket'. However, Mr C.H. Lockhart, a former club treasurer, said if a man held views that were distasteful to the vast majority of the members it was usual to ask that member to resign. The matter was eventually laid to rest when one of the lady member told the press, 'the remark she had passed that if the member was allowed to remain in the club she would serve no more tea was made half-jokingly.'

There was no doubt about cricket's alignment with the Allied cause in the mind of E.A. 'Manny' Martindale, the West Indian fast bowler who had played for Burnley as a professional before the war. Martindale attended a dance in Brierfield to award prizes won during an Ambulance Charity Cricket Competition. He asserted that there would not have been a war if Germany 'knew and played cricket in its truest sense'. The fact that many cricketers were devoting their skills to charity games showed the game was 'doing its bit', for they felt cricket and other sport was almost as essential in these difficult days as in times of peace. Mr W.J. Morton, president of the competition, said some players, including Martindale, were devoting between five and seven days a week for Red Cross games.

Some clubs sought to provide playing opportunities for troops stationed nearby. The *West Sussex County Times* carried a photo of two of the four newly formed Observer Corps cricket teams affiliated to the Horsham Cricket Club. 'It is not expected that any serious cricket will be played, but it is felt that an occasional game would do much to dispel the ill-effects of many daylight hours spent indoors.' Up in Yorkshire's North Riding, at the Oxford Road Ground in Middlesbrough, a sum of £3 3s was collected for the Gazette War Fund in a match between the Dorman's Club and an Army XI, bringing the total amount raised by this appeal to £1,180 0s 3d.

* * *

By early summer, German successes across the Channel had placed the whole southern and eastern coastline under threat. Beach defences of barbed wire, trenches, mines and scaffolding-pole obstacles were erected. By late May, open rural spaces were being covered with poles and wires and giant steel hoops were erected over roadways to prevent landings by German gliders. At the start of June, it was announced that the quintessentially English sound of church bells was to be stilled, only to be heard in the event of an invasion. Road signposts were removed in the hope that they would render any German paratroopers ignorant of their location. Cricket played its part in these invasion preparations. On 3 August, an appeal was made in *The Cricketer* by H.G. Dormon, the chairman of the Club Cricket Conference. He had been contacted by the Ministry of Home Security to request clubs' assistance in rendering cricket grounds useless for enemy aircraft landings. Since hundreds of clubs had ceased operating during 1940 it had been impossible for the Ministry to make contact with all club secretaries. The magazine noted that many clubs had already taken the necessary precautions. Lord's had been rendered unusable by placing obstacles across the playing area when a match was not in progress.

It was announced that MCC would charge only 6d for entrance to Lord's for matches between the services: North *v* South, and Under 30 *v* Over 30. Sadly, some of the proposed fixtures would not materialise due to the exigencies of war. The ground's opening fixture came on 4 May when the City Police played the London Fire Service. Saturday, 3 August saw 500 runs scored in a day for the loss of fifteen wickets as the RAF drew with the London Fire Service, and 6,000 spectators raised funds for King George VI's War Fund for Sailors. The future stalwart of England's post-war bowling attack, Alec Bedser, recently returned from Dunkirk, took four for 22.

The fine weather enjoyed through the summer of 1940 would normally have afforded a glorious season of runs, wickets and catches. Festivals at Folkstone and Scarborough would have brought the curtain down on another round of cricketing marvels. However, for the match at Lord's between Sir Pelham Warner's XI and the West Indies on 22 August, there was cold wind and little sunshine for the 7,000 spectators. Five days later, *The Times* reported: 'For the first time probably in the history of cricket "raid stopped play" at Lord's on Saturday.'

* * *

Countless thousands of cricketers would lose their lives on active service during the six horrific years of war, and 1940 saw the start of the entries into that sorrowful scorebook. Robert Nelson, who as county captain in 1939 had lifted Northamptonshire off the foot of the championship table for the first time since 1933, returned as master to his old school in Harpenden. In July 1940, he answered an advertisement in *The Times* inviting applications for commissions in the Royal Marines. He played in a match for Northamptonshire *v* Leicestershire at the Spinney Hill Ground in Northampton in August. Nelson had already pledged, in a letter to the Northamptonshire committee, to 'thoroughly erase' the 'barbaric underside of European civilisation' that Nazism represented.

Nelson appeared for the British Empire XI *v* the Buccaneers at Lord's on 31 August, a match eventually abandoned due to repeated air-raid sirens. In his final innings he made 45 before being dismissed by Freddie Brown. On 29 October 1940, Second Lieutenant Nelson was in the officers' mess at the Royal Marine barracks in Deal when it received a direct hit from an enemy bomb. Nelson was amongst the thirteen fatalities. Sussex's Hugh Bartlett, later to win the DFC serving with the Glider Regiment, wrote, 'I was desperately sorry to hear of the death of poor Bob Nelson – what a grand fellow he was and what a loss he will be to all those lucky enough to have known him … a very even tempered fellow who kept things on a steady level.' His parents chose to have Bob's love for the game permanently recorded on his gravestone: 'A Love of Cricket: He Maintained in his Life the Spirit of the Game.'

R.P. Nelson. (*Courtesy Northamptonshire CCC Archive*)

Kent and England batsman Geoffrey Legge, just six days after having been promoted to the rank of lieutenant commander in the Fleet Air Arm, was killed in a flying accident in Devon on 21

November and buried at St Merryn in Cornwall. Legge was the first of five English Test cricketers to die while on active service. The second fatality followed soon afterwards. Former Yorkshire off-spinner George Macaulay perished in mid-December while serving in the RAF on the Shetland Islands. Although contemporaneously ascribed to pneumonia, it was in fact cardiac failure linked to alcoholism that had done for the volatile 43-year-old Yorkshireman. Following the end of his first-class career in 1935, Macaulay had opened a sportswear shop, which soon folded, and he was declared bankrupt. After a couple of seasons in league cricket and perhaps looking for a fresh outlet for his energies, he volunteered for the RAF in early 1940 despite being well past the age of compulsory military service. Sent to the Sullom Voe to serve as a junior mess orderly, on

George Macaulay.

9 December he was admitted to the camp hospital, it being reported that he had been drinking heavily for the previous ten days. He died in his sleep on 13 December, his death certificate citing ten years of alcoholism as a contributory factor. Due to these circumstances his wife Edith was denied a war pension.

Forfarshire Cricket Club, one of Scotland's foremost clubs, mourned the loss of a former vice-captain who was one of the Battle of Britain 'few'. Flying Officer W.J. Moir Scott had been a member of the University of Cambridge Air Squadron and commissioned into the RAFVR in January 1938. Scott joined 41 Squadron on 13 July 1939, and on 7 September 1940, destroyed a Messerschmitt 109, the enemy pilot being captured. The next day, Scott's Spitfire was downed off Dover. He was reported missing, and on 1 November, his body was washed up on the Kent shore. His remains were taken to Scotland and buried in the Dundee Western Cemetery.

W.T. Whewell, who had played Minor Counties cricket for Cambridgeshire, was a victim of a German air raid in early October. Whewell had also played amateur association football and was a sports master at Haberdashers' School at the time of his death. Lieutenant Claude Jones RAMC, who had played for Bristol University and captained Chipping Sodbury CC, died in France on 21 May,

Flying Officer W.J. Moir Scott.

J.F. Boughey.

according to his gravestone, 'succouring the wounded'. Harrow School mourned the loss of Air Vice-Marshal C.H.B. Blount, who was killed in an air accident in October at the age of 46. He had captained Harrow in 1912, scoring 137 *v* Eton at Lord's, and had been a regular member of the RAF XI in their annual match with the Navy.

A match between A.E.R. Gilligan's XI and an RAF XI at Lewes in early May was watched by Sir Home Gordon. Writing on 25 May, he optimistically noted the match was taking place 'whilst the French seventy-fives were being rushed up to devastate the ponderous German tanks'. No charge for admission was made, although a collection from the 500 spectators to cover players' expenses yielded £8 9s. The difficulties in raising teams during those uncertain dark days was demonstrated by the fact that twenty-five invitations had to be issued before a full XI could be confirmed, with J.F. Boughey of the Coldstream Guards arriving at noon having been on duty until half-past ten.

For 21-year-old Lieutenant Boughey, who had captained Eton College in 1938, this would prove to be his final major cricket match. While serving on board HMS *Express* off the east coast on 31 August that year, the vessel struck a mine and Boughey was reported as having been killed instantly. He had written a premonition of his death shortly beforehand:

Last Night I Dreamed

Last night I dreamed that to my bed there came
A heavenly vision, calling me by name
Who, standing in the moonlight, softly said
'Arise and follow me, for you are dead.'
Then in a sudden, timeless flash unfurled
Before my eyes, the compass of the world;
Before me lay eternity revealed
And all the secrets in earth's bosom sealed.
Thus, for a space I stood and watched, supreme
Wrapt in the matchless splendour of my dream,
And, suddenly I knew that time and death
Were but the fable on man's lying breath.

Peter Eckersley had captained Lancashire from 1929 to 1935 in an era in which an amateur whose cricketing output would not have warranted a place in the team would be appointed to lead a team of professionals. Despite his modest first-class batting average of just under 20, Eckersley had led the county to the championship title in 1934. He had given up his playing career after being elected MP for Manchester Exchange at the 1935 general election. A member of the Lancashire Aero Club, he was known as the 'Cricketing Airman', frequently arriving at cricket matches by air. Eckersley joined the Fleet Air Arm during the war and was based at HMS Raven. He was killed in a flying accident near Eastleigh on 13 August 1940. At his funeral at St Ann's, Manchester, Canon Paton-Williams remarked that he died as he would have wished, 'playing for England. ... Life for him consisted of playing the next stroke, and whether at Old Trafford, at the House of Commons, or in the air he always played the game – a clean game, a good game.'

Cricket counted the loss of Leyton bat-maker William Breeden, killed in a German bombing raid on 10 October. A long-established firm, Breeden's had an outlet under an arch at Leyton's London Midland Railway Station. Alan Ross recalled, 'Near the Leyton ground there had been a batmaker's shop, W. Breeden, which supplied many of the Essex players with their bats.' Despite Mr Breeden's extermination by Nazi bombs, the business continued through to the 1960s, with Ross noting, 'Beautiful bats are still made in the little shop, and it is moving to find it still there, and still in the family, under the shadow of the big railway arches of Leyton Midland station; only a few yards from one of the most famous cricket grounds in the world.'

* * *

During the course of the 1940 season, English county clubs altered radically in their playing composition, capacity for competition and financial footing. For many counties, the necessity of maintaining the infrastructure of staff and premises for the duration meant that members were still encouraged to pay subscriptions. Some counties who had been in a precarious financial state at the outbreak of the war actually saw their fiscal positions greatly improved by 1945.

Derbyshire, who had reported a loss of £905 the previous year, managed to play just one match in 1940, against Nottinghamshire in May, but could not raise a team for the return fixture in August as their leading professionals had accepted contracts in the Bradford League. In the match that did take place, across 11 and 13 May, the Reverend Wilfred Payton scored 25 and 0 for Derbyshire against Nottinghamshire, for whom he had played during the 1935 season. He would later take a commission as a chaplain in the RAF, one of nearly 1,000 clergy appointed to provide for the spiritual needs of Britain's flyers. Despite the dearth of cricket, Derbyshire managed to turn a profit of £530 in 1940.

It was Nottinghamshire who were able to maintain the most semblance of pre-war normality, as many of their players were called up into local territorial units or taken on as physical training instructors at nearby recruitment centres. Six matches were played; three against the RAF, one each against Leicestershire and Derbyshire, and one against a Notts and Derby Border League Select XI. It was during one of the RAF matches that the season's highest individual score was made, with Joe Hardstaff amassing 183 for the flyers' team against his erstwhile teammates. The same match saw the emergence of the young Reg Simpson, who scored 134 not out for the county. County men were doing their bit. Walter Keeton was in the Police War Reserve in Mansfield, Hardstaff, Charlie Harris and Harold Butler were all sergeants in an Anti-Aircraft unit stationed within reasonable distance of Trent Bridge. Bill Voce and George Gunn were in reserved occupations, whilst rising star Simpson, having refused an offer to join the groundstaff at Trent Bridge before the war, worked in administrative support for Nottingham City Police CID. The county's net annual profit was £43.

Kent were fortunate that 1,212 members continued to pay part or all of their subscription, allowing essential work to be carried out and allowances paid to members of staff called into the armed forces. Wages for existing staff continued to be paid. However, infrastructure repairs had been deferred until after the war. Despite this resilience, some members expressed disappointment that the club had not arranged any county fixtures. The committee pointed out that 'throughout the summer, Kent suffered from frequent air attacks, and it was not considered advisable to take the responsibility of causing crowds to collect when no adequate shelter was available. 35 Club and Army matches were played on the St Lawrence Ground, which is in good condition.' Bryan Valentine, W.H.V. 'Hopper' Levett, Doug Wright and Godfrey Evans joined the Army, whilst Les Ames and team captain Gerry Chalk joined the RAF.

Now they're
PLAYING FOR ENGLAND

IN THE GRIMMEST TEST OF ALL

Most cricketers were ready to put aside their whites and sign up for the Grim Test match against Germany.

Glamorgan were not able to fulfil the three fixtures they arranged, with eight of their regular first-team players – Maurice Turnbull, Wilf Wooller, Jack Mercer, Johnny Clay, Haydn Davies, Allan Watkins and Phil Clift – serving in the forces by the summer. Many Welsh league clubs also found it difficult to carry on. Similarly, Gloucestershire had suffered from a migration of players into the services, including Walter Hammond, Charlie Barnett, Basil Allen, Grahame Parker, Desmond Eagar, Arthur Brodhurst, Arthur

Wilson, Jack Crapp, George Lambert and Colin Scott. Tom Goddard, Reg Sinfield and William Neale were in the Civil Defence Service.

Hammond, the England captain, had immediately joined up, receiving a commission as a pilot officer in the RAFVR. He was posted to the No. 3 Initial Training Wing, serving in Hastings, then Torquay. In both locations he was able to play some cricket, including an appearance alongside Les Ames and Leonard Crawley for an RAF XI *v* Sussex. In late 1940 Hammond was posted to RAF Middle East Headquarters at Cairo, remaining there for three years. Given his public profile, he was responsible for promoting sporting and entertainment facilities for officers and men across Africa, a fact that in later years would cause Hammond some regret, leaving a lingering feeling that his war, although a 'good' one, had not challenged him as much as many of his playing comrades.

Hampshire were another county unable to field a side in 1940, whilst considerable damage was done to the pavilion at Southampton by enemy bombing. The southern county provided four recruits for the Army; Cecil Paris, Gerry Hill, Richard Court and George Heath, whilst George Taylor, Percy McKenzie and Alister McLeod joined the RAF. Notably, Neil McCorkell was the only player to take to the seas with the Royal Navy from this most nautical of counties.

Worcestershire's sole fixture was a fundraising match against Warwickshire in aid of the Worcester Fighter Fund in front of a crowd of 2,000 at New Road, and a sum of £45 15s was raised. Roly Jenkins took seven for 40, his third seven-wicket haul in three days, following performances for West Bromwich and Sir Julien Cahn's XI. Pre-war Worcestershire regulars Hon. Charles Lyttleton, Eddie Cooper, Roly Jenkins, Phil King, Dick Howorth, Peter Jackson and Hugo Yarnold joined the forces. The club's committee had called in their groundsman, Fred Hunt, to request that he carry on his work. Hunt had wished to relinquish his role, facing difficulties in obtaining sufficient petrol to power the mower to roll and mow the New Road Ground. He was persuaded to continue for the sum of £150 p.a.; 64-year-old Hunt said he did not want to let the club down.

For Warwickshire too this was their solitary 1940 fixture, with club captain Bob Wyatt having joined the RAF and leading professional Tom Dollery in the Army. The club's Edgbaston headquarters was damaged by enemy bombing, when the bowling shed was destroyed, as Birmingham's armaments industry was a high-profile Luftwaffe target. The county managed to run a small surplus, with 680 members contributing £1,106 in 1940 to give a surplus of £21. Somerset drew a complete blank, playing no cricket in 1940. Leicestershire managed three matches; two against Northamptonshire and one against Nottinghamshire. Sussex played some early season games under the name of 'A.E.R. Gilligan's XI' before the threat of invasion from across the Channel curtailed their activities.

Similarly, Essex fell victim to invasion anxiety, with some of their first-class grounds being located within defence areas. Denys Wilcox, Tom Pearce, Peter

Smith, A.B. Lavers and J.W.A. Stephenson served in the Army, whilst Frank Rist, Reg Taylor, Ken Farnes and Frank Vigar were in the RAF. Ray Heaven was in the Royal Navy. Star all-rounder Stan Nichols became, like many professional cricketers, an Army PTI. Despite these exigencies, six matches were played by 'an Essex XI' in 1940. In one such fixture, against Ilford on 11 May, the county team defeated the club outfit by 165 runs, chiefly due to 100 runs, four wickets and two catches by Ray Smith – this despite Essex fielding nine men, with 'Captain T.N. Pearce, Cadet T.P.B. Smith absent'.

Of the northern counties, Lancashire's Old Trafford Ground was taken over by the Army and used as a transit camp for men returning from Dunkirk. Bombing during the winter of 1940/41 left a crater by the front gate and two of the stands were badly damaged. It therefore proved impossible to raise a team in 1940, or to use the ground the season after, although many of the professional players engaged on war work in Manchester and Liverpool were engaged to play in the strong leagues in the county. County stalwarts Cyril Washbrook and Norman Oldfield joined the RAF, and Dick Pollard joined the Army.

Their Roses rivals, Yorkshire, saw Brian Sellers, Hedley Verity, Herbert Sutcliffe, Norman Yardley and Bill Bowes given Army commissions whilst Maurice Leyland and Frank Smailes were appointed sergeants in the Army Physical Training Corps (RAPTC). Paul Gibb, Cyril Turner and Ellis Robinson joined the RAF. Several of these cricketers played in a trio of matches between Captain Sutcliffe's XI v Sergeant Leyland's XI at Sheffield, Leeds and Bradford. Even during the nation's darkest hour, the future health of the game was being nurtured. In July, young cricketers were invited to attend the Headingley Ground

for coaching from the celebrated former England all-rounder George Hirst. Hirst also attended a Leeds young players' match at the ground. The near-septuagenarian was also commissioned to tour the ridings to coach boys from elementary schools through June and July. From Hull to Redcar, from Barnsley to Bradford, the sagacious coach cast his experienced eye.

Aside from Yorkshire, efforts were being made to ensure boys from state school backgrounds could be provided with the opportunity to learn the rudiments of the game. The Playing Fields Crusade had its most active season ever, as more than 1,000 London Boy Evacuees who had been evacuated to Oxford to continue their education were afforded the chance of organised cricket. The Oxford Scheme had been established in the early 1920s to allow local elementary schoolboys

Stan Nichols.

to receive cricket coaching at the city's university colleges. It was considered that ordinary boys would, according to the 1925 Club Cricket Conference handbook, 'learn the value of discipline [and] develop *esprit de corps*' from the influence of the privileged milieu. This facility was extended during the war as grounds and equipment were provided for matches between the evacuees and teams from Oxford Boys' clubs.

The London-based counties, Middlesex and Surrey, were severely denuded by the spring of 1940. Some of the former county players were involved in matches organised by the Lord's authorities. High-profile Middlesex players in the armed forces included Gubby Allen, Ian Peebles, Jack Robertson, Denis Compton and George Mann in the Army, whilst Walter Robins and Bill Edrich had joined the RAF. Grenville Stevens joined the Royal Naval Volunteer Reserve (RNVR). Surrey managed to play nine matches on club grounds as their pre-eminent players, including Errol Holmes, Freddie Brown and Alf Gover, all joined the colours.

Northamptonshire's County Ground pavilion was requisitioned by the National Fire Service and only a few local club games were possible on the pitch, so most of the county's games took place at Spinney Hill, a mile away from the club ground. In May 1940, Northamptonshire played London Counties in front of a Sunday crowd of 3,500. Their captain, Robert Nelson, joined the Royal Marines for a tragically short military career and Dennis Brookes became a physical training instructor in the RAF.

Sergeant Denis Compton in his army greatcoat.

Walter Robins in RAF uniform.

Of the Minor Counties, Hertfordshire forewent the opportunity to play any cricket in 1940 due to the deprivations of war. Bedfordshire, Durham, Northumberland and Devon did manage some fixtures, with the last of these drawing a large crowd for a match against a team led by Wally Hammond at Torquay. Another member of the RAF stationed in the county was Bill Edrich. Having scored a bright 49 to help an RAF XI defeat Torquay on 3 August, the Middlesex man was presented with a silver cigarette case during the interval to mark the support he had given to cricket in the English Riviera town. Edrich had scored 44, 68, 102, 40 and 49 in five matches, as well as taking many wickets, including bowling out the first nine batsmen in a match against Paignton. In the same match, Les Ames hit 104 in forty-seven minutes, with eight sixes and eight fours. The presence of so many first-class players in Torquay had given the game a fillip in a district where the support has been somewhat lukewarm in the past, commented *The Cricketer*. Both of the universities that had first-class cricket status, Oxford and Cambridge, managed to play some three-day fixtures, but the traditional fixture between the two institutions did not materialise.

The bank holiday weekend in early August saw a feast of entertainment. At Bramall Lane on 3 August, Captain H. Sutcliffe's XI took on Major G.W. Ferrand's XI; £350 was raised for the Red Cross Fund, with Sutcliffe, the neat and commanding former England opener, scoring 35, and Maurice Leyland and Paul Gibb making good contributions for Ferrand's XI. Sutcliffe's erstwhile opening partner for England, Jack Hobbs, was the proprietor of a sports shop in Fleet Street. He was told about a 7-year-old batsman who had scored 93 in a prep school match. Impressed by the feat, the great man sent a bat to the youngster, with a congratulatory letter:

Dear Mr Cowdrey,
I hear you are very keen on the game so I feel sure you will score many centuries in the years to come.

Young Master Colin Cowdrey would indeed emulate two of The Master's feats by completing a hundred first-class centuries and becoming England's highest run-scorer.

* * *

As the Battle of Britain reached its height during August, the Luftwaffe turned its attention to attacking RAF stations in the south of England, causing some dislocation of planned matches. By 7 September, Hitler, angered by British bombing raids on Berlin, set his destructive sights to London. On that day, the match between a Middlesex XI and a Lord's XI was delayed for some time by a long air raid, but the Luftwaffe planes were intercepted over the Thames, with only one getting through to drop bombs on the capital. The match was eventually completed in the gathering autumnal gloom, when 51-year-old Patsy Hendren, who had made his first-class debut as far back as 1907, scored 45. On 16 September, bombs fell on Wellington Road, close to Lord's Cricket Ground, whilst on 16 October an oil bomb fell to the left of the nursery. A synagogue opposite the rear of the tavern was destroyed on 1 November, before, on 9 December, a 1,000lb bomb dug an enormous crater just short of the north-east stand.

Across the Thames, the Kennington Oval was the scene of a bizarre and ultimately tragic sequence of events. On 15 September, during a large blitz raid, Oberleutnant Robert Zehbe's Dornier plane developed engine trouble and was set upon by RAF fighter pilots. Zehbe bailed out, his parachute coming to rest on a telegraph pole outside the famous ground on Harleyford Road. In order to protect the badly injured pilot from a gathering lynch mob, Superintendent Gillies of Kennington Road Police arrived to place him in a police van, which then drove off over the revered Oval turf, and across Vauxhall Bridge to Millbank Military Hospital. Zehbe died from his wounds the following day and was buried in Brookwood Military Cemetery.

The contribution of the Spitfire to the prospect of success in the Battle of Britain stirred the British public into action. Donations ranging from children's pocket money to substantial sums from the wealthy poured into an appeal instigated by Minister of Aircraft Production Lord Beaverbrook, and 1,400 councils, workplaces and voluntary organisations set up their own Spitfire appeal funds. Eventually the money to build approximately 2,600 Spitfires was raised by public appeals. Pelham Warner was determined that cricket should be seen to be playing its part in the fundraising drive. Whilst acknowledging the grand work already ongoing in raising money for the Red Cross and other war charities, Warner reckoned, 'our great national game should now plan to purchase a fighter plane'. The cost of a Spitfire, £5,000, should be raised via clubs. Each person who had had the 'very good fortune' to play or watch cricket should pay one shilling, amounting to between £1 and £3 per club. Warner took up his own suggestion by setting up a Middlesex CCC Fighter Fund, arguing that a county XI would only be able to grace Lord's once the Royal Air Force had been successful: 'how better could the arms of the County Club – three scimitars – be carried than by a Fighter of our incomparable Air Force?' Warner followed up the appeal in *The Cricketer*, quoting Churchill's 'Never in the field' broadcast of 20 August. It was noted that a cheque of £500 had been received from Mr Norman Webb.

Others argued that the fund should be better employed in providing scholarships to the universities after the war for officers and men of the RAF or their sons, or in contributions to the RAF Benevolent Fund. Warner remarked that a scholarship was a luxury and may be left to the future, once the immediate necessity of winning the war had been accomplished. By the time *The Cricketer*

609 Squadron play cricket in front of a Supermarine Spitfire at RAF Biggin Hill, Kent.

Winter Annual came out, Warner had raised £1,300 – £1,000 of which had been sent to Lord Beaverbrook.

Across the country a close alignment between the justification of playing cricket and the raising of money for charity was maintained. Horsforth Cricket Club in north Leeds hosted a Red Cross charity match at their Old Ball Ground between two scratch sides. In the West Country, a 'Wings *v* Fuselage' match took place on the Wellington School ground in September in aid of the Wells and District Spitfire Campaign. Also in September, the Sussex County Ground at Hove hosted a match in aid of the Spitfire Fund, with a Sussex XI including Arthur Gilligan, Maurice Tate and the Langridge brothers taking on a scratch team from the Brighton, Hove and District Cricket Association. The *Morecambe Guardian* reported on a thrilling end to a Spitfire Fund game at Charney Hall in Lancashire in a fixture between Grange-over-Sands ARP services and the Home Guard. When the last man went in, the Home Guard required three runs to win. After hitting a single, R. Clark was nearly caught off the next ball, and in the same over he sent the ball 'flashing to the boundary' to win the game. The Club Cricket Conference sent a cheque for over £600 to the Sports Section of the Red Cross Fund.

'Bright Cricket Helps Bomber Fund' was the headline in the *Nottingham Journal* when Sir Julien Cahn hosted a match at his ground in West Bridgford

Reg Perks.

in early August. Over £70 was raised for the City of Nottingham Bomber Fund as Cahn's XI and a team raised by W.H. Sherwin of the Nottinghamshire CCC committee 'produced thrills, surprises, some fine batting and a remarkably fine bowling performance by Reg Perks, the Worcestershire fast bowler', who took seven wickets. New Zealander Stewie Dempster hit a six and ten fours in his 85.

* * *

As English cricket adapted to a new wartime normal through 1940, across the Atlantic the game showed similar stoicism in increasingly adverse conditions. The Chicago League continued with nine teams, but a projected tour of Canada and the eastern states was abandoned due to the war situation. According to *The Cricketer*'s correspondent, 'cricket in this part of the world lost some of its cheery appeal as many times the thoughts of the participants and spectators conflicted with the cricket field in Chicago and the battlefield in Europe ... [but was] a splendid antidote for the horrors of war.' Two teams from the Detroit area visited Chicago, one representing white clubs and one of those of Caribbean heritage. It was a low-scoring league, with just one century attained, and H.L. Sims topping the batting averages with 25.60 from his seventeen innings, whilst the top six men in the bowling averages averaged under 5 per wicker. M. Green of Hyde Park, an Australian national, claimed thirty-two wickets at 2.75 each. The Rochester Club of New York arranged twenty-six fixtures for the season, including competition in the Buffalo and District League. American cricketers were reported to be contributing to the Middlesex Fighter Fund, with members of Merion CC donating.

North of the border, the planned celebrations for the centenary of Ottawa Cricket Club were abandoned but as much cricket as possible continued. Englishmen visiting the city were advised that Cathedral CC would 'be able to provide them with plenty of cricket'. A normal season of cricket was possible in the city, with the championship being won by New Edinburgh CC. Ottawa CC suffered severely through enlistments into the fighting services but managed to clinch the Confederation Cup. In Argentina, Buenos Aries won the first division championship, with thirteen rounds of matches played. The game in the country was predominantly the preserve of the English-speaking community.

H.G. Stephenson, honorary secretary of the Guernsey Island Cricket Club, evacuated the island aboard one of the last steamers to leave before German bombardment. H.V. Stone, the club captain, had taken up an appointment at a Scottish public school. Others were not so fortunate. Major E.R. Morres, captain of the club for many years and the major driver of cricket on the island, remained to suffer the privations of German occupation. On the island of Ireland, the various leagues and cup competitions continued as usual, although in Ulster many prominent players were on active service. However, *The Cricketer* reported 'a lack of real zest' as most representative games had been abandoned, excepting the one between Leinster and Munster.

* * *

On Saturday, 7 September, air-raid sirens had sounded at Lord's. When the all-clear rang out, the players re-emerged onto the field. The last four wickets fell in seven balls to bring the match to a conclusion. Pelham Warner stood on the pavilion balcony, watching the fires raging in the docklands as sirens wailed and anti-aircraft gunfire echoed around the city. Cricket at Lord's had ended for the summer.

By the end of 1940, non-professional sport in Britain had adopted the pattern that would continue throughout the war – locally based events between clubs and service sides. The latter were particularly popular as often they could furnish a more lavish tea than the exigencies of rationing would allow. Also, should a wicket need to be prepared, forces sides could sometimes provide scarce petrol for the mower. Contemporary commentators thought that English cricket had had a good 1940. Home Gordon wrote:

> The war will set an indelible alteration on the future of our beloved game. … We have learnt to be undaunted in national reverses. … The love for the game all over England has been abundantly demonstrated in recent months … the turn of the tide is already evident and we can face the future with confidence.

However, he was unable to avoid his customary swipe at the northern professional. Whilst praising the brighter cricket of 1940, he found space to criticise Len Hutton for his pre-war obduracy at the crease, and called Lancashire's batting 'lethargic'. He then turned to his pet themes of the future of university cricket and its throughput from public schools. The war against fascism was no reason for him to drop his private war against the state-educated professional cricketer while eulogising about his beloved public school and 'elite' university game.

Other commentators admired the bravery and stoicism of cricketers great and unknown who continued playing during the summer of 1940, but questioned whether the English game as a whole was innovative enough. Eric Midwinter argued that during a summer in which most of Britain's forces were still at home, cricket could have been less laissez-faire and arranged 'something more attractive and compelling'. He claimed that, with many sportsmen deployed in training depots as physical instructors, eleven counties could have fielded sides of close to first-class standard for one-day matches. If only half a dozen of these had produced regular XIs, the competition could have been augmented by a Bradford League XI, Birmingham League XI and the London Counties and British Empire XIs. The availability of a Dominions XI, the RAF, the

Army and an Oxbridge XI would have provided further consistent competition. Midwinter retrospectively suggested that four groups of four teams could have played on a home and away basis, with knockout semi-finals and a final, when 'an interesting little tournament could have emerged'.

Accepting that some matches might have been ruined by an air raid or absence of players at short notice, Midwinter reckoned it unfortunate that the cricket authorities limited their thinking to either a County Championship or nothing in terms of competition, comparing them unfavourably to the Football League, which, during the 1940/41 season, ran northern and southern leagues, with over thirty teams in each. However, given the restrictions on the availability of petrol, the turning over of much of the rail network to the military, the acute anxieties of the threat of invasion for much of the year, and the fact that the German attack on the Low Countries only began once the season's programme had started, it is perhaps a little harsh to blame the authorities for not having a competition ready to start in late April. Furthermore, some of the combinations suggested as part of this competition, notably the British Empire XI and London Counties XI, were only formed once the season started. In the case of the former, with the remit to play entertaining cricket for charity purposes, there may have been resistance to taking part in a more formalised structure. The northern and midland leagues already had their own established fixture list, and clubs may have been loath to agree to the release of their star players.

Indeed, the success of the 1940 programme of one-day fixtures and the strength of the northern leagues was already causing consternation among the game's powerbrokers. Pelham Warner warned:

> On the strength of one-day charity matches which have brought great contentment to those who have seen their favourites in action once again, some people appear to think that all the cares and problems confronting county cricket when the war is over may be brushed on one side by introducing leagues and cup competitions and reducing all matches to a single day. But is it as easy as all that, and are not those who advocate such a violent change with the past confusing the hectic hurly-burly of professional soccer – with which we have no quarrel – with its 90 minutes of intense excitement with the leisurely warfare of cricket which never can be and indeed was never intended to be 'hotted' up?

Warner stated that cricket was not meant to appeal to 'those who revel in Americanised sports gossip and the vitriol into which many of the pens are dipped'. He was sensitive to criticism of MCC, asserting that 'no cricketer wants any other organisation in control of the game'.

R.C. Robertson-Glasgow ended his *Wisden* notes on this season in a melancholy manner: 'And so to a close. If little has been said, little enough was done. We hope for more; much more, and soon. But first a task falls to be completed. *Delendus est hostis.*' More than a little was indeed done by clubs across the land. Matches at Lord's alone raised £843 for the Red Cross, £150 for the King George's Fund for Sailors and £100 for the Cricketers' Friendly Society. Collections were taken by ladies who were, according to Warner, 'charmingly persuasive'. The northern leagues continued their competitions, albeit sometimes in a slightly revised format, whilst in the south, several teams played, often little resembling their peacetime iterations. It was anticipated that the calling up of a large number of men during the winter months would have a detrimental influence on club cricket in 1941. Indiscriminate bombing had naturally resulted in some grounds being unlucky, with one famous London club's ground coming in for what A.W.T. Langford called 'a special dose of hate, with the result that their heaviest roller just disappeared from the face of the earth'.

During one of the darkest periods in British history, the sound of bat on ball and the sight of white-clad figures in sunlit fields had provided a very welcome relaxation from the sweat and toil of war.

* * *

Just as the English game had to adapt to emergency circumstances, so did its Australian counterpart. The season of 1940/41 saw the suspension of the Sheffield Shield competition, with a series of eleven friendly fixtures taking its place to raise money for patriotic funds. Meanwhile, a Test tour of India which had been mooted by Frank Tarrant had failed to materialise, and 18-year-old Arthur Morris scored a hundred in each innings of his first-class debut for NSW against Queensland in December 1940. At the opposite end of the seniority spectrum, Clarrie Grimmett, nine days before his forty-eighth birthday, bowled thirty-eight eight-ball overs, seventeen of them in succession, taking seven wickets at the Melbourne Cricket Ground. For South Australia *v* Victoria, both Ron Hamence and C.L. 'Jack' Badcock scored a century in each innings, the first such occurrence in Australian cricket. In the same month, in a one-day match on behalf of the Soldier's Cigarette Fund, donors gave 2/6 for every run scored by Don Bradman, who made 109. However, The Don endured a lean spell in first-class cricket with consecutive scores of 0, 6, 0 and 12.

Neville Cardus – frequently cited as the finest cricket wordsmith ever, who would spend most of the war in Australia, many miles from his native Manchester – found the talk in bars to be of Bradman rather than Hitler, the war being an 'abstract idea' to a country holding at bay the grim prospect of being drawn into the Empire's conflict. Cardus had made the decision to sojourn in Australia following an invitation from media mogul Sir Keith Murdoch to cover Sir Thomas Beecham's concert tour of the country for the *Melbourne Herald*. Cardus had grown depressed in England, with little cricket and few classical music performances about which to write: 'I was imprisoned in Manchester, useless to anybody.' In old age Cardus tried to excuse his extended hiatus from England: 'I thought Australia soon might be needed as another sort of Noah's Ark for the preservation of remaining European culture.'

In the same way England captain Walter Hammond had set an example to the nation and its sportsmen by stepping forward quickly to serve, so Australia's greatest sporting celebrity, Don Bradman, enlisted with the RAAF in June, saying he 'felt the urge of all patriotic citizens to do my duty in a sterner sphere'. Adelaide's Lord Mayor, Arthur Barrett, who had been a First World War pilot, commented, 'Let us hope now that Don will get centuries in the air as readily as he got them on the ground.' Regrettably, it was not to be. Having attended training classes, he was released by the RAAF and transferred to the Australian Army in October as a student at the School of Physical and Recreational Training at Frankston, Victoria, with a view to him becoming a physical training supervisor.

One future Australian cricketing star who had little hesitation in joining up was Keith Ross Miller. On 20 August, the up-and-coming Australian all-round sportsman joined the Militia (Australian Army Reserve) and was assigned to the 4th Reserve Motor Transport Company. In late September, with his Australian Rules Football Club St Kilda already eliminated from the season's competition, Miller attended his first army training camp at Caulfield Racecourse in Melbourne. A perennial thorn in the side of authority, Miller had the first of his many clashes on 4 November, when he was charged with 'using insulting language to a superior officer' and was fined 10 shillings.

The volunteering urge had been less pronounced in South Africa than in Australia and New Zealand. Nevertheless, 1940 saw several prominent players join the forces, including Alan Melville, W.W. 'Billy' Wade, Bruce Mitchell, A.W. 'Dooley' Briscoe, E.S. 'Bob' Newson and Ronnie Grieveson. They did so against a backdrop of domestic civil strife, which led Prime Minister Jan Smuts to decide against a fully national war effort, relying instead on volunteers to make up the national army. In the end, two-thirds of the South African Army was comprised of men with British surnames. India had been thrust into war without consultation from the British Government. Much of the population was outraged at this high-handed approach, with political leaders such as Nehru and Gandhi seeing the war as an opportunity to throw off the shackles of British rule. However, 2.5 million volunteers had joined the British Indian Army by 1945. Apart from Assam in 1944, India would remain free from military action. Cricket would prosper during the war years, despite the cancellation of the 1939/40 England tour and the abandonment of plans of a tour by Australia a year later. Heavy scoring became the order of the day in first-class cricket, with Maharashtra scoring 675 against Bombay's 650 at Poona in November, the only two innings to take place over five days.

By the end of 1940 most cricketing nations had been affected by global warfare to a greater or lesser degree. The Grim Test was well into its first innings.

Chapter 3

1941: Playing the Game

'He died as he lived, Playing the Game.'
Ken Farnes' gravestone inscription

The new cricketing year was ushered in with a four-day match between Stan McCabe's XI and Don Bradman's XI at the MCG, the former team emerging as convincing winners by an innings and 103 runs. Sid Barnes and Jack Badcock, formerly known as the 'Tasmanian Bradman', made centuries for the McCabe XI. The decision to suspend the Sheffield Shield drew stinging criticism from some quarters. According to Ray Robinson, writing in *The Cricketer*, the Interstate Cricket Conference 'bowled a wrong 'un to itself and the public by suspending the Sheffield Shield competition (12 matches) and arranging 11 "patriotic matches" for the same players'. He labelled the decision 'emotional' as it was 'difficult to find anything unpatriotic in competitive cricket that does not hinder the war effort'. State and national leaders had emphasised the national benefit of keeping sport going to fulfil its normal purpose in people's lives, as far as war's demands permitted. Indeed, 'When I read of Englishmen playing on during air-raid alarms, stopping only when the enemy is sighted, I feel that the Conference is, in Robertson-Glasgow's phrase, "wearing mental sackcloth in advance".'

Horse racing and football enjoyed large attendances but exhibition cricket matches failed to attract the crowds due to the lack of competitive flavour. Match profits for war funds slumped, with a mere £8 17s 6d taken at the gate when Victoria snatched a win from NSW, with Cec Pepper declaring it was like 'playing in a cemetery'.

The Australian game could hardly have been accused of shirking, with eight of the sixteen players who had toured England in 1938 having joined the armed forces. Sid Barnes made the most of the matches on offer, passing 100 in five of his six first-class matches by the end of January. In Sydney First Grade Cricket, 19-year-old Arthur Morris scored a record 890 runs, and Bob Cristofani, also 19, set a record with his fifty wickets.

Across the Tasman Sea, New Zealand's Plunket Shield competition was also suspended on 3 March after the completion of six matches, as many prominent players slipped away into the military services. Nevertheless, the nation's thirst for cricketing competition remained unabated. By the spring of 1941, members of the NZEF based at Maadi Camp near Cairo had established a full cricketing infrastructure to support an inter-unit competition. Gear was made available to the teams and two cricket nets were established for practice.

In the Caribbean, a strong Barbados team led by Herman Griffith played two matches against Trinidad in aid of the Red Cross in February. In the second match, the Stollmeyer brothers were to the fore for Trinidad, Victor making 40 and 86 not out and Jeff 84 and 93, with stands of 127 and 172. Across the 1940/41 season, in successive innings Victor made 207 not out, 146 and 174, and Jeff scored 114 and 241 not out. In consecutive opening partnerships the brothers put up 288 and 372, the latter being a record for Trinidad.

For South African cricket writer Louis Duffus, it mattered less what format of competition was on offer during wartime, but more the significance of players and followers being able to refresh their souls by immersing themselves in the game when circumstances permitted. He reported on the return of a group of veterans from the battlefield to Durban:

> A few days later a match was arranged for [the] men. Indian groundstaff refreshed a turf wicket lying fallow at the back of the Kingsmead ground, famous for the last illimitable pre-war test. I don't know when I have seen a game of cricket that gave more personal enjoyment to a single player than this match did to the major, whose last match had been played a year previously at Gibraltar. Now for one whole day he lived again in the setting of his youth, the setting of green English fields with worm-casts, and tents around the boundary, and players in old Varsity caps ... and of soothing drinks at sundown. ...
>
> As it happened he won no particular distinction that day, but he revelled in the game with a wartime hunger for cricket, and observed its ritual as faithfully and as gracefully as though it were played somewhere in the heart of Surrey.
>
> For at least a day his mind was freed from thoughts of the hazardous journey he was making daily over the seven seas. To him and his men the game was a refreshing tonic.

For those left at home engaged on vital services and for the many cricketers scattered about the Union in military training camps, the 1940/41 season brought forth a magnificent response. Closer attention than usual was given to the fostering of cricket in the schools, with the Nuffield Week taking place in Cape Town. Senior cricket was confined to friendly matches, with the Currie Cup suspended. In January, a Rest of South Africa XI took on Transvaal at the Wanderers' ground in a one-day match, with both sides largely comprising cricketers in the services. The Rest made 314 for six, with 107 from Desmond Fell, who had been on the fringe of Test selection in 1938–39, whilst Eric Dalton's six for 42 skittled out Transvaal for 119. The match was played in aid of war funds and attracted the largest cricketing crowd of the South African summer.

One player unable to take part was Alan Melville. Watching from the stands, Melville had suffered a severe fall in training and was confined to a steel jacket for eleven months. Each movement was carried out gingerly and was accompanied by a metallic clang. At the time it was feared that the injury would terminate his playing career. However, following demobilisation in 1945, an intensive physical regimen brought about such a good recovery that Melville was able to resume playing, leading his country on their 1947 tour of England.

All over the Union there was an admirable readiness shown by old players to help the game along. Dave Nourse, the grand old man of South African cricket, remained hale and hearty. Nourse had been born in Croydon in 1878 and bred in the atmosphere of English village cricket. He had gone to South Africa as a drummer with the West Riding Regiment in 1895 and settled there. Herbie Taylor (51) and Claude Carter (59) also came out of retirement. Taylor had won the MC in the First World War and had scored the last of his thirty first-class centuries back in 1934. Carter, whose first-class career had begun in 1898, played several matches for Natal, bowling with considerable skill. Frank Elworthy, playing his first match for ten years, took a wicket with his first ball. Other veterans who dusted down their old cricket bags to do their bit included Charlie Frank (59), Bob Catterall (40) and Fred le Roux (57).

These players helped enliven what might have been a dull season. Duffus reflected, 'I cannot help feeling that the country's post-war cricket will be the richer through their action in returning to cricket. Many schoolboys and other young players ended this season cherishing vivid memories of playing against and receiving friendly tips from these famous players.'

* * *

Captain A.B. Hamer RAMC is not a widely acclaimed personality in cricketing history, but his skill helped shape England's fortunes in the first post-war decade. Sergeant Len Hutton came under his care in March, having slipped and fallen on his left arm while conducting a training class, fracturing the radius and dislocating the base of the ulna at the wrist. Hutton, an Army PT instructor, had his arm encased in plaster. Hamer then wrote a note to the specialist unit in Wakefield, which would attempt to return full use of the arm: 'In view of the great importance of this man's left arm in batting, we trust that you will attend to his further treatment and admit, as arranged by telephone.'

Coming under the care of distinguished surgeon Reginald Broomhead at Wakefield, who had to perform three operations on the crucial arm, Hutton was eventually discharged from the Army in 1942. With a left arm almost 2 inches shorter than the right, he was considered fit merely for civilian work for the Royal Engineers. However, sufficient skilled work had been done that Hutton was able to resume batting for Pudsey St Lawrence in 1943 and regain his status as the pre-eminent Test opening batsman in the post-war period.

During Hutton's long convalescence from his arm restructure, he immersed himself in Neville Cardus's *Days in the Sun*, removing his mind from anxiety over his cricketing future to luxuriate on evocations of players and grounds that seemed a lifetime away from the grind of war. The master batsman wrote to the master wordsmith to thank him for writing such an inspiring book. The Yorkshireman was fit enough to turn out for Sir Pelham Warner's XI *v* RAF at Lord's on 16 August. Despite scoring 19, Hutton concluded that his arm had not set satisfactorily and required further treatment.

* * *

The English season began under a cloud with the loss of Essex all-rounder Laurie Eastman in April. During the previous war this popular professional had served in Egypt with the London Regiment, twice being wounded and issued with a disability pension and Silver War Badge. Eastman had volunteered as an ARP warden when war broke out and had appeared for London Counties XI in the 1940 season. In January 1941, a high-explosive bomb burst close to him, causing shock and severe injuries. Eastman fought for his life for three months before slipping away in Harefield Sanatorium on 17 April 1941 following an operation. Home Gordon bade farewell in *The Cricketer*: 'May the grass rest lightly on the grave of a good fellow.' The 43-year-old had intended to begin a career in medicine before the Kaiser's war had intervened. He died leaving two unusual cricketing legacies, firstly having filled every batting position from 1 to 10 for Essex. At Leyton in 1932 he had been the 'lucky' bowler who had ended Holmes and Sutcliffe's record opening stand of 555 as the latter sacrificed his wicket assuming the milestone had been reached. Eastman's funeral in Romford was attended by his former Essex teammates Jack O'Connor and Reg Taylor.

It was decreed that play could continue until 8.00 pm at Lord's and other grounds as, due to daylight saving time regulations, the clock would be two hours in advance of the sun. MCC also agreed at its AGM on 7 May to admit members of first-class and Minor County clubs to the Lord's pavilion at no extra charge. The London Counties XI entered the spring of 1941 aiming to

Laurie Eastman.

Arthur Fagg.

keep their flag flying. Undismayed by bombs and barrage, Charles Jones, their founder and honorary secretary, had been busy all winter making arrangements and building up a fixture list. There would not be much change in the side's make-up, drawn as it was from stars over military age and those engaged in civil defence and munitions. One leading light, Kent's Arthur Fagg, had been rejected by the Army due to the lingering after-effects of rheumatic fever contracted on the 1936/37 Ashes tour. One highlight of their summer was the lavish hospitality provided at Sir Julien Cahn's West Bridgford Ground in Nottinghamshire on 1 June. The host raised a strong side, including C.B. Harris, F.C. Newman, G.F.H. Hearne, Stewie Dempster, Reg Simpson and Reg Perks. In a drawn game, Arthur Fagg, Jack O'Connor and Arthur Wellard put in strong performances for the visitors. Later that month the XI racked up a mammoth 446 for seven in only 210 minutes against Gravesend, with Fagg top scoring with 131, in a match in aid of the local Mayor's Prisoners of War Fund. In a rare wartime two-innings match in June, London Counties XI drew with Northamptonshire. The biblical supplication of 'Am I my brother's keeper' was applicable with Denis Compton scoring 0 and 92, being denied his century in the second innings, 'stumped Compton, L.', as Leslie appeared as a guest for Northamptonshire.

The set piece Lord's encounter between London Counties and their fellow wartime combination British Empire XI occurred on 19 July. The match was notable for the appearance of 54-year-old Frank Woolley. Home Gordon noted the great man arrived:

> with hardly any weight put on though having many silver threads among the dark ones on his bare head. A rapturous welcome from six thousand admirers greeted the famous left-hander as he walked to the wicket. He turned his first ball rather tentatively, but then despatched three straight to the pavilion rails, each just skimming the turf all the way. The master had lost none of his graceful skill though his footwork is slower.

London Counties had mixed fortunes during a mini-tour of Lincolnshire and Bedfordshire. Against Grantham on 5 July, Leslie Compton's century set up a target of 262 before Alf Gover and Peter Judge ripped through the host's top order, eventually being taken out of the attack before they could, as *The Cricketer* put it, 'wage total war against the opposition'. The following day, Bedford Town brought off a good victory thanks to the bowling of E.D. Markham, who claimed five for 29.

The British Empire XI too had compiled a good fixture list. As the XI's founder, Desmond Donnelly, had been called up to the RAF, secretarial duties had passed to the popular Essex all-rounder Ray Smith. Rarely has there been a more underrated servant of the game than Smith. His unflagging enthusiasm no matter what the state of play, and his ability to see the wider context of cricket made him the ideal candidate for such a morale-sustaining role. Donnelly was still able to play in one nail-biting match against Gloucestershire at Newnham on Severn, with

Ray Smith.

Harry Crabtree and Bertie Clarke – two stalwarts of the wartime game. (*Courtesy Peter Crabtree*)

Charlie Barnett in his RAF uniform outside Lord's.

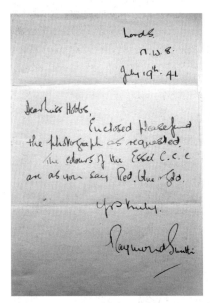

Letter from Ray Smith to a Miss Hobbs responding to her request for a photograph and an enquiry about Essex CCC.

the host's Tom Goddard ensuring a tie with his four for 56, his tally including Donnelly's wicket. Goddard was also the scourge of the Empire XI when he appeared for Evesham, taking six for 20 in a low-scoring victory.

The Empire side ventured to the Midlands, taking on Nottinghamshire on 21 June, with New Zealander spinner Bill Merritt bamboozling the Robin Hood county with figures of eight for 48. The following day many of the same players appeared at Sir Julien Cahn's ground as the Essex duo of Harry Crabtree and Sonny Avery enjoyed an opening stand of 219 against an invitational XI. A total of 613 runs were scored in the day as Cahn's XI valiantly chased a huge target of 324, ending on 289 for five. Crabtree, a native of Yorkshire who had served as a schoolmaster in Westcliff-on-Sea before the war, would go on to become the British Empire XI's leading run-scorer across the war.

In June, the British Empire XI played a two-day match against a Chelmsford and District XI, raising a sum of £450 for the Red Cross. Crowds of over 2,000 were present each day and on the Saturday night a most successful dance was held. An exciting match took place between the RAF and British Empire XI on 5 July at Lord's. The Empire XI won with eight minutes to spare and at least 10,000 spectators saw Charlie Barnett in good form with 67. The British Empire XI was indebted to an unbroken eighth wicket stand of 75 between W.M.F. Bebbington and Bev Lyon.

Ray Smith often had to cope with the last-minute unavailability of players. Denis Compton had played in England's victory over Scotland in the Red Cross Soccer International at Hampden Park on Saturday, 3 May before being due to turn out for the

British Empire XI at Slough the following day. He was unable to fulfil the latter commitment due to the near impossible logistics.

The encroachment of the wartime football season into June 1941 was criticised by Sir Home Gordon. Football clubs invariably insisted on having first call on the players and many counties would risk losing their staff for large portions of post-war seasons. Plum Warner expanded on this theme: 'Soccer is a splendid game and we have the greatest admiration for it, but is there any real need for such inordinately long seasons?' Stating that May 'is definitely a date for cricket', he observed the competing demands on players such as the Compton brothers. Stanley Christopherson, MCC Secretary, contacted the Football Association in June expressing concern at the encroachment of their season. Stanley Rous of the FA agreed to urge clubs to arrange fixtures with as little interference as possible to 'summer sports, such as cricket and tennis'.

The two-day match at Slough which Compton was forced to miss still proved a big attraction as it coincided with the opening of the town's War Weapons Week. Both teams were presented at the inaugural function and were given a speech by the energetic and diligent Mr A.V. Alexander, First Lord of the Admiralty. Alexander gave the first details of 'the miracle' achieved by the Royal Navy in the evacuation of Allied forces from Greece. The Labour politician then spent half an hour at the match and revealed a 'first-rate' knowledge of cricket. He commented that it was most refreshing to be able to relax for a moment from the sterner issues at hand and he ended his visit by delighting a small group of boys by signing their autograph books. The presence of so many first-class cricketers attracted large crowds both days and it was estimated that the Red Cross and the local War Weapons fund each benefitted by at least £50.

* * *

The controversies surrounding the position of conscientious objectors within cricket clubs continued into 1941. Although the British Government was far more lenient in its treatment of objectors than had been the case in the previous war, allowing for them to engage in a wide range of occupations as directed by the tribunals, many employers still drummed objectors out of their posts. Even some church congregations turned their backs on objectors in their midst. Therefore, cricket clubs faced a tricky dilemma: whether to continue to allow such men to play a full part in playing activities, or to discourage or even prohibit their presence as bad for team morale. April's annual meeting of Buckingham Cricket Club passed a resolution 'that we do not entertain the idea of giving any conscientious objectors an opportunity of a game' . As the club was short of playing members and facing the new season with trepidation, it had been suggested that amongst the significant number of objectors who had been assigned to agricultural work in the county, some useful cricketers might be found. When one member, Mr J.S. Butler, argued that they should not be welcomed, he was accused of being 'narrow-minded' by Mr H.B. Toft, although the latter's more tolerant attitude was tempered by the view that 'Personally I think they are fools; but the Country has decided that they are quite sane.'

Mr Bell had heard that COs working in bomb disposal units 'were the best body of workers' who had been through the 'thick of it'. Mr Figgins argued that if the club had to be kept going by allowing COs to play, 'it was time they closed down ... men who could not fight for their country ought not to be allowed to play for Buckingham'. Figgins declared: 'Send them to Germany and let Hitler do what he likes with them.' Alderman Busby went further, saying if he had his way, COs would have 'no grub'.

A greater degree of sympathy was extended to Desmond Rought-Rought for his conscientious stance. Rought-Rought was one of a trio of cricketing brothers from Brandon on the Norfolk/Suffolk border who all played first-class cricket in the 1930s. The eldest brother, Basil, had turned out in Minor Counties cricket for Norfolk and Cheshire and had appeared for H.D.G. Leveson Gower's XI and a combined Minor Counties XI in four first-class fixtures. Receiving a commission in the Royal Norfolk Regiment and joining the British Expeditionary Force on the Continent in 1940, Basil was captured during the fall of France and spent most of the war as a prisoner of the Germans. After one unsuccessful escape attempt, he triumphed in 1945 and made his way back to England.

The second brother, Rodney, had played thirty-four first-class matches, predominantly for Cambridge University, whilst Desmond had also earned his blue as well as appearing for Free Foresters and the Minor Counties XI. However, it was Desmond's stance on war service that set him apart from the majority of his generation. In August 1941, as Churchill and Roosevelt committed to the Atlantic Charter, agreeing British and American peace goals for the post-war period, Desmond Rought-Rought stood determined to play no direct part in that war. It was reported that Desmond, a 'jobbing gardener' of Amersham, had applied for exemption from military service. This placed him amongst the 0.5 per cent of conscripted men and women who chose this path after the fall of France in June 1940. Those who wished to claim exemption, usually on the grounds of religious principles, ethical beliefs, political persuasion or the liberty of the individual, had to appear before a regional tribunal to put their case. The chairman of the tribunal would

Desmond Rought-Rought.
(*Courtesy Stephen Musk*)

then direct the appellant as to what work they must undertake for the duration of the war.

Desmond's argument for exemption was based on 'Christian and humanitarian grounds'. Although raised an Anglican, he claimed to worship at a range of Free Churches, attending on a weekly basis. He also argued the sincerity of his position was based on the fact that he had given up a good job as a manager in the family hat-making business in order to be of more service to his country in the production of food. This genuineness was affirmed by a written submission from Rodney Rought-Rought who, whilst disagreeing with his brother's position, did not doubt his earnestness. Desmond had been one of 140,000 members of the Peace Pledge Union, an organisation that had attracted significant attention during the late 1930s and which continued to campaign against the conduct of the war throughout the 1940s.

Desmond stated that he did not wish to enter into non-combatant military service in the Non-Combatant Corps, Army Pay Corps or Royal Army Medical Corps 'as it was too much part of the military machine'. Challenged by a tribunal member that engaging in civilian work would make him 'part of the machine', Desmond reiterated, 'I feel that my witness for Christian pacifism must keep me from any part of the army or military service.' The decision given by the tribunal chairman, Judge Maurice Drucquer, was that Desmond Rought-Rought was to be registered for full-time land work, but that his current position would fit that requirement.

The sincerity of the position held by many conscientious objectors was recognised by their contemporaries. Bill Edrich, a member of another renowned Norfolk cricketing dynasty, who had the won the DFC for his role in flying bombing raids over Germany, wrote shortly after the war that 'many a time [the Rought-Rought brothers] gave me a quiet hint or bit of advice that was invaluable, and which occurred to me many a time afterwards, in the strenuous, hard grind of a Test match'. Edrich clearly bore no ill will to the man who had chosen a very different path to his own.

Another pair of close cricketing friends who had chosen to invoke the conscience clause were Yorkshiremen Johnny Lawrence and Miles Coope. Lawrence, a committed Methodist who would later resign his membership of Yorkshire CCC over the involvement of leading players of a so-called 'Rebel' tour of South Africa, and Coope, a member of the Baptist Church, appeared before the Yorkshire tribunal in Leeds in 1940. Coope had proclaimed: 'The military put their faith in guns but not in God.' Employed as a piano tuner at the time, in addition to playing in the Bradford League at the weekend, Coope was challenged by Judge Stewart that several Baptist chaplains were currently in France ministering to the spiritual needs of the British Expeditionary Force. Coope replied that Christians were taught to be prepared to suffer, leading Stewart to conclude he had 'the attitude of a person who would like to be a martyr burned at the stake'. Both Coope and Lawrence were ordered to undertake forestry work. Although many conscientious objectors found themselves driven out of their jobs, and shunned by friends and family, it would appear that the positions of Lawrence and Coope were accepted by their teammates as they both carried on playing league cricket before moving to the South West to play for Somerset CCC after the war.

* * *

Another ethical issue that presented itself to cricket's administrators was the subject of Sunday play. Prior to the war, a decision by London County Council to allow recreational cricket on the Sabbath had drawn strong condemnation from the Reverend Frank Gillingham, the former Essex batsman. He feared the 'slippery slope to competitive sport, and even to the opening of cinemas on the Sabbath'. In 1930, Bev Lyon, captain of Gloucestershire, had suggested that some County Championship matches should include Sunday play. The churchgoing Jack Hobbs had disagreed, stating that whilst he had no objection to Sunday club cricket for those unable to play during the week, the Sabbath should remain free from the necessity for professionals to earn their keep. Hobbs refused to play Sunday cricket during a privately organised 1930/31 tour of India. The *Sydney Morning Herald* had reported:

> Hobbs said that he was sorry, but that nothing would induce him to play cricket on Sunday. He had been brought up in a religious atmosphere and taught to respect the Sabbath. He did not wish to do anything which might injure Christianity in India. His wife also objected to his playing on Sunday.

Since the end of the First World War, Sunday play in club cricket had increased, particularly in the Home Counties. In the North, where the nonconformist churches still had a great influence on people's behaviour, league cricket was confined to Saturdays. Whilst London County Council had voted in 1922 to allow Sunday sports on its municipal pitches, councils in Birmingham, Brighton, Leeds, Leicester, Liverpool, Northampton and Swansea rejected pleas to do the same. Home Gordon argued that Sunday play would have to be considered post-war: 'one financial salvation for county cricket is to play on Sundays from half-past one or two o'clock, with Saturday and Wednesday starts, leaving Tuesday blank. I anticipate the commencement of the innovation will be some championship matches between the Southern counties.'

Jack Holmes, the Sussex captain, who had already won a DFC, contemplated the circumstances in which first-class Sunday cricket might be made more palatable to Christians. Play should begin at 1.30 pm so as not to interfere with the morning service. Holmes also proposed that immediately at the conclusion of play, there should be a short open-air service on the ground:

I should get a tip-top parson or army chaplain to give a short address and have three or four popular hymns accompanied by the best military band in the neighbourhood. The size of the receipts would render it easy to afford the band and people would remain to join in this sort of hearty worship who would never dream of entertaining church or chapel. So actually in this way people might be attracted to religion through Sunday cricket.

According to Malcolm Gunn, founder of Gravesend CC, Sunday cricket had been increasing at a phenomenal rate in the 1930s, particularly amongst the nomadic teams. Gunn contrasted the unseemly and frantic rush a Saturday cricketer faced in getting from his office to the ground for the start of play, 'with his bag in one hand and a banana in the other', with the leisurely preamble to the game enjoyed on a Sunday. 'Business cares are banished for the day [the player] can so order his day that transport can be made to wait on man and not vice versa; the home Sunday player can earn valuable domestic marks, having time for some good husbandry before he takes leave of his spouse.'

Gunn reckoned that the war would demolish any lingering 'Victorian prejudices against honest, healthful recreation on the Sabbath'. Sunday cricketers, some of whom had been accused of failing to observe religious norms, were 'a section of the community who value the Sabbath as deeply as their neighbours and in many cases put it to better use. … The last of the critics will then concede that a cricket ball is a far more beautiful thing to have about than an explosive bomb.'

Gunn's piece drew a response from J.M. Swift, stating that the suggestion that the playing of cricket rather than attending church on a Sunday was 'an unfortunate statement'. In Swift's experience those who played cricket were unlikely to have attended church beforehand. 'Whether the work and witness of the Church are of much value is a matter of opinion, but it is a fact of experience that Sunday games are a hindrance to the Church's work.'

In the North of England, many parts of which were previous bastions of Methodism, and in Scotland, with its Presbyterian aversion to Sabbath frivolity, Sunday cricket was slower to take hold. The war, however, was providing an impetus for change. On Sunday, 13 July, a match was played on the County Ground at Alloa, when an Army XI led by Captain Vaughan-Thomas met a Scottish Counties XI captained by J.M. Fleming of West Lothian. C.J. Reichwald wrote to *The Cricketer* about his baptism in Scottish cricket: 'Scotland is not cricket-minded in the same sense that any of the English first-class counties are, but there is good, keen cricket to be had.' He was impressed by the grounds and standards of play at Fettes and Loretto schools.

One who did not see Sabbath Observance and cricket as mutually exclusive was RAF clerk L.W. Hall, who was able to nourish both body and soul one Sunday in Risalpur:

The cricket match was over by 6.40 pm and just gave me time, without stopping for a shower, to get my bicycle and dash down to church for Evensong which commenced at 7 pm. This church has only just reopened after being closed for a spell and things need reorganising. It has therefore been arranged for a group of us to form a committee to see what can be done.

Whilst post-war Sunday cricket matches would become a regular feature of a county professional's benefit season, it would be nearly three decades later, with the launch of the John Player League, that professional county-level cricket would be played on the English Sabbath. The first Sunday play in a Test match in England would be a full forty years after this wartime ethical examination.

L.W. 'Laurie' Hall. (*Courtesy Mike Hall*)

* * *

The Luftwaffe did its level best to prevent the publication of 1941's *Wisden Cricketers' Almanack*. Much editorial material was lost, due to the destruction of the publishers' premises by enemy action at the end of 1940. The venerable cricketing institution soldiered on, albeit with a reduced print run of 800 hardback copies and 3,200 softback editions. The printer's office was burnt in another attack as the number of pages fell from 871 to 426, with the report on public schools cricket having been destroyed by the Luftwaffe in transit, whilst the original also perished in a simultaneous air raid. For the first time, all players, amateurs and professionals alike, were accorded the same status on scorecards, appearing with their military rank, or initials if they did not hold such a position. Partly to compensate for the loss of the public schools information, but also in recognition of their enhanced status in the wartime game, for the first time reports of the northern and midland cricket leagues were included. The volume did not appear until December. Stoically but incongruously, the fixtures for the season that had already passed were included.

One precious copy of the 1941 edition somehow made it into the hands of Keith Jackson, an officer in the Durham Light Infantry. Jackson had been captured by the Germans during the Battle of France and served some of his incarceration at Oflag VII-B in Bavaria. Upon liberation of the camp by the US Army on 15 April 1945, Jackson made his way back home with the *Wisden* amongst his possessions. It was probable that the cherished volume had ended up in the camp library, either sent there in a parcel from home, or taken there by a prisoner captured at a later date. Jackson would go on to make thirty-three appearances for Durham, including one against the 1950 West Indians, in which he took the wickets of Roy Marshall and Jeff Stollmeyer amongst his four for 120.

* * *

English cricket faced the 1941 season with a greater degree of certainty than had been the case in 1940. Unfortunately, this included an inexorable dwindling of resources and rising challenges. The grassroots game faced major difficulties as clubs struggled to survive with conscription and war work biting deeply into their playing and administrative resources. With a falling number of clubs in operation there was a corresponding decline in playing standards, with lads and greybeards being pressed into service. Petrol rationing put paid to distance fixtures. Despite these deprivations, cricket joined in the general mood of defiance against the Nazi menace. A notice pinned to the gates of a leading south coast ground that had been slightly bomb-damaged read:

> Local cricketers are as pleased as you. Each peardrop which fell on this ground saved lives and property. We shall carry on. Nothing which falls from the skies will deter us, except RAIN.

The famous Trent Bridge Ground fell victim to German blitzkrieg on the night of 8/9 May. The practice hall and other buildings were destroyed and the playing

Bomb damage at Trent Bridge, 9 May 1941. (*Courtesy* Nottingham Evening Post)

area was scarred by incendiaries, causing a crater on the Fox Road side. *The Cricketer* reported that 'at one time it really did appear as if the Huns had ruined all possibilities of cricket for the season … the position seemed hopeless.' Due to magnificent work by the groundstaff and other willing volunteers, cricket was played on the ground a day after the bombing.

Meanwhile, Lord's, as it had during the previous war, played host to a baseball match as a group of Canadian war correspondents defeated their American counterparts. The event drew a comic representation of the reaction of cricketing traditionalists in the *Toronto Daily Globe*: 'Egad! Most Extraordinary! What! Baseball at Lord's?'

Efforts were made to ensure the next generation of cricketers would have some opportunities to develop their skills in the disruption that war brought. G. Rollo Walker organised eleven matches for the Gentlemen of Herts against schools. Southgate Cricket Club set up a scheme to help young cricketers, with twenty boys being 'hard at it' in the nets in May. During the school summer holidays the club organised a series of matches, with a somewhat limited invitation extended to 'any boys from Public Schools staying in the district' to take part. Joe Hulme of Middlesex was engaged to coach a small number of the most promising boys. Whilst the offer of coaching must be applauded, the class-based exclusion of the next potential Compton, Edrich, Robertson or Smith demonstrated that parity of esteem between those from the state and private education sectors was still an elusive dream. Winchmore Hill Club in London ran a more inclusive initiative, charging boys aged from 10 to 16 five shillings – about £10 in 2021 value – for a weekly Tuesday coaching session and Friday match. Their colts section numbered thirty-three, despite the constraints of war.

Cricket administrators in Staffordshire had given serious thought to bridging the great gap between elementary schools and the senior clubs. For a long time school cricket had been well organised in the Potteries, with a popular league bringing many youngsters into the game, but on leaving school there had been a hiatus of about four years during which facilities were lacking to enable boys to play. The creation of several boys' clubs during the first year of the war sought to bridge this gap. The City of Stoke-on-Trent Boys' Sports Federation was formed and organised cricket leagues arranged for males of ages 14 to 20. Schools, Scout associations and youth groups joined, with 400 to 500 boys playing weekly, with good facilities.

Public school cricketers continued to be afforded the best opportunities. On 31 May, Edward Spooner, the younger son of the Lancashire and England batsman Reggie Spooner, scored 113 for Eton College against the British Empire XI, his century coming in just ninety-five minutes. Sadly, the Spooner family would experience tragedy two years later when Edward's older brother, Captain John Spooner DSO, 2nd Battalion Royal Fusiliers, was killed in Tunisia aged just 22.

* * *

As the blitz on English cities and the fighting across Africa escalated during the spring of 1941, cricketing casualties were inevitable. With the Christian names Arthur Wellesley, Captain 'Dooley' Briscoe was perhaps always destined for military eminence. His Test career for South Africa had been brief and unsuccessful, but upon the onset of war he joined the 1st Battalion of the Transvaal Scottish Regiment, alongside fellow Test players Bruce Mitchell and Ronnie Grieveson. Having seen action against the Italians in Ethiopia, Briscoe was awarded the MC before being killed in action near Dessie in Ethiopia on 22 April. He had gone forward to reconnoitre a position before leading his men into action, exposing himself to fire. He was 'prepared to take the risk rather than get his chaps into trouble', according to Grieveson. Briscoe was hit in the chest and died almost instantaneously.

William Basil Wilberforce.

Another cricketing name with noble antecedents was that of Lieutenant Colonel William Basil Wilberforce. Playing for C.J. Lyttleton's Army XI at The Circle in Hull against a team that included Major Herbert Sutcliffe, Wilberforce took two for 34 and made 21. Two years later, Wilberforce would be killed in action in Tunisia. He was the great-great-grandson of the instigator of the abolition of slavery in British colonies in 1833. As head of the family, William Basil had been involved in the centenary celebrations of this great historical event in Hull.

Harold Gimblett.

Captain P.F. Seagram of 48th Highlanders of Canada was killed by enemy action in London at the beginning of March while dining at the Café de Paris. He belonged to a famous Canadian family that had been intimately associated with cricket and had been a member of the Hon. R.C. Matthews' Canadian team that visited England in 1936. Meanwhile, Somerset's Harold Gimblett had a lucky escape during a raid on Bristol. A member of the Auxiliary Fire

Eric 'Budgie' Dixon.

Service, Gimblett was in charge of a trailer pump squad when two of his men were killed and another wounded. Gimblett himself was fortunately physically unhurt. Nevertheless, a perpetually troubled soul, Gimblett carried the mental scars of his experience long after war had ended. In 1947, he confided in umpire Frank Lee, 'every time a bomb fell there was a lovely, pink glow and it blew up a piece of someone.'

Yorkshire-born Eric 'Budgie' Dixon had made his home debut for Northamptonshire *v* Somerset in July 1939, scoring 128. Thriving on hard work, in the same term in which he captained Oxford University at cricket he took a Second Class in the Honour School of Modern History. Whilst serving as a sub lieutenant in the RNVR, his plane was lost near Libya on 20 April. A man who always put his team above himself, in his farewell letter he wrote, 'please think of me with smiles not tears'. Across the land club cricket mourned the loss of several of their number. Major John Huskisson had managed a batting average of 31 for the Buckhurst Hill Club in 1940, including one innings of 135 not out. He was killed in action in Crete on 27 May. His body was never identified, and he is remembered on the Athens Memorial. One survivor of the evacuation of Crete was Surrey and England's Freddie Brown of the Royal Army Service Corps, who was awarded an MBE for his efforts in the evacuation of the British Army. Twenty-five-year-old Private Robert Christie had won *The Mail* Cup in 1939 for scoring the fastest century during the Adelaide cricket season, his 100 coming in fifty-eight minutes. He died of wounds in Egypt on 7 May. His grieving mother recorded on his gravestone:

GOD HAS YOU IN HIS KEEPING, WE HAVE YOU IN OUR HEARTS.

* * *

The Cricketer reported that 'The war is causing well-known players to appear in all sorts of strange places.' Norman Yardley and Hedley Verity played for Strabane *v* Sion Mills in a Northern Ireland league match. Yardley made 57 and took three for 20 whilst Verity secured six for 62. Yardley also recalled a charity match, during which he and Verity posed for the latter's final ever cricketing press photograph. The commanding officer of the 1st Battalion Green Howards,

Lieutenant Colonel A.L. Shaw, was keen that his men were afforded the opportunity to play cricket whenever possible. He ordered the future England captain to 'nose round the locality' whenever they moved area to identify a ground on which to play. On one occasion the only suitable ground was at the local mental hospital near Omagh. Yardley, Verity and hospital manager Louis Walsh produced their own wicket, 'a very fine one'. The ground was tiny, about 40 yards wide, with a running track outside. Yardley recalled, 'In Ireland, while Europe was falling to pieces, we spent many pleasant months of a perfect summer.'

Norman Yardley and Hedley Verity during their service in Ireland.

It was rare for a side to reach three figures against Verity's bowling. Home on leave in late June, Verity turned out for Rawdon v Earby in the Airedale and Wharfedale League, taking all ten wickets for 51 runs. Across the island of Ireland, cricket became completely localised. No regional representative matches were played and there was only one match, Dublin University v Queen's University, between a Leinster and an Ulster club. Leinster CC won both their league and cup competitions.

As Verity, unbeknownst to him, was playing what would be the tail end of his cricketing career, a match in June between a Fathers' XI and Kimbolton School saw the last of 244 recorded centuries scored by 'The Master' Jack Hobbs. His friendship with the headmaster, William Ingram, also saw the great man coaching pupils at the Huntingdonshire school on Wednesday half-days. As arguably the greatest English batsman of all brought the curtain down on his own playing career, 28-year-old Pilot Officer Donald Fezard 'Hooky' Walker of 58 Squadron took off with his four-man crew in a Whitley bound for a raid on Cologne. On the return journey the aircraft was intercepted by a Messerschmitt BF 110 and shot down near the Dutch village of Best. Walker had been a popular member of the Hampshire team of the late 1930s, establishing a county 5th wicket partnership record of 235 with Gerry Hill. Walker's erstwhile county teammate, Army chaplain the Reverend John Steele,

D.F. 'Hooky' Walker.

recalled, 'he communicated to all he met his vitality, optimism, faith and his simple belief that life was there to be lived.' In addition to his cricketing prowess, Walker had captained the Dorset County Rugby Union team and the RAF rugby XV, and was a popular member of Bournemouth Sports Club.

* * *

As Winston Churchill sought to involve the USA more directly in the war through the summer of 1941, with MI6 planting fake news stories of British successes in the American press, Trinity College in Hartford, Connecticut, indicated solidarity with Britain's struggle with the staging of a match between English Students and the President's XI, held on 24 May, British Empire Day. King George VI's speech was relayed onto the field. A band of twelve Scottish pipers and drummers in kilts enlivened the proceedings by marching about during the intervals. When the match was over, headed by the pipers the whole assembly marched in procession round the field to the chapel, where a service was held, including an emotional rendition of the national anthem.

One of the match organisers, David Sexton enthused:

A banquet was held afterwards. As the United States does not suffer from such handicaps as rationing, it may be taken as read … that the concluding junketings included some 'swell eats'. The match programme included reference to cricket in England being 'not a mere game like golf, ancient and honorable though it be, it's an institution – like Oxford, Parliament and Tea'.

A toast was raised to 'The King'. W.S. Hinchman – an old Philadelphia cricketer who had been one of twenty-two Philadelphia Colts who had taken on K.S. Ranjitsinhji's XI during their 1899 North American tour – made a speech. Proceeds of the match, amounting to several hundred dollars, were donated to the British War Relief Society. Sexton reckoned, 'It is testimony to the genuine spirit of friendship for, and sympathy with, the British cause that so many people attended who had no knowledge of the game of cricket.'

Regrettably, cricket in New England was in a parlous state. Thirty years previously, a league of fifteen clubs existed, but that had dwindled to a mere trio, with boys preferring baseball or golf. Another factor in the decline was the decision taken on the formation of the Imperial Cricket Conference in 1909, that membership be confined to countries that accepted the British monarch as head of state. Inadvertently this forestalled the potential development of the game in Philadelphia, which had previously enjoyed several reciprocal tours with English teams. Cricket in the USA was left isolated in the march to align the international game with British Imperial interests. As the effects of global warfare hit the American game, the River Forest Club of Chicago was forced to disband, whilst the remaining nine clubs were forced to scratch fixtures owing to players being engaged in National Defence Programme work. The season extended from the beginning of May to the middle of October, with Winnetka CC winning all their league and cup matches.

The presence of British service personnel in the United States did lead to some fleeting reawakening of the game. In what was believed to be the first cricket match played in the state of Mississippi, Commander F.M.R. Stephenson RN, elder brother of J.W.A. Stephenson, led an Officers' XI against a Ship's Company XI. The chairman of a local shipbuilding firm kindly manufactured bats, stumps and bails. Spalding of New York sent down some proper cricket balls for the occasions whilst another local firm made pads and gloves. Gallons of Coca-Cola was provided for the spectators, who numbered about a hundred American ladies, all beautifully dressed, and 200 men. The pitch consisted of mud and sand and would have been treacherous had any bowler of significant class been present. During the Officers' innings, Commander Stephenson used a loudspeaker to explain to the spectators the rudiments of the game. The consensus from the crowd was that it was on the slow side and would never replace baseball.

RAF cadets arriving in Lakewood and Arcadia in Florida were surprised to find a high standard of cricket played by local inhabitants. They were soundly beaten by the former by 100 to 44 runs. Cricket in Arcadia dated back to 1936, when British residents raised a side to play HMS *Orion*. This novelty was so successful that the weekly cricket match became a commonplace feature of local life. Across the 49th Parallel, a match took place at Rideau Hall, Ottawa, between teams comprising British servicemen and local civilians. Robert N. Stuart played for the Peterborough Cricket Club of Ontario in a match against an RAF team when a week short of his 79th birthday. Stuart had played for Christ's College, Finchley, as a young man, against a team that included 69-year-old Charles Absolon, who had begun his career in 1838. Thus, more than a cricketing century was spanned. In Vancouver on 29 July, Bob Chamberlain took six wickets for six balls playing for Pro-Rec CC against Rowing Club CC, and all ten wickets for 13 runs.

* * *

Elsewhere in the British Empire, Brian Castor, secretary of Essex CCC, who was serving in Singapore, played some cricket with a former Essex wicketkeeper, Lieutenant Colonel Hugonin. Other cricketers on the island included D.V. Hill of Worcestershire and J.R. Cole of Surrey 2nd XI. Castor described the level of play of good London club standard, with two grass wickets at the Singapore Club and the Singapore Recreation Club. Cricket was popular throughout the country with excellent grounds at Kuala Lumpur, Ipoh and Penang. Castor and his colleagues would not long enjoy these facilities, as three and a half years of miserable captivity awaited them.

The Cricketer mused on the noble spirit shared by cricketing nations great and small:

> It is a significant fact that the most strenuous opposition to Nazi aggression has been provided and is still being provided by countries in which cricket is played. Apart from the various members of the British Commonwealth, the United States and Holland are two countries in which cricket has been played for many seasons. … The whole underlying spirit of the game is antagonistic to Teutonic regimentation. Had the Germans played cricket they would probably have been guilty of fewer enormities of which it is possible to say 'That's not cricket'.

* * *

Despite holding the line during the challenges that 1940 presented, English cricket entered the 1941 season with understandable trepidation. The Club Cricket Conference's AGM in March sounded a resolute note, with a determination to 'overcome all difficulties and carry on', but the number of functioning clubs had already fallen from 681 to around 400. Quite apart from the difficulties of raising eleven players each week, the preparation of reasonable wickets and general ground maintenance was proving to be considerable challenges. Lack of petrol and a shortage of labour meant infrequent cutting of the outfields, whilst one north London side had their motor mower blown to pieces during an air raid. The wandering Buccaneers Club had lost all their correspondence due to enemy action, so the secretary, W.G. Goodliffe of Gipsy Hill, had to appeal to clubs with whom they had arranged fixtures to contact him.

Another logistical problem was the transportation of bulky cricket bags. For away fixtures, most teams eked out their combined petrol allowances by squeezing as many men as possible into a few cars, thus leaving no room for luggage. The British Empire XI was fortunate when one of their honorary members, Mr Paget Bowyer, presented the side with a small trailer that could be attached to any car and hold a dozen bags comfortably. Despite the problems, much cricket did take place in the South East, with Ealing Dean CC winning thirty-six of the seventy-eight matches they played in 1941. Trevor Bailey, whose performances for Dulwich College were attracting favourable attention, turned out for Beckenham against West Kent Wanderers in August, taking seven for 9, including a hat-trick. Frank Edwards, the 56-year-old former Buckinghamshire bowler, was playing as an amateur for Slough as well as for a works team. Over the season he took nearly 200 wickets at single-figure average. Against Ealing Dean on August bank holiday he performed the hat-trick. London Counties played one of the prominent amateur London clubs, Southgate, in a match on behalf of the Army Comforts Fund. This was the their first visit to the famous ground and to enable the spectators to follow the game a special scoreboard, the work of one of the members, had been constructed. Forty-seven-year-old Jack Durston, one of the heaviest cricketers ever to appear at Lords, took five for 7 for the visitors.

The Conference's Emergency Fixture Bureau managed to arrange 783 matches during the season, and after two wartime summers a sum of £1,326 14s 0d had been raised for the Red Cross Fund. However, threats to the continuing existence of several conference clubs came from internal as well as external actors. The annual report stated:

> The preservation of all existing amateur cricket and other sports grounds has become a matter of serious importance and urgency. Schemes of great magnitude for reconstruction and rehousing are under Government consideration and prompt action in furtherance of these purposes will without doubt be inaugurated as soon as conditions permit.

It was argued that amateur sports grounds needed to be preserved for the use of people resident in cities and towns as, at the end of the previous war, many grounds were taken over and utilised for public and private building development. The Club Cricket Conference had joined forces with the London and Greater London Playing Fields Association to press the government on this matter.

Whilst many clubs and players kept calm and carried on, G.D. Martineau presaged the season's programme by bewailing how the horrors of modern warfare had meant the 'disappearance of the loveliest of athletic spectacles from so many green fields'. His article, 'Life Without Cricket', saw matches that were taking place that had an 'absence of the deep, full-throated ring' and were 'symptomatic of a barren age'. The turning over of many grounds for military use meant 'the tender turf blows uncared for, and the pavilion, used as an office by drab-uniformed warriors, assumed the hideous patter of dazzle-painting'. What playing fare was on offer was not 'real cricket', but a 'dim figure dressed in the glittering pageantry of remembered splendour'. Martineau's bleak conclusion was that the spring of 1941 brought 'sterile fields, life without cricket, a living death'.

Despite these challenges, practical and spiritual, the game went on, providing not just a window of relief from the stresses of war for players and spectators, but valuable monies for war charities. The newly appointed Club Cricket Conference secretary, Miss Joan Charmley, would ensure that the show went on in 1941. Some clubs were attracting well-known players, with Laurie Fishlock scoring 122 for Merton against the RASC in May, and Eric Bedser making 57 of Guildford's 121 against Malden Wanderers.

Whilst such players injected an extra layer of class into CCC matches, E.W. Swanton managed to stir up a controversy over the contrast between competitive

Laurie Fishlock.

league cricket in the North and Midlands, and the friendly fixtures that formed the fare of southern club cricket. A captain in the Bedfordshire Regiment, Swanton had been stationed in Liverpool. He reported in June: 'It has been a happy experience to play Northern cricket. They say it's fairly tame now compared with peace standards, but I can tell you there's a bite in it we too often miss in London.'

Swanton mused on the reasons why league and cup club cricket were so frowned upon in the South: 'it has never been clear to me what a man whose excitement mounts high over the chances of Middlesex beating Yorkshire in the County Championship may take as an almost personal affront the suggestion that his club, be it Hampstead, Highgate or Harringay, might for part of a league.' Talent in southern clubs was 'undisciplined and some unrecognised'. Swanton was particularly irked by the lack of punctuality in some matches, 'the outward and visible sign of slackness'.

Having played in the Liverpool and District League, a competition of relatively modest standard, with the club professionals acting as groundsman and playing on Saturdays without being outstanding stars, Swanton reckoned that the league system brought a higher standard of play. The fielding was more mobile, the bowling more accurate and the batting less inclined to slapdashness and the leadership more discriminating. Swanton wished to see southern cricket 'gingered up' by starting a league system. In a stinging conclusion, he claimed: 'But I know there are many who take cricket as an easy social relaxation, and they will like things as they are. I can never understand why these people do not play lawn tennis – which has the additional advantage of the ladies.'

Swanton invited A.W.T. Langford, a leading light of the Club Cricket Conference, to provide his views. The latter agreed there was 'unnecessary slackness' in the South and that many London club players would look favourably at a league system, many of them exasperated at the lack of keenness in some matches. However, the Conference Clubs as a whole would not vote in favour of it. 'There is no doubt that the Northern cricketer takes his cricket more seriously than the Southerner and league matches appear to suit his temperament.'

Further views were added to the discussion from correspondents to *The Cricketer*. One pointed out that during Esher War Weapons Week, several Surrey clubs had organised an evening knockout competition of twenty overs per innings. 'The competition of course was only a war-time expedient – but was it a case of coming events casting their shadows?' Another expressed surprise that so many southern players were in favour of competitive matches, but rejected the notion that gate money should be charged and collections made for individual performances. V.I. Robins was more withering in his response to Swanton: 'It may be that the atmosphere in competitive cricket provides some moral and intellectual uplift which is absent in non-competitive cricket and that sinners come to repentance. Or are they just cast into outer space?'

Second Lieutenant S.C. Spicer argued that southern league cricket would be 'a most retrograde step'. Club Cricket Conference matches were 'bright and keen'. A league programme would lead to 'a "win at any cost or failing that a draw" and the best goes out of cricket at once'. Spicer thought that the result was of minor importance in club cricket, and competition would kill the spirit of the game. He exhorted the innovators to 'Leave well alone and let those who are gallantly keeping the clubs running during the war carry on in the same spirit when peace comes'.

The exchange of views provoked no immediate change of organisation in the South, but it did lay the way for a more robust soul-searching of the gap between club cricket and the county game in 1948, in the wake of England's pummelling by Bradman's Invincibles.

* * *

Aside from the continuing divergence between the competitive North and pleasure-seeking South, 1941 English season's prominent fixtures again focused on raising money for war charities. R.J.O. Meyer took a strong XI to play Marlborough College in aid of the local War Weapons Week. The team included Stan Nichols, Arthur Fagg, Frank Lee, Harold Gimblett and Leslie Compton, and £22 10s 0d was raised. The keen alignment between the national summer game and the national cause was evident in a match in aid of the Royal Artillery and Royal Air Force Welfare Fund, held at the King's Heath Ground. The fixture had received the enthusiastic support of Ernest Bevin. The British Government had strained considerable sinews to evaluate the impact of morale on the conduct of the war, and the Minister of Labour and National Service fully endorsed the raising of funds for recreations and furnishings for anti-aircraft gunners and Royal Air Force men in isolated districts. A generous anonymous sponsor had already guaranteed £200 for the match, between a combined RAF and Royal Artillery XI and C.C. Goodway's XI. A festival feel was provided by the band of the Royal Artillery. Eventually, £392 was raised for the cause.

Despite the fact that the weather frequently interfered with cricket in 1941, some £1,075 was given to various services charities as a result of the big matches at Lord's. This was based on admission to the stands of sixpence, free for service members in uniform and MCC members and following deductions for entertainment tax, umpires' fees, payment to scorers and gatekeepers, provision of lunches and teas and players' expenses. The British Empire XI amassed over £2,000 during the course of the season, turning in some particularly fine performances. An almost full-strength Nottinghamshire side was overwhelmed at Trent Bridge, whilst Yorkshire, including nine county players, were forced to lower their colours at Bradford. Bertie Clarke claimed all ten wickets for 29 against the Metropolitan Police on 3 August and Ray Smith performed the hat-trick against Northamptonshire.

Jack Appleyard, secretary of the Leeds & District League, arranged several matches in the city, which raised over £1,000, a sum that paid for the endowment of a cricketers' bed at the Leeds General Infirmary. In one match, his invitation XI took on the RAF, with eighteen of the twenty-two players on show having played first-class cricket. Tommy Lodge, the Slaithwaite CC professional, took five for 51 for the RAF.

* * *

A great crowd revelled in a splendid Saturday's cricket at Lord's on the summer's longest day as the Army took on the RAF. The pavilion was thronged with members and a large party of generals lunched in a private room. Percy Perrin, the England selector, came from Norfolk for a few hours' spectating, the first match he had seen since hostilities began. Les Ames made his first appearance of the season. Having arrived at the ground with no cricket gear, he was quickly provided with a complete outfit and top scored in the match with 127 not out. The match was played under the backdrop of blue skies, newsboys calling out the latest editions and the turnstiles clicking merrily as 14,000 spectators enjoyed the occasion. This was the first in a four-match series between the two services. In July, the Army drew level in the series with victory at Trent Bridge. The RAF had racked up an impressive 259 for five due to a century from Paul Gibb and contributions from Charlie Barnett, Les Ames and Stan Squires. In reply, Joe Hardstaff and Maurice Turnbull steered the Army to victory. Of the 520 runs scored, none were in the form of byes thanks to the duumvirate of Kent keeping competence of Ames and 'Hopper' Levett.

The tournament moved on to the Yorkshire spa town of Harrogate in August, with Sergeants Len Hutton and Maurice Leyland scoring half-centuries on home turf and Peter Smith tweaking out five for 22 as the Army edged 2-1 ahead. Smith had previously been the victim of a cruel hoax, receiving a message summoning him to The Oval for his possible Test match debut in 1933. He arrived at the ground to face a bemused captain Bob Wyatt. Smith had also been selected for the abortive MCC 1939/40 tour of India. Justice would eventually be served as Smith achieved four Test caps immediately after the war.

The fourth match at Aigburth, Liverpool, as the city reeled from a week-long blitz pummelling in May, saw Peter Smith top score for the Army with 52 out of a total of 151. A sporting declaration by Brian Sellers allowed just enough time for the RAF to knock off the runs at a high tempo, which they duly did to draw level in the series.

To settle the competition, an additional fixture was arranged at Sheffield's Bramall Lane Ground, with the RAF clinching the series. Over 600 people had been killed in blitz raids on the Steel City, with the King, Queen and Prime Minister all paying visits to witness the devastation and sympathise with the bereaved. The deciding match saw the RAF win by 77 runs in the final over of the second day's play. Irish amateur cricketer J.A. Macdonald took nine for 70 in the RAF's first innings.

Another badly blitz-ravaged city, Coventry, staged a fundraising match between London Counties and Coventry and District in June. Over 1,000 people had been killed in major bombing raids in November 1940 and April 1941, and two thirds of the city's buildings had been damaged. As three hospitals were among those afflicted, the match was in aid of the Coventry Hospital Appeal Fund. Bob Wyatt scored a century for the Coventry XI, as did Leslie Compton for the southern visitors.

Service matches ranged from representative whole-service teams featuring many Test and county players down to the humble unit scratch fixtures. On Whit Monday, a strong RAF batting line-up including Charlie Barnett, Bill Edrich and Cyril Washbrook was bundled out for 51 by The Rest XI, with Essex duo Ray Smith and Stan Nichols claiming five for 11 and three for 18 respectively. Whilst top players received invitations to Lord's and other first-rate grounds, players lower down the pecking order often had to follow the wartime maxim of 'Make Do and Mend'. E.W. Swanton experienced at first hand the problems surrounding cricket in the Army: 'One ingredient you can take for granted: enthusiasm. When, last summer, the troops started work daily at 0330 Hours and carried on, breakfast intervening, until dinner, they were still happy to play cricket in the afternoon. The other two, ground and equipment, are often harder to come by.'

Swanton went on to recommend a concrete pitch with matting overlay in every village whilst recognising the hullabaloo this would cause amongst traditionalists.

August saw the Lord's debut of the Royal Naval College, Dartmouth, against the RAF's Air Training Corps. *The Cricketer* reported: 'It is good that the young members of our Sure Shield and of that Force to which "so many owe so much" should meet on the cricket field. They get to know one another, and this helps liaison.' Further down the scale, a match between the Second XIs of two unnamed RAF stations resulted in a total of one (scored by the last man) and bowling analyses of five for 0 (including the hat-track) for Balcombe and four for 1 for Paxton.

* * *

Action from Gezira Club *v* Australian Imperial Forces, October 1941. (*Australian War Memorial*)

Cairo's Gezira Sporting Club was the scene of many famous wartime matches. The facilities were laid out on the southern end of Gezira Island on land given by Khedive Tewfik to the British and included gardens, polo fields, a golf course, cricket pitches, squash courts, tennis courts and croquet lawns. A new clubhouse had been built in 1938 fronted by a swimming pool. A guide to Cairo for men in the services stated that that for 'All Soldiers, Sailors and Airmen of the British and Imperial Forces' part of the ground had been 'set aside … where you will find the green grass and shady trees a pleasant change, where you can watch regular Cricket matches, and take part yourself'.

The club employed the services of a cricket and tennis professional, Abdou Hassanein, a right-arm spinner considered by many to have been of English county standard. The main cricket ground was lined with exotic trees and had a large scoreboard and sightscreens. An immaculate outfield enclosed the matting wicket. The club was described as 'an oasis in Cairo' with a typical English pavilion complete with decorated afternoon tea tables.

General Archibald Wavell, at this time Commander-in-Chief Middle East, had played cricket at Corps HQ in Palestine during the Great War. Described as a more than useful batsman, and leg-break bowler of some skill, bowling faster than many of his type, he was keen that men under his command would have ample opportunities for playing and spectating. In July, a fully representative NZEF Base XI contested a two-day match against the Gezira Sporting Club. Despite containing many first-class players, including double international Eric Tindill, the Kiwis were defeated by over 100 runs thanks to some skilful bowling by Freddie Brown. In August, England captain Walter Hammond, serving in the RAFVR, scored a century in a match for the Gezira Club against a 1st South African Infantry Brigade side, which included Test players Dudley Nourse and Athol Rowan. In December, a Transvaal XI played the RAF at Johannesburg. Hammond gave spectators a taste of his powerful driving on the off-side, smashing the ball between mid off and cover and cover and point with terrific force during his 130. The Wanderers Club shouldered the entertainment expenses and the gate of £150 was divided between the RAF Benevolent Fund and South African War Charities.

Eric Tindill.

Bob Crisp described the mood at the Gezira Club during one July match: 'Rommel stood confident and menacing beleaguered Tobruk.' The South African quick took two wickets in one over, including that of Wally Hammond, 'the applause rippled round the khaki-crowded ground. The applause was for me, and I enjoyed it, as I always have done, but it could not drown the sound of distant gunfire.' Many of the soldiers sitting under the jacaranda trees had recently returned from Wavell's brief failure to regain the initiative in the Western Desert in Operation Battleaxe, 'as abortive as it sounded obsolete'.

In a further encounter between the NZEF Base XI and the Gezira Sporting Club on 19–20 September, Freddie Brown and Bob Crisp skittled the Kiwis out twice to record a comfortable victory, but the match was more notable for Maori troops entertaining the crowd with a song of welcome at the conclusion of proceedings. Elsewhere in Egypt, the Port Said International Sporting Club hosted a match between Navy House and an XI from a naval vessel. With the scores of all four innings totalling 76, it can be concluded that fun and frivolity rather than high skill levels were the order of the day.

Crisp had been involved in the Greek campaign and the retreat through Crete. In 1960 he wrote a classic war memoir about this experience – *The Gods Were Neutral*. He recalled his tank unit being poorly equipped and supplied, with the Allies having inadequate numbers to meet the Axis onslaught. He survived what he reckoned to be a hopeless task against overwhelming forces, persevering with honour to fight another day. In September, Crisp was among the wickets for the Gezira Club against a New Zealand Base XI. The Kiwis included Eric Tindill, Bill Rainbird and Jim Blandford, while Gezira had Charles Bray of Essex and Freddie Brown alongside Crisp, who took eleven for 67 in the match, which Gezira won by six wickets.

Away from the luxuries of the Gezira and other famous sporting clubs in Egypt, service personnel based at home and abroad were in need of fresh equipment in order to pursue their love of the game. The eminent entertainer and cricket fan Bud Flanagan wrote to *The Cricketer* on 28 June to appeal on their behalf:

Dear 'First Ball-Outers and Duckers'

… irrespective of how badly we play, or how badly we field, we love the game – there must be millions more like us in the Forces who are of the same opinion.

'Tis all right for us to sit up at Lord's seeing first-class cricket, but it must be heaven to have the cricket gear and play with the desert as a pitch – or even on some foreign plain – but how can you play the game anywhere if you haven't got the gear? So WE APPEAL TO YOU as sportsmen of the game that means so much to England – PLEASE SEND US SOME GEAR – CRICKET GEAR. If you have already magnanimously given – PLEASE SEND A DONATION, so that the FRANCES DAY'S PENNY FUND can buy some more to meet the many demands made upon Miss Day for these items!

The American actress Frances Day's Penny Fund provided the forces with sports equipment and other comforts, raising £10,000 by the summer of 1941.

An appeal was also made on behalf of a group of 'aliens' serving in the Royal Pioneer Corps. The was a group of various nationalities, mostly refugees from Fascist oppression, who had been permitted to join this corps. Having done fine work at Dunkirk, they were scattered across various parts of Britain, and

Cricket gear was in short supply, as this advertisement from *The Cricketer* suggested.

Australian troops play cricket in Tobruk. (*Australian War Memorial*)

several had watched some cricket. The game had appealed to them and they were anxious to start their own team but lacked equipment. The Central Office for Refugees, National Service Department, was the organisation to which spare equipment could be sent.

The keenness with which any opportunity for an impromptu knockabout match was seized by Australian cricketing troops was evidenced in the war-torn streets of Tobruk in 1941. While one of their number, Harold Pullman of 2/5 Australian Heavy Anti-Aircraft Battery, kept watch for enemy aircraft on a balcony, five of his comrades improvised a quick competition. The state of the wicket made batting a challenge.

* * *

Wartime cricket continued to play host to the unusual and bizarre. In a match between Carlton Hayes Hospital and Narborough in Leicestershire, a batsman was 'ploughed out'. The allocation of part of the cricket field for agricultural purposes led to this novel method of dismissal. A rule introduced by the hospital authorities stated, 'All balls hit over the new fence erected at the end of the ploughed portion of the ground are a penalty against the batsman. He will score four runs thereby but be adjudged out.' Sir Ronald Campbell, His Majesty's Minister in Belgrade, while awaiting rescue from the advancing Axis armies by the Royal Navy led his staff in a cricket match. Those who played in this remarkable match autographed a bat, fashioned from a piece of wooden packing case, which was presented to MCC by his brother, Sir Guy Campbell.

Cricket broadcasts, both live commentary and special features, continued on the BBC. On 25 July, in the series *The Crowd Roared: Famous Sporting Occasions Recalled*, Percy Chapman broadcast memories of the MCC Australian Tour of 1928/29. The following day a commentary on the London Counties *v* Northamptonshire match was given by Captain E.W. Swanton during the afternoon, with an account of the Ulster *v* Army XI match on the same day provided by A.D. May.

The thin gruel of county fixtures during the previous English summer prompted the organisation of a combined counties match as Middlesex and Essex took on Kent and Surrey at Lord's during the August bank holiday – the first such double county encounter since 1878. The former side struck 412 for six, with Middlesex's Bill Edrich making 102 and Essex's Sonny Avery 96. The Surrey and Kent side had reached 65 for three before rain ruined the contest. However, with a crowd of over 16,000, someone suggested a photo of Lord's should be taken and sent to Hitler to show, as Home Gordon related, 'how thousands in the most bombed town in the world stayed put and revelled on their Bank Holiday'.

Wartime matches often saw feats of fast and high scoring. However, there were examples of bowler-dominated games. On 16 August, a low-scoring affair at Lord's saw Pelham Warner's XI skittled for 87, with Glamorgan's Austin Matthews claiming six for 31. In reply, the RAF could only muster 61, with Surrey's Alf Gover and Stan Nichols of Essex amongst the wickets.

* * *

What was incorrectly reported as being the first women's cricket match to be played since 1939 was staged at the University Ground, Harrow, on 4 August. It was a one-day fixture between teams captained by the England all-rounder Myrtle Maclagan, serving with the ATS, and Megan Lowe of the ARP. Ten of the players were among those selected for the aborted 1939/40 tour of Australia. The putative captain of that touring side, Betty Archdale, was serving as a wireless operator with the WRNS in Singapore. Arriving in July 1941 at the head of a group of forty Wrens, Archdale was awarded the OBE for her work in assisting nurses to escape from the terror of the advancing Imperial Japanese Army. Lieutenant Colonel G.H.M. Cartwright, Secretary of Eton Ramblers, suggested that MCC should invite the WRNS, ATS and WAAF to play a triangular tournament at Lord's, but this proposal was not taken up.

By 1941, the women's game was restricted to charity, fundraising, or morale-boosting matches, with league competition suspended. The BBC women's team was discontinued but Nottinghamshire women beat Leicestershire women at Victoria Park, Leicester, the visitors scoring 65 to the hosts' 32. Over £300 was raised by WCA teams for the Red Cross. Following a break in 1940, the series of women's cricket matches instituted in 1938 in aid of Hounslow Hospital resumed on 6 September 1941. A Gunnersbury XI drawn from players from various clubs met a similarly constituted Wagtails XI. Future England player Megan Lowe starred with the match's top score of 27 and five for 24 for Gunnersbury. The evening saw a dance, cabaret and an auction to augment the hospital's proceeds.

The *Worthing Gazette* reported that the women of the town's ARP first-aid posts had taken up cricket, playing their first match at the Rotary Ground. Haslett Ladies took on workers from the Cissbury and Cresta posts. It was a low-scoring match, with the Cissbury

Betty Archdale.

Women from the ATS pose for the camera at Lord's.

and Cresta team winning by seven runs, the totals being 29 and 22, with extras being the top score in each instance. Miss Waites took six for 5 for the Cissbury and Cresta team whilst Haslett's star bowler was Mrs Paris, with five for 3. In the return fixture in August, the Cissbury and Cresta XI was again triumphant, with Miss Haynes scoring 25.

* * *

August 1941 marked the centenary of the Kent County Club's first appearance at Canterbury, a defeat against 'England' by 74 runs at the Beverley Ground in the Cavalry Barracks. To mark the occasion, the St Lawrence Beverley Club arranged a match against an Army XI, which took place on the August bank holiday. Before play began, the captains, H.F. Reed and Brigadier Robertson, laid a wreath at the memorial to Colin Blythe, the Kent and England bowler who had fallen in the previous war. Despite the lack of star names, 4,000 people attended. The band of the Buffs played in the afternoon, providing what one spectator recalled as 'quite a Cricket Week atmosphere'. The Mayor of Canterbury entertained 250 National Savings Group workers in the tea interval.

Kent CCC continued to accrue financial advantage from the war as 932 members' subscriptions enabled a profit of £359 6s 5d. Allowances continued to be paid to members of the staff in the services. The St Lawrence Ground remained intact, though increasingly threadbare, with post-war painting and repairs reported necessary. The ground had played host to seventy-three matches, mainly involving military or civil defence units against the St Lawrence and Beverley Clubs, who had amalgamated for the remainder of the war to pool resources. The collective spirit of the game was evident in the fact that Kent CCC members were permitted by MCC to use the pavilion at Lord's.

In one of the eight matches Nottinghamshire played at Trent Bridge, the former scourge of Australian batsmen Harold Larwood emerged from his cricketing purdah to help raise funds for war charities. Bowling at rapid pace, he took three wickets in four overs and was then taken off to prolong the match. His erstwhile county and England opening partner Bill Voce, who was appearing regularly for Hucknall, provided left-arm venom from the other end. Voce had made his first wartime appearance on a cricket field on 19 July, against Notts Amateurs, taking two wickets and scoring 40 runs. As one thrilling duo played out the twilight of their careers, young stars were on the rise. Cyril Poole, an 18-year-old from Mansfield Woodhouse, made 101 not out, alongside Reg Simpson (100 not out) against an RAF XI. Both men, valuable wartime finds, would go on to be county stalwarts in the post-war years and represent England. Simpson, whose night-time service with the Nottingham City Police left him free to play most weekends and many weekday evenings, scored 2,750 runs during the season. He shared another large partnership with Joe Hardstaff against Leicestershire at Trent Bridge, each recording centuries. As summer turned to autumn, some Nottinghamshire clubs were determined to wring the last drop of daylight from the season. Gedling Colliery played four matches during October, with their 60-year-old bowler H. Bettison claiming 177 wickets in the season.

Other counties managed a few token fixtures. Sussex were able to arrange five matches in 1941. Despite a combined age of over 90, Maurice Tate (three for 24) and Arthur Gilligan (four for 38) reduced the RAF to 133 at Hove on 31 May. It was not enough to stop the flyers winning on the first innings. John Langridge and Jim Parks were available to open the batting for the county against an RAF XI on 2 August. Despite an opening partnership of over 100 runs, the county, hampered by having to play with ten men, still slumped to a narrow 8-run defeat against an RAF XI led by their former captain, Arthur Gilligan.

Derbyshire managed just one match, against Nottinghamshire. Edgbaston was badly damaged by bombing, the practice shed being completely destroyed, but this did not prevent Warwickshire playing a few fixtures there, including an August bank holiday match against Midlands rivals Worcestershire, which formed part of the Holidays at Home drive. A reciprocal match took place at the New Road Ground, which was also used for numerous school and Civil Defence Service matches that summer. The programme aimed to reduce pressure on overcrowded transport services and coastal areas. Local authorities became the local agents for the government, and it fell to the clerks of the councils to liaise with entertainers, the committees and the public in order to create a successful programme of events.

Leicestershire also provided a series of matches to support the programme. Northamptonshire played against London Counties and, on 27 July, the British Empire XI in a memorial match in honour of the late R.P. Nelson. As the county won an exciting encounter by 2 runs, Mr Robert Nelson snr was present with members of his family. Before the tea interval a short ceremony took place when tributes were paid to 'Bob' Nelson by Desmond Donnelly, the Empire captain, W.C. Cooke, Northamptonshire chairman and Jack Webster on behalf of the Cambridge University Cricket Club. There were written tributes from Pelham Warner and R.C. Robertson-Glasgow. Cooke stated, 'Northamptonshire has had many gallant captains, but never a more gallant one than R.P.'

Ian Phillips, who had played a handful of games for the county under Nelson's captaincy, wrote a poem in his honour:

The Memory
The roared appeal rang round the crowded stand,
And in the hush that followed every head
Was turned, all eyes were focused on the hand
Of him who would pronounce the verdict dread,

The hand was up – the batsman came away with smiling face, nor any sigh
   of hate.
Fighting for runs throughout a desperate day
He too a chance and lost – that was his fate.
But he did more than hit a six or two
In that brief happy knock, to help his side;
His jaw was set, his bat was straight and true
When patient strength was all could stem the tide
He taught us how to play the game we love
And when the umpire's finger said him nay,
A lesson of importance far above
All else he taught – he smiled and came away.

Essex CCC returned a profit of £355 6s 4d in 1941, with about 600 members
paying full or part subscriptions. The club played twelve matches with district
sides, mostly schools. Arrangements were made for coaching juniors in April
at the Chelmsford Ground under the supervision of Jack O'Connor. A county
match occurred at the Clifton College Ground near Bristol between teams
representing Gloucestershire and Somerset in July. Sides comprised servicemen
stationed in the two counties. Somerset stalwarts Harold Gimblett and R.J.O.
Meyer were boosted by the presence of Essex's Tom Pearce and Frank Vigar,
and Kent's Tom Spencer, who thirty-five years later would umpire the first-ever
World Cup Final at Lord's.

Lancashire played a talented West Indian XI at Fazakerley near Liverpool.
A crowd of 10,000 saw Learie Constantine smash 39 from thirty balls. The
match was not played at the county headquarters as Old Trafford had suffered
significant war damage. However, an increase in revenue from subscriptions

Jack O'Connor.

(£1,814 in 1941 and £2,269 in 1942) ensured that Lancashire would be able to emerge in a strong position to face the post-war era.

Surrey continued with their Colts XI. On 30 August, Alec Bedser dominated the match against East Molesey, top scoring with 53 out of a total of 175, then dismissing the opponents for 50 with eight for 10. P. Wingate of Weybridge, playing for Surrey Colts, took five wickets in consecutive balls in early June. 'Bosser' Martin, the groundsman responsible for The Oval featherbeds of the interwar years, retired after fifty-one years' service, whilst across the Thames, MCC generously halved Middlesex's rental for using Lord's to £350, even though Middlesex played no matches.

Such county matches as did take place were insufficient to pay the wages of their playing staff. When the Cricketers' Fund Friendly Society met on 3 September at Lord's, Stanley Christopherson suggested that counties subscribe £5 or £10, as: 'People who are employing professionals have a definite duty to look after them and their health.' Christopherson also suggested that professionals should be made to join, at the cost of a guinea, when they received their county cap – a practice already in place at Yorkshire. One famous Yorkshire professional of a bygone era passed from the earth. August marked the death of legendary left-arm spinner Bobby Peel, aged 84. Peel had been famously sacked by Lord Hawke back in 1897 for presenting himself intoxicated on the field at Bramall Lane.

The popularity of county, military and scratch XI one-day fixtures led to a brief questioning of shibboleth that county cricket should be a three-day affair only. Plum Warner wrote, 'it is not easy to visualise the world after such a tremendous upheaval, but rightly or wrongly, there appears to be a general impression that it will not be feasible to devote three whole days to a county match.' He recalled that two-day matches had been a failure in 1919. Another suggestion doing the rounds was to reduce County Championship matches to one innings each. Warner invited comments but warned, 'The one-day match would play havoc with our time-honoured weeks and festivals and raise many financial and staff problems.'

R.C. Robertson-Glasgow, writing in *The Observer*, was typically acerbic in his condemnation of such sacrilege:

> No greater nonsense could be put forward. … During the war there has been a number of one-day matches between teams of first-class cricketers, and these matches have sometimes been called 'first-class'. They are not first class cricket, though they are often first-rate fun. … To think that such matches could provide in a County Championship in peace-time a proper test of strength or first-class cricket worth anything much is to think in a most substantial fog. …
>
> There are some advocates of such matches who point to the success of the Saturday League cricket matches, in the North and Midlands. Success

as what? As shows, featuring one or two stars and providing half-holiday fun, yes. As cricket in the sense of a first-class game, of complexity, of mental as well as physical effort, no.

First-class cricket stands or falls on standards evolved by past cricketers who knew what they were about ... not be show-men ... needs two, and possibly three days to unfold.

A leader in *The Times* concurred:

These one-day matches have been good to watch; but ... to be fond of the hedgerow is not to wish to abolish the beauty of the garden. There is room for every kind of cricket – the league cricket of the north, the three-hour match of Yorkshire villages at the end of the day's work, the two-day matches, the three-day matches and even the 'timeless' Test matches.

A letter to *The Cricketer* from James D. Coldham put forward the view that if one-day matches did continue after the war, the game of cricket would degenerate into 'The English Baseball, with no science remaining in it, brute force taking

its place, in order to force a result'. A desire not merely to stop the clock advancing but to turn it back to pre-First World War time was articulated by Edward C. Lee, who suggested that exciting play would be maintained by ensuring that amateurs provided the backbone of the post-war county game.

Home Gordon was more emollient about the nature of wartime cricket: 'It ... required Hitler with his satellites to regenerate our national game. At long last, in the past delightful season, has been demonstrated that the object of cricket is to make runs. However, he could not resist a swipe at pre-war professional batsmen for playing too dourly. Gordon's compilation of statistics from the 'big' matches saw Joe Hardstaff at the top with an average of 58.00 from his eleven innings, closely followed by Denis Compton and Sonny Avery. Yorkshire off-spinner Ellis Robinson topped the bowling averages with 21 at 11.09.

Joe Hardstaff.

* * *

The Bradford League continued to provide the most consistently high standard of cricket on show anywhere in England, with stars such as Learie Constantine, 'Jim' Smith, Manny Martindale, Alf Pope, George Pope, Bill Copson, Arthur

Wood, 'Buster' Keeton and Eddie Paynter on regular show. Enjoying the limelight previously shone on the Lancashire Leagues, spectators were plentiful. On one high summer Saturday, gate receipts from crowds paying 7d per head included £42 at Keighley, £41 at Undercliffe, £21 at Bowling Old Lane, £20 at Victoria and £22 at Saltaire. One match between Windhill and Lidget Green, with four renowned players in each side, ensured a gate of 5,000 and receipts of £91.

By and large, the professionals fully justified their contracts. In Saltaire's first three matches, Bill Copson and Alf Pope bowled unchanged, the combined totals of their opponents amounting to a paltry 123. Copson claimed sixteen for 48 and Pope twelve for 66. Lidget Green set a record for the two-and-a-half-hour time limit rule with 320 for four, with Sidney Martin, Worcestershire's South African batsman, making 122. West Indian Manny

Bill Copson.

Martindale had been appointed captain of Bingley. Playing in the Priestley Cup in June against Eccleshill, *The Cricketer's* Bradford correspondent eulogised: 'runs came with easy grace and rhythm. Martindale's beautiful display was inspiring, and the spectator could feel the joy each stroke gave to the batsman.' His 87, scored in an hour, included two sixes and fourteen fours. Relying more on ruthless efficiency, Eddie Paynter and Wilf Barber battled it out to be the season's highest run-scorer.

Wartime conditions meant that league affairs sometimes ran far from smoothly. One tragi-comic match took place between Saltaire and Great Horton. The former's three star bowlers – Copson, Pope and Townshend – were delayed by car engine trouble. After Saltaire had made 209 for three, their bowling trio had still not arrived, and Saltaire took the field with only two bowlers, neither of whom had been pressed into service thus far in 1941. However, a certain J.C. Laker stepped up to the mark, taking five for 37 as Saltaire won by 106 runs.

Stars from the league, including five Test players, turned out for a charity match against a Yorkshire XI at the city's Park Avenue Ground on 11 August. Receipts of £220 were handed over to the

Paul Gibb.

British Red Cross Fund. Batting first, the Bradford League scored 192 for nine, Eddie Paynter top scoring with 54. When stumps were drawn the Yorkshire side had scored 147 for four, with Paul Gibb (75) the principal contributor.

As the Bradford League entered its final phase, Windhill appeared to be closing in on a fifth consecutive league title, with a convincing win over Baildon Green. John Timms of Northamptonshire held their innings together with 86 not out, whilst Jim Smith and Learie Constantine bundled out the opposition for just 48 runs. However, nerves began to fray as Windhill then collapsed against Idle. Constantine and Smith had dismissed the opposition for 96 but Lancastrian Robert Rae took eight for 39 in eighty balls. A complete choke was avoided as in their final league match Constantine and Smith once again bowled right through the innings to restrict Keighley to 112 for two (Paynter 57 not out). This defeat consigned Keighley to relegation.

Saltaire were masters of all they surveyed in Division Two, claiming 52 out of a maximum 54 points. Bill Copson took fifty-nine wickets at 6.59 whilst Alf Pope headed the league averages with 69 at 6.49. The Roberts Park-based club also won the Priestley Cup, thus ending the season undefeated in league and cup cricket. The cup final between Saltaire and Undercliffe on 13 September was a tense and well-attended one. Nearly 8,000 people witnessed the low-scoring match, and the gate realised £236. Saltaire, electing to bat, were reduced to 27 for six before the captain, G.B. Haley, and Bill Copson put on 52 for the seventh wicket. This proved the turning point of the match as the total was hoisted to 102. Copson and Pope duly bundled out Undercliffe for just 44. The end-of-season tally saw Eddie Paynter topping the league batting averages with 838 runs at 52.37, just ahead of Wilf Barber with 704 at 50.28.

Cricket followers in the West Riding town of Huddersfield enjoyed an extensive sporting summer. The Huddersfield and District League's programme ran from April to October. Tommy Lodge was highlighted as a notable rising star, not yet 20 years old at the start of the season. The Slaithwaite CC professional, having made 140 not out against Marsden on 5 July, was called up to the forces. For the match against Elland on 16 August, Learie Constantine was engaged as a replacement professional but unfortunately there was no play possible and, as the Slaithwaite CC Centenary booklet put it, 'like the gentleman he is "Connie" waved his fee'.

The outstanding bowling performance of the season came from Fred Haigh of Dalton who returned ten for 11, nine bowled out and one caught and bowled. A different Fred Haigh, the

Alf Pope.

professional with Marsden, also managed a clean sweep of wickets, his ten for 66 against Huddersfield on 19 July including two hat-tricks. Bradley Mills played host to the twilight of Percy Holmes's career. The 54-year-old former Yorkshire and England opening batsman often batted alongside 14-year-old W.H. Bolt jnr, who scored a pair of not out fifties, benefitting from the mentoring of his veteran partner.

The white rose county's tradition of fine slow left-arm bowling was upheld with Fred Metcalfe taking nine for 23 for Primrose Hill and Speight eight for 23 for Kirkburton. With Elland winning the league championship and Holmfirth the Sykes knockout cup, members of the forces stationed in the area were able to play in the competitions, most notably Jack Buswell of Northamptonshire, who headed Kirkheaton's bowling averages with forty-seven wickets at 13.99 each. Freddie Jakeman, the future Yorkshire and Northamptonshire batsman home on leave from the RAF, scored 54 in Holmfirth's Sykes Cup semi-final win over Paddock.

To support the Holidays at Home scheme a match was played at Huddersfield's Fartown Ground on 6 August between sides collected by George Hirst and Wilfred Rhodes, the eminent sons of the town acting as umpires. Their influence brought together several well-known players, including Percy Holmes, Wilf Barber, Arthur Wood, Ellis Robinson, George Duckworth, Eddie Paynter, Denis Smith, George Pope, Learie Constantine and George Cox. Paynter, for Hirst's XI, top scored with 91 not out. A crowd of 3,000 paid £126 in gate receipts, with a draw for a bat autographed by all the players and the umpires bringing in £35. A very successful 'do', as they say in Yorkshire.

To allow all clubs to continue competing, it was agreed by the Birmingham League that players not required by their parent club could play for another league member, with each club limited to one professional per match. Both Aston Unity and Moseley were compelled to play all their matches away from home as one ground had suffered in blitz raids and both clubs felt unable to raise the necessary funds to keep their grounds open. Although fewer professionals were available, those who did play put in some fine performances. Not normally renowned for his run-scoring, with a first-class batting average of under 10, Tom Goddard

C.S. 'Stewie' Dempster held commissions in the Royal Armoured Corps and the Pioneer Corps. (*Courtesy Rob Franks*)

made consecutive scores of 140 and 106 for Kidderminster in May, whilst Kiwi Stewie Dempster proved a great acquisition for Smethwick in the seven matches he was able to play.

West Bromwich Dartmouth won the league largely thanks to the leg spin of Eric Hollies whilst Joe Mayer, the Warwickshire fast-medium bowler, topped the league averages playing for Walsall.

Several of the North Staffordshire and District League clubs had been hard hit by the demands of the war. Caverswall saw the tenancy of their ground, beautifully situated under Caverswall Castle, suspended. Neighbouring Longton agreed to the use of their ground for the homeless club's fixtures. A further challenge was a large-scale training exercise that took place in July. Several players who were members of the Home Guard and other Civil Defence organisations were unavailable for selection, causing mass postponements. Clubs often struggled to field a serviceable team. On one occasion in May, Stone were dismissed for just 9 by Great Chell, who ended up as winners of both the Eastern Group and the overall honours, beating Western Group's Bignall End in a play-off.

* * *

London Counties XI ended the season having chalked up thirty-eight matches. Many contests against club XIs were one-sided but the county players did slide to defeat on three occasions. One such was at Bedford on 6 July, when the local team was assisted by Les Berry of Leicestershire and Vernon Grimshaw of Worcestershire. In addition to the joyous entertainment the XI brought to cricket fans, £1,200 was handed over to war charities, including £350 to the Coventry Hospital and £296 for the Bexleyheath War Weapons Week. Denis Compton topped the batting averages, with Jack Lee leading the bowling averages with 47 at 8.19.

As the 1941 English season drew to a close a crowd of 10,000 saw the Army score 235 for nine on 6 September in the last of seventy matches played at Lord's, with Denis Compton contributing a century. This match was notable for the brief but glorious appearance of Compton's Middlesex compatriot Bill Edrich, who had recently been awarded the DFC. Squadron Leader Edrich was cheered all the way to the wicket, scored 4, then was caught by Compton on the boundary. He was cheered once more on his journey back to the pavilion. The match ended as a draw in fading light,

Bill Edrich.

reflecting the passing of one more English summer. Edrich might have owed his presence at Lord's that day, and on many subsequent gloriously successful days, to Worcestershire's Reg Perks. On the MCC 1938/39 tour of South Africa, Perks, sympathising with Edrich's loss of form, had given him a white elephant as a lucky charm. Edrich wore it on all his wartime missions.

In his memoirs, Edrich reflected on the incongruity of a pastoral cricketing setting amidst the devastation of war. One Saturday, his RAF squadron were due to play Massingham, a Norfolk village side. That morning the planes had been called out to assist with some shipping in the North Sea. Two had been lost. Substitute players were found, but the match seemed like a strange dream to the Middlesex man:

> The elms, the roses, the caw of the rooks; these joined the familiar sounds of ball on willow, and the cry of 'Owzatt?'... a sudden vision, as real as the other, of a 5,000 ton ship heeling over with pathetic little black figures scrambling up her tilting deck.

Edrich's mind flitted between the play and his fallen comrades:

> One's mind would flicker off to the briefing, and to joking with a pal whose body was now washing in the long, cold tides, and one saw again his machine cartwheeling down, flaming from nose to tail; and then a ball would roll fast along the green English turf and in the distance the village clock would strike and the mellow echoes would ring through the lazy air that perfect summer afternoon.

* * *

As whites were washed a final time before being packed away for the British winter, in North Africa cricket continued in the searing heat. By October, the North African campaign had suffered serious reverses with the failure of Operation Battleaxe to relieve the siege of Tobruk, with General Wavell being replaced by General Auchinleck. In the midst of this grave situation, British and Australian cricketers were dispatched from Libya to play in a series of matches in Cairo. It was considered that the morale that could be inspired amongst troops by watching the great cricketers of the peacetime years offset any organisational difficulties caused by their temporary absence.

Similar encounters took place between players from the Antipodes. On 7–8 October an AIF XI sought to gain revenge for the defeat inflicted on them by a NZEF Base XI the previous year. The Aussies were now bolstered with three Test match players – Lindsay Hassett, Ray Robinson and Alec Hurwood – and five Sheffield Shield players. The team had been provided with fresh flannels and long trousers for each of their tour matches and proudly wore an official tour blazer. Such was the interest in the contest that the Egyptian State Broadcasting

Cricket was a popular relaxation for Australian troops, whatever the conditions. Members of the 9th Division enjoy a match in the Alamein Sector, 1942. (*Australian War Memorial*)

Service provided ball-by-ball commentary across the two days. The meticulous preparations by the AIF were rewarded with a seven-wicket victory, in which Hassett scored a century. The future Australian captain was also in form during a tour of Palestine, scoring 107 and 63 not out whilst Alec Hurwood took five wickets against Palestine Police.

Tasmania's *Advocate* newspaper proudly reported on the AIF side's unbeaten tour, which ended in a resounding victory by an innings and 81 runs in a match billed as a 'test' between them and 'a crack eleven from the Gezira Sporting Club', which included England Test players Freddie Brown and Bill Bowes. Optimistically it was reported that 'the new A.I.F. team should offer almost as valuable a nucleus for future Australian Test sides as the historic team captained by Collins'. A 'large and exuberant contingent' of Australian troops enjoyed the entertainment; their 'barracking and cries of advice often brought roars of laughter from the rest of the spectators'. The tour saw success for Lindsey Hassett as he averaged 89.66 in his three innings. Sadly, this tour would mark the apogee of Australian cricketing success in North Africa. As Hassett himself recalled decades later: 'After beating Freddie Brown's side, we returned to our units – Bert Cheetham to Tobruk, Hassett, White and Hurwood to Haifa and later Beirut, Tripoli, Syria and Port Moresby: others to the Western Desert and eventually the Battle of Alamein, Jack Rymill ... of what was then Java.'

Members of the AIF XI relax at the Gezira Sporting Club.

Elsewhere on the African continent cricket took place wherever and whenever the opportunity presented itself. Walter Hammond took part in a charity match in between Kenya Kongonis CC and the Southern Rhodesia Armoured Car Regiment. The Kenyan club's historian recalled: 'The sun shone, the grass was green, never before had so many spectators congregated at a cricket match in Kenya and lastly but most importantly Hammond scored a typical and chanceless hundred … and by his modesty and charm made himself deservedly popular with all who met him.'

The Kenyan cricket season ran from July to March, when the long rains began, with C.V. Braimbridge, honorary secretary of the Kongonis Club, reporting that matches had proved an ideal method of providing hospitality for the troops, with half-day matches on Saturdays and full day matches on Sundays. Most matches were played at the Gymkhana Ground at the Nairobi Club, with boots with studs or nails prohibited on the matting wicket. The war had been a 'grand thing' for Kenyan cricket, with many famous players appearing, including Bruce Mitchell, Ronnie Grieveson, 'Dooley' Briscoe and Athol Rowan.

Many of those joining the South African military had been members of the 1935 tour of England. They had given themselves the moniker of 'The Sticklebacks' to perpetuate the good fellowship of that side and, according to Louis Duffus, to 'keep alive for all time those priceless things that England taught the South African cricketers: tolerance, patience, laughter, sentiment and above all, freedom'. Several had joined the Transvaal Scottish Regiment and won distinction in the South Africans' capture of El Wak on the border of Italian Somaliland. Herbie Wade took a commission in a Rand regiment and Ronnie Grieveson was to reach the rank of major and receive the OBE. Bruce Mitchell was in an infantry regiment whilst Dudley Nourse was stationed at Durban. A.B.C. 'Chud' Langton was a pilot in the SAAF and Eric Rowan was in the Tank Corps. 'It is the story of every man who prizes above life's material things those priceless possessions, liberty and fair play,' eulogised Duffus.

Two players who would have a significant impact on post-war Ashes cricket were keen to play their part in this sterner conflict. Disillusioned with life in the Australian Militia, Keith Miller quit on 8 November 1941. He and a friend attempted to join the Royal Australian Navy as stokers. When the navy would not take his friend, Miller tore up his paperwork in protest, left the recruiting office, and walked around the corner to the

Jim Laker.

Royal Australian Air Force recruiting office. Meanwhile, the 19-year-old Jim Laker volunteered for army service, giving a false age to speed through his application. After a period of infantry training in Leicestershire, he set sail from Greenock on the SS *Mooltan*, bound for service in Egypt with the Royal Army Ordnance Corps.

One player who could reasonably have hoped to have sparred against Miller and been a comrade of Laker's in post-war Ashes Tests was the popular Essex fast bowler Ken Farnes. Although teaching duties at Worksop College had limited his appearances somewhat, Farnes had still managed to take sixty Test wickets in his fifteen appearances for England. Having joined the RAFVR on the outbreak of war, Farnes had recently been commissioned as a pilot officer when, at 2310 hours on 20 October, his Vickers Wellington crashed shortly after an unsuccessful landing attempt at RAF Chipping Warden. The plane hurtled into the village, bursting into flames and killing Farnes on impact. Another of the crew died of his wounds the following day whilst a lucky third survived his injuries. *The Cricketer Winter Annual*'s valedictory read:

> It is indeed sad that never again shall we see stalwart Ken Farnes in the cricket field. Quiet by disposition and gentle, though so manly, in his outlook, his exceptional modesty about his own skill was a characteristic part of his attractive personality. ... He was an unobtrusively noble and valiant Englishman, deeply mourned.

The tragedy was felt around the world. Corporal L.W. Hall, serving with the RAF in Delhi, wrote to a friend:

> I wish to say how very sorry I was to see that Kenneth Farnes had been killed in action. This will prove to be a very big loss to Essex and England

cricket which has already suffered a hard blow in the death of Eastman. Farnes had given us much enjoyment and I share your regret at his passing.

Farnes's gravestone in Brookwood Cemetery simply reads, 'He died as he lived, Playing the Game.'

Although two seasons of wartime domestic cricket had been possible in Australia, the summer of 1941/42 saw the Imperial Japanese Army invade New Guinea. The ominous threat of the Imperial Japanese Army Air Service patrolling the northern Australian coastline meant that Australia's war effort was intensified. On 9–11 December the new Prime Minister, John Curtin, met with the state cricket associations of South Australia, Victoria, Queensland and New South Wales and it was decided to abandon attempts to continue inter-state matches for the remainder of the war. Two weeks later, laws were passed that banned the playing of organised sport on weekdays. This marked the end of any first-class cricket in Australia until the end of 1945.

The only first-class tournament that remained regularly contested throughout the war was India's Ranji Trophy. The 1940/41 iteration was won by Maharashtra, who in the three rounds amassed totals of 798, 518, 460 for three and 798 before vanquishing Madras in the final with a more modest 284 and 210 for four. The powerhouses of their batting were S.W. 'Ranga' Sohoni, Vijay Hazare and D.B. Deodhar, who scored over 1,800 runs between them. Deodhar's 508 runs at an average of 84 was all the more remarkable as he was 50 years old. George Abell captained Northern India against Southern Punjab in his final first-class match, a Ranji Trophy fixture at Lahore on 27–29 December. Abell had played for Worcestershire and Oxford University as well as a variety of Indian XIs, becoming the first man to score a double-century in his Ranji Trophy debut, back in 1934–35. Abell would later serve as private secretary to the final two Viceroys of India, Lords Wavell and Mountbatten.

Cricketing provision for ordinary service personnel stationed on the subcontinent was plentiful. On arrival in India, L.W. 'Laurie' Hall was posted to RAF Risalpur on the North-West Frontier, now part of Pakistan. 'Sport plays an important part here and there are facilities for cricket, tennis, soccer, rugby, golf, swimming, table-tennis and billiards. Bicycles can be hired by the day.' This pleased Hall, who commented, 'Personally, I should be very content if I am left here for the duration.' The cricket pitch was quickly put to use: 'On Friday evening a cricket trial match was held … As L.W. Hall retired pavilionwards after receiving one ball, he sorrowfully wondered what had induced him to flick that one ball into the wicketkeeper's hands! His own wicketkeeping was rather uncertain and a flick by one of the opening batsmen was deposited on the ground. Most unsatisfactory!'

Hall's knowledge of the game was put to good use over the following weekend:

On Saturday a team was selected to meet another bungalow in a knockout competition. This game was umpired by L.W. Hall. Another team was

selected for a further game on Sunday and L.W. Hall was in this team...
Owing to his innings of one ball in the practice, he found himself in last.
Wickets fell rapidly and the biggest stand was that for the last wicket,
which added ten runs. The closing score was 32 – L.W. Hall not out 3. Our
opponents had a strong batting side and passed our score with four wickets
down. There were no byes – the game was played on a matting wicket and it
certainly helped my wicket-keeping. It was much easier to judge the bounce
of the ball than on the bad grass pitch we played the practice game on.

Later in the year Hall was transferred to New Delhi and soon ingratiated himself
with a local club, Delhi CC. He had gone to the Delhi Cricket Ground to watch
the action and enjoyed a close encounter that swung the way of both sides.

The standard of play was quite good, being up to the average Saturday
afternoon game at home. Last Sunday afternoon part of another game was
witnessed. After the game, L.W. Hall was introduced to the Secretary and
was immediately told that if he liked to turn up in time for the start of next
Sunday's game, he would be in the team! It is not yet known whether Delhi
C.C. will be thus honoured, as Hall is right out of practice at the present
time and, incidentally, the class of play is rather above that to which he is
accustomed – still, one never knows!

Hall was indeed included in the team, which played away against Commercial
College on 30 November. The match was played on a matting wicket. The
outfield consisted of thick, dry dust, which made fielding difficult. Often the
fielder running in to gather the ball would scoop up a handful of dust as well as
the ball. The home team batted first and, aided by dropped catches, scored well.
Hall then took on the narrative, describing his contribution in the third person:

Before lunch Hall got his hand to a sizzling drive, shoulder high, but was
unable to hold the ball. Lunch was taken with the score at 110 for 6. After
lunch the innings was continued and Hall dropped an easy catch at point.
The innings eventually closed at 120 and Delhi were left with just two
hours batting. The bowling of the College side proved deadly and wickets
went as follows: 0 for 1, 11-2, 11-3, 13-4, 13-5, 21-6, 21-7. At this stage
Hall came in (he had asked to go in late as he was out of practice) and soon
settled down to play a back-to-the-wall innings. Meanwhile, the batsman
at the other end started scoring well and the first stand of the innings
developed. This stand lasted for 20 minutes during which 33 runs were
added. Then, with 54 on the board, a brilliant piece of fielding resulted
in Hall being easily run out and the scoreboard read 54 for 8, Last Man 5.
The innings closed a few minutes later for 59. Hall was invited to play the
following week but, unfortunately, was working on that Sunday and was,
therefore, unable to play.

L.W. Hall with Delhi CC. (*Courtesy Mike Hall*)

Aside from the joy of playing the game, Hall wrote of an evening cricketing companionship he enjoyed while stationed in New Delhi:

> L.W. Hall, together with two other airmen accepted the invitation of a certain Mr Abell to supper. The invitation, as set out in Orders, stipulated that those accepting should be interested in cricket – hence L.W. Hall's presence. On entering the drive to the house, it was observed from a nameboard that Mr Abell's initials were G.E.B., which seemed familiar. Later in the evening, it was discovered from the conversation that our host was G.E.B. Abell, the Worcestershire county cricketer. Upon enquiry it was ascertained that Abell had played against Essex at Leyton, Chelmsford and Colchester and knew most of the Essex players quite well. He mentioned Cutmore, O'Connor, Russell, Nichols, Freeman and others. A thoroughly enjoyable evening was had. The supper was excellent.

Hall would subsequently play his part in the development of a new generation of Essex notables. Running a primary school team in Leyton in the 1960s he had under his charge one young player who was 'really good – he'll be playing for Essex one day', the schoolboy in question being Graham Gooch. On Hall's final visit to a cricket ground shortly before his death, a fixture between Devon and Essex in 1991, Gooch organised tickets and sought out his old teacher to reminisce about those times.

Chapter 4

1942: Good Fellowship and Camaraderie

'A millionaire couldn't buy the friendships we built up.'
Geoff Edrich

The new cricket year began brightly in the Caribbean, with two matches taking place between Barbados and Trinidad at Port-of-Spain, half the proceeds of which were given to Authorised War Charities. The first match was played over four days in delightfully fine Caribbean weather. The large crowds could hardly have hoped for a more exciting finish with fluctuating fortunes. Trinidad had the final day to score 285 with all wickets intact but slumped to 59 for four. Then Gerry Gomez and Rupert Tang Choon put on 139 for the fifth wicket, Trinidad eventually squeezing home by two wickets. Gomez, the young West Indian, was carried shoulder-high into the pavilion by an excited crowd. The match was also notable for the first-class debut of 17-year-old Frank Worrell, a slow left-hand bowler who, according to *The Cricketer*'s West Indian correspondent, 'should make a very good cricketer. … He is quite a good bat and if taken in hand should get lots of runs.'

The start of the Barbados season saw the Trinidadian team make the reciprocal journey by air, their first experience of this method of transport. Kensington Oval's hard and fast wicket oozed runs, with 100 scored in the final hour of play by two schoolboys, Clyde Walcott and Frank Worrell. Derrick Sealy's eight for 8 dismissed the visitors for 16, setting a new record for the lowest first-class score in West Indian cricket, and paving the way for a comfortable victory by an innings. A second match between the two sides was reduced to a farce when a home umpire repeatedly no-balled the Trinidad spinner Mobarak Ali. In protest, Ali resorted to bowling underarm creepers. After calling Ali thirty times, the umpire relented, and the match was restored to normality. Trinidad maintained their unbeaten home record, which stretched back to 1906. By scoring 286 not out in the last match of the Trinidadian domestic season, Jeffrey Stollmeyer beat the previous record of 262 not out made in 1925. In Jamaica, the 'Black Bradman', George Headley, was working for the government's Labour Department while captaining his club, Lucas, with some success.

Australia had cut its projected programme of first-class matches for the 1941/42 season from eleven to eight. It transpired that only one would be completed before the Far East theatre of war erupted into life. State cricket associations swiftly showed themselves equal to the occasion by wiping out the remainder of the interstate programme, but the decision drew some criticism. Ray Robinson argued: 'The Australian people had long been working harder, under wartime strain and – taking a line from good attendances at football and horse racing – they would have liked to see first-class cricket, provided it had genuine competitive flavour.'

Prime Minister John Curtin expressed the hope that Ashes cricket would resume as soon as the war ended as 'a demonstration to the world of the characteristics of the British race'.

Most state players who had not volunteered for overseas service with the AIF were called up into the militia. Sid Barnes, who had made six centuries during the previous season, dropped out of cricket entirely to work in the aircraft industry. The eminent leg-spinner 'Tiger' Bill O'Reilly availed himself of the opportunity to play Sydney Grade Cricket, amassing the first of what would be a triumvirate of 100-wicket hauls in a season.

The New Zealand domestic season was similarly disrupted. The Otago Cricket Association had to abandon plans to play home and away matches with Canterbury and Southland. The Christmas season match between Auckland and Wellington was not played but the two sides were able to meet at Eden Park in early February, the former winning a high-scoring match by eight wickets. Canterbury too replaced their yuletide programme with a match against NZ Representatives. First-class status was awarded to some matches between military-based teams, such as North Island Army, South Island Army, New Zealand Army and Air Force teams. Other inter-services games also took place between Northern Military District, Central Military District and Combined Services sides.

* * *

The grimness of the war situation following the fall of Singapore and reverses in North Africa also threatened to restrict cricket in England. Sir Stafford Cripps, the recently appointed Leader of the House of Commons, announced on 25 February that certain sports, including boxing and greyhound racing, would be considerably curtailed as they were interfering with the war effort. 'Personal extravagance is to be eliminated. All wastage, all unnecessary expenditure is to be ended,' he declared. Pelham Warner took up the cudgels in defence of wartime cricket. Citing the positive impact that the previous two seasons had provided for morale and charity fundraising, he argued that many matches at Lord's and elsewhere featured services teams and people in service uniform were admitted free at the home of cricket. Prominent British Army, Royal Navy and RAF chiefs had stated that such arrangements were good for morale. All big matches raised money for service charities whilst careful planning of fixtures placed no extra strain on the railways: 'Cricket in these grim days is not of the slightest importance, but it has a definite use as a diversion in a very pleasant atmosphere for sailors, soldiers and airmen and those engaged on war work.'

Sport was one of the tools utilised by the British Government to maintain a sense of national identity, and therefore national purpose. Ernest Bevin's secretary had written to Warner requesting he send a team to the 'industrial north' after the fall of Dunkirk, and such compliance stood the game in good stead as restrictions increased. The government spent £50,000 on a poster campaign urging cheerfulness, and many agreed that a decent weekend's sports programme was worth a great deal more than that. The alignment of cricket and the coalition government's war effort was further amplified in a report in the *Manchester Guardian* of 12 March: 'First-class cricketers stationed or otherwise working in the North of England are co-operating with the welfare section of the Ministry of Labour, in providing a North of England cricket season in aid of funds to provide men in the forces with parcels and other comforts.' Matches had been arranged in Manchester, Liverpool, Preston, Blackburn, Stockport and Sheffield. A Lancashire XI would play against XIs of West Indies, RAF, Yorkshire, Cheshire, Derbyshire, South of England and Manchester and Division.

Wartime shortages meant that restrictions were placed on the manufacture of sports impedimenta. As clubs faced an impending shortage of cricket balls, R.W. Kelly of Ealing offered a 'Cricket Ball Renovation Service', which claimed to re-polish balls like new, at a cost of 2/6 each. His 'satisfied clientele' included Surrey CCC and members of the Lancashire League and Central Lancashire League. Stringent paper restrictions meant that *The Cricketer* had to reduce its frequency of publication from weekly to fortnightly. To compensate, eight additional pages were added to each edition.

On 15 February 1942, Lieutenant General Arthur Percival signed the surrender of British and Commonwealth forces in Singapore. Percival, the most senior officer amongst 140,000 troops who would endure three and a half years of degradation and misery, had previously been admired for his cricketing skills during his time at Camberley Staff College in 1923–24.

About 25 per cent of those taken prisoner by the Japanese did not survive the war. The victors had not anticipated such large numbers of men surrendering in 1942 and cared little for their new captives' welfare or indeed survival. Despite the constraints of captivity at Changi Camp, prisoners formed resilient communities which enabled morale, and therefore physical resilience, to remain at a level that would ensure the survival of a higher proportion of men. One of the unfortunate captives was E.W. Swanton. He recalled:

> In the days that followed shortly on the fall of Singapore … there was a certain amount of play on the padangs of Changi camp that really deserved the name of cricket. It is true that one never seemed able to hit the ball very far, a fact probably attributable about equally to the sudden change to a

particularly sparse diet of rice, and the conscientious labours of generations of corporals in charge of sports gear, for whom a daily oiling of the bats had clearly been a solemn, unvarying rite.

These Changi bats must have reached saturation point in the early thirties, and I never found one that came up lighter than W.H. Ponsford's three-pounder. However, the pitches were true – matting over concrete – and there were even such refinements as pads and gloves.

As the Japanese authorities saw little humanitarian urgency in informing captives' families of their fate, *The Cricketer* reported on 6 June that no news had been heard of Swanton, Brian Castor the Essex CCC secretary, or Francis Hugonin, who had played for Essex and The Army. It would not be until December that Castor's family would learn he was still alive. In mid-July, news reached Australia that Captain Ben Barnett, the Australian and Victorian wicketkeeper, had been reported missing: 'Indications are that he is a prisoner of war in Japanese hands.'

Cricket ball made by a civilian internee at Changi camp. (*Australian War Memorial*)

Olga Edrich was another spouse who endured a prolonged period of anxiety waiting for news of her husband. Geoff Edrich had played for Norfolk against the 1939 West Indies, scoring a half-century against the pace of Manny Martindale. Signing up for the 5th Battalion Norfolk Regiment at East Dereham, Edrich arrived in Singapore in January 1942 and was captured when the island fell in mid-February. Sent to Changi camp, Edrich and his fellow inmates would work for six days, having Sunday off. His battalion sports officer, Dick Curtis, had managed to carry a bag full of cricket equipment into camp. During the ensuring 'Test series' against Australian prisoners, Edrich scored 65 in one of the matches. Curtis even managed to access a typewriter and produced beautifully typed team sheets for the occasions.

In March 1943, Edrich was placed in a working party and sent to Thailand to toil on the Death Railway. He recalled many decades later: 'That was the worst time. Go out at daylight, come back at dusk. Every day. We didn't know what day it was.' Life became a repetitive cycle of 'Work,   Ben Barnett.

sleep, bit of rice, work', with fever, dysentery, tropical ulcers and cholera ever present to sap physical energy and morale. Things became so grim that Edrich was forced to sell his wedding ring to a Japanese guard in exchange for quinine to treat himself and other prisoners for malaria.

E.W. Swanton.

On liberation, the slight-framed Edrich weighed a mere 6 stone. Returning to England, the 27-year-old took the winter of 1945/46 to rebuild his strength and stamina, with fresh food from his father's farm and plenty of Guinness. As Lancashire were bereft of players, only four of their 1939 team being available, Edrich was given a chance by coach Harry Makepeace and gave the county sterling service for over a decade.

Another unfortunate captive was Len Muncer, then a useful lower-order batsman and occasional leg-break bowler for Middlesex. Muncer, a sergeant serving with the 1/5th Sherwood Foresters, was sent 'up country' on 1 November to work on the notorious Thai-Burma 'Death Railway'. Also assigned to the railway working parties was E.W. Swanton. Despite the inadequate diet and tiring and exhausting work, Swanton and his comrades still managed to find the energy to organise a cricket match. This took place on Christmas Day at Wampo camp, the first holiday the men had been granted. The camp guards thought that the match, which was played during the afternoon, had some kind of religious significance and so were reluctant to grant future requests:

> This particular game was notable, I remember, for what is probably the fastest hundred of all time. It was scored in about five overs by a very promising young Eurasian cricketer called Thoy, who, with graceful ease, kept hitting the tennis ball clear over the huts! Nothing, of course, could have been more popular than the victory of the Other Ranks over the Officers, but the broad lesson of the match was that the merit of any contest depends on the preservation of the balance between attack and defence. … For Jungle cricket our bat, surreptitiously made by the carpenter, was obviously too big.

Lieutenant Colonel Denys 'Hooky' Hill, who had played a few dozen matches for Worcestershire in 1927–29, was also captured. Later he would entertain fellow captives with a talk about county cricket from the captain's point of view.

The most prominent Australian cricketer captured was Ben Barnett, who had toured England in 1934 and 1938, the latter as first-choice wicketkeeper.

Barnett had been serving with 8th Division Signals in Singapore when he was taken. He would be incarcerated in Changi jail and then sent to work on the Thai-Burma Railway. A camp library was established, with works by J.B. Priestley, Evelyn Waugh and H.V. Morton included. E.W. Swanton's battered copy of the 1939 *Wisden* was donated. It had to be stamped by a camp official as being 'non-subversive'. Swanton would use the volume to recount tales of the 1938 Ashes series to prisoners yearning for a psychological connection to home and the good things of life.

Ern Toovey. (*Australian War Memorial*)

Ern Toovey, an ordinary seaman serving in the Royal Australian Navy, may have considered himself fortunate to escape with his life, having been on board HMAS *Perth* when it was struck by four Japanese torpedoes, sinking in the early hours of 1 March. Reaching the Javanese shore aboard a ruined lifeboat, Toovey's fortunes took a turn for the worse when he was captured by the Japanese. Of the *Perth*'s company of 686, only 218 would eventually make it back to Australia, their comrades being killed during or soon after the sinking, or succumbing to the ravages of Japanese imprisonment.

Toovey had the ingenuity and skill of Australian Army medics to thank for his post-war cricketing career. While suffering from a leg ulcer, it was recommended to Toovey that he undergo a leg amputation to save his life. He replied, 'You can't take my leg off because I've got to play cricket for Queensland.' During his time in camp, Toovey played association football against the Japanese, under strict instructions to allow the opposition to win. He also played some cricket with an ersatz cricket ball and baseball against some American troops. Beatings were common. One senior Japanese officer would kick men to the ground for refusing to bow to him.

Despite the physical and psychological privations he underwent, Toovey was able to reflect on those terrible years with clarity, dignity and humour when interviewed by David Frith in 1998. Commenting on the poor diet men were provided with, he quipped, 'I still like rice.' He refused to denounce the Japanese nation as a whole, stating, 'I would never hold it against the kids.' Finally, for a man who was a sportsman and a comrade to his core, he drew strength from those youthful years that were taken from him: 'A millionaire couldn't buy the friendships we built up.'

* * *

Conditions in German and Italian prisoner-of-war camps were considerably better than those run by the Japanese. Article 17 of the Geneva Convention stated: 'Belligerents shall encourage as much as possible the organisation of intellectual and sporting pursuits by prisoners of war.' A standard Red Cross sports parcel sent to prison camps would typically include two composition cricket balls among its contents. As the war progressed, cricket bats and stumps were added to the ensemble, with an average of 400 standard units sent annually from 1942 to 1944. Cricket would prove to be an extremely versatile and adaptable game, and a firm favourite in the camps. One survey of 173 inmates for an in-house camp magazine revealed that 76 per cent had taken part in a cricket match during incarceration. Whilst wickets were mostly concrete, Stalag VII-A, near Warburg, boasted a grass wicket and equipment donated by the De Flamingo club of Holland.

In March 1942, prisoners held at Oflag IX-A/H in Spangenberg Castle, Hesse, began to create a cricket pitch. A detailed description of the cricketing facilities in the camp was smuggled out and published in *The Cricketer* in June 1944. Its author, Lieutenant Terence Prittie, had been captured during the siege of Calais in May 1940, and had previously experienced two distinct varieties of prison cricket – one in the constricted parade ground of a Polish fortress, the other in a broad gravelled yard on the windswept Swabian plateau.

Oflag IX-A/H camp, located on a steep hill, seemed to afford very little opportunity for any form of cricket. A small courtyard 50 yards in length and 12 yards in width was the largest open area. However, its surface consisted of 'irregular and protuberant cobblestones'. Several rows of windows faced on to it and the damage caused would 'have levied a terrible toll on their glass panes'. Therefore, during March and April 1942, a levelling out of the 40-foot wide castle moat was undertaken. Around the inside wall of the moat flower beds bounded by a raised path were built. Prittie provided a sketch showing the dimensions of the impromptu 'cricket pitch'.

Wickets of the correct measurements were made from plywood boards propped up by stones. There were proper bats available but just one tennis ball, which bounced excessively on the earthen wicket. Soon wooden stumps were constructed, and Elastoplast was added as a covering to the tennis ball to minimise the high bounce and make it more receptive to spin. Lime was acquired and mixed with water to draw proper creases. Rain was infrequent, meaning the wicket had to be regularly watered.

The rules of matches played were largely the work of Flight Lieutenant Aidan Crawley, the amateur Kent batsman and future Labour and Conservative MP. Initially, eleven-a-side tip-and-run was played. Then ordinary cricket was played in two-hour chunks of two innings per side, each of thirty minutes, with any individual batsman retiring once he reached 20. A system of scoring was devised – one run into a flower bed. Hitting the ball over the wall incurred automatic dismissal. Straight drives were awarded four or six runs. Bowlers were limited to

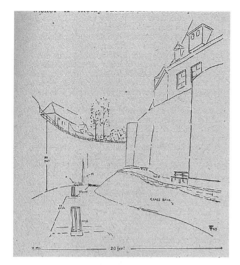

Spangenberg Castle PoW cricket pitch, drawn by Lieutenant Terence Prittie.

three overs per innings. To avoid excessive use of leg theory in such a restricted space, any ball more than a foot wide of leg stump was called 'wide'. During 1942 and 1943, cricket was played on at least 140 days per year, between April and October. More than 75 per cent of the camp played, 50 per cent of them regularly.

The terrace would be packed with onlookers, and 'club' fixtures arranged between Gunners, Green Jackets and Commando officers. Prittie wrote of some exciting encounters, summarising, 'Whatever we are missing, we might, after all, be worse off, for with a cricket-bat in his hands, the prisoner of war is rather nearer home than at any other moment of his existence.'

Donald Jones, captured by Italian forces and despatched to PG78 camp at Fonte D'Amore, near Sulmona, amplified the morale boost that cricket could bring: 'When I entered [the] camp ... very low-spirited, I was greeted by the sight of the inmates playing cricket. As a modest but enthusiastic club cricketer, my morale was sent sky-high.' Jones was later forced to abandon a planned cricket match to seize his chance to escape.

On 20 June 1942, the bespectacled Bill Bowes, whose demeanour was that of a kind university professor than a hostile Test match fast bowler, was one of 20,000 prisoners taken at the Fall of Tobruk. Also taken were Lieutenant C.G. 'Tim' Toppin, formerly of Worcestershire, G.J. Whittaker, a young Surrey 2nd XI batsman who achieved a Minor County average of 100 in 1939 for eleven innings, and Lieutenant D.H. Biggleston, captain of St Lawrence CC in the years preceding the war. From South Africa, 41-year-old Test veteran Bob Catterall and Threlfall Baines of Transvaal were taken prisoner.

Despite the privations of the ensuing years, 'grand team-work' would ensure the majority eventually reached freedom to enter a post-war life. Bowes reckoned the art of survival as a prisoner of war was the ability to live on one's wits and a not-too-full stomach – no mean feat for a man of his muscular 6ft 4in frame. Ingenuity and comradeship amongst men from diverse backgrounds formed the basis of survival and the flourishing of the human spirit.

Upon taking them prisoner, the Italian guards removing Bowes and his comrades from the front line to the back area carried out looting searches, stripping the prisoners of valued personal items such as rings, watches and cigarette cases. Entering a transit camp at Bari, it was time to 'face facts'. One of the dismal facts for Bowes was the diet, consisting of an ersatz coffee at 6.00 am, a bowl of soup with fruit for lunch and a further bowl of soup at 6.00 pm. This fare lasted for eight weeks before Bowes was moved on to PG 21 at Chieti, notorious for overcrowding and poor sanitation.

Bill Bowes.

Even in the grim struggle to defend the Libyan port, some troops were determined to find opportunities to play cricket. One serviceman contacted *The Cricketer*:

> Nowadays one associates Tobruk with tanks, dive-bombers, ships and guns, but one of our keenest supporters wrote not long ago to say that despite the fact that 'Jerry' was overhead he had 'had a darned good game of cricket'. Conditions were somewhat primitive and our correspondent informs us that the pitch was concrete, the bat a sawn Italian rifle and the ball a tennis ball.

Alongside Bowes in PG21 were Surrey and England all-rounder Freddie Brown, future Yorkshire batsman Harold Beaumont and C.G. 'Tim' Toppin. Bowes was appointed Sports Officer for the prisoners at Chieti, facing problems such as an initial lack of equipment and suitable space for most ball games. When it was possible to arrange organised sport, the periods of play had to be kept very short, since their diet denied the men any real energy. Initially, the Italian guards refused to supply tools, wood or nails that would enable sports equipment to be made, and scant supplies came through from the Red Cross. To make balls, torn or damaged clothing was collected. A competent leather worker was found amongst the prisoners. As illness, cold and lack of food reduced the appetite for sport through the autumn and winter of 1942/43, it would not be until the spring of 1943 that organised sport became a major pastime in camp. In the meantime, Freddie Brown agreed to give talks on cricket when asked, and later captained one of the sides that played in Chieti.

* * *

For Dominion troops who remained free from enemy capture, cricketing competition continued in North Africa. A South African Base Depot had been established at Helwan, within easy travelling distance of the New Zealand camp at Maadi, and in May the first of three international matches took place between the NZ Base XI and the South African 6th Division. It had been ten years since the countries had met at Test level. The first match, at the Maadi Sporting Club in May resulted in a narrow win for South Africa by two wickets. The second match took place at the Maadi Sporting Club ground, with Eric Rowan's 70 securing another victory for the Springboks. The last in the triumvirate of matches occurred on 11 October, with Verdun Scott's 109 not out salvaging some pride for the Kiwis. In the spirit of comradeship that characterised these encounters, Ray Mardon, captain of the South African side, presented his personal bat to Scott, who would go on to play in the first post-war test match in March 1946. The NZ Base XI completed fifteen matches that season across Egypt.

An inter-unit competition took place at the NZEF camp at Maadi, which saw Headquarters Company 'A' top the table, having won eighteen of their twenty-one fixtures. Bill Putt, who played for the NZ Field Ambulance team, achieved the double of 1,045 runs and 100 wickets in the series. Towards the end of September a match took place between New Zealand and South African First World War veterans. South Africa's Eric Rowan scored five consecutive centuries in Egyptian service cricket whilst Walter Hammond scored 129 and Bob Crisp took five for 26 in a Gezira Club v RAF XI match. S.K. 'Shunter' Coen of the Orange Free State scored 50 in two overs, finishing on 118 not out.

Also appearing in services cricket in Egypt was the Reverend G.L.O. Jessop, son of the explosive 'Croucher' of the Edwardian Golden Age. Jessop, in whose Fordington vicarage his famous father resided, had volunteered his services as a Royal Marine chaplain. He followed his father's fast-scoring batting approach, scoring 85 for the Marines against the Gezira Sporting Club on 21 June, and six days later, 149 not out in a Royal Marines total of 177 against a South African XI.

Across the Arabian Sea, in New Delhi, L.W. 'Laurie' Hall, a keen but modestly talented Leyton club cricketer serving with RAF Central Registry, came across a match being played at a school for deaf and dumb children. Writing in the third person, he recalled:

> Some of the boys, under the supervision of a master, were having a game of cricket and L.W. Hall became an interested spectator. He was soon recognised, however, and was invited by the master to have a look around the school. After this the master asked L.W. Hall if he would give a batting demonstration. This request was readily acceded to and L.W .Hall proceeded to the wicket. He scored eight runs and then, to the delight of the boys, he was bowled. He was then asked to show his bowling skill. Although he was out of practice, he agreed to bowl a couple of overs. His

cunning slows soon had the batsmen in difficulties and with his third ball he secured a wicket – caught & bowled. His final figures were 2-0-4-1. It is expected that the boys will long remember this visit.

Hall had become a popular member of the local Delhi Cricket Club and played for them against his own RAF Headquarters team, from which he had previously been omitted. He exacted his revenge with gusto:

The RAF batted first and, after an opening partnership of 15, they collapsed so badly as to be all out for 33 runs. Delhi started off with 27 for the first wicket and were soon past the RAF score. L.W. Hall was No. 6 on the batting list and, with the score at 122 for 4, to play the last ball before lunch. After the interval, Hall got off the mark by turning his first ball to fine leg for a single. At the other end he faced a left-arm slow-medium bowler and promptly sent him to the fine-leg boundary. He again had the left-armer for his next over and found him so much to his liking that he drove his fourth, fifth and sixth balls to the boundary. Such hitting is very unlike Hall but he was obviously feeling at home with the bowling and was intent on showing Air Headquarters that they had made a big blunder in not selecting him. We have never seen him use his feet to such advantage. The same bowler was still on for the next over and again Hall sent the ball flashing past him to the ropes. Later in the same over, he tried to repeat the shot but this time did not connect properly and merely skied the ball for point to take a good catch. The scoreboard read 166 for 5, Last Man 24. The partnership with Nain had added 44 runs in less than 20 minutes and Hall's 24 contained five boundaries. ...

L.W. Hall was congratulated by the members of the Delhi Club on his performance and was told how proud the club was to have him as a member. He was asked to make an especial effort to accompany the team to Meerut next Sunday but unfortunately he will not be able to make the journey. However, he hopes to have a few more games with them this season.

A subsequent match did take place, in which Hall represented RAF Headquarters against Roshanara Cricket Club. The club had hosted previous MCC sides including players of the stature of Jack Hobbs and Herbert Sutcliffe. Hall wrote: 'This ground is situated amidst semi-tropical woods and boasts a splendid pavilion.' Hall was also able to appear at the Delhi No. 1 Ground, described as the third-best turf wicket in India, for Delhi CC *v* India Sports. The opportunities the war provided for players of modest ability to tread in the footsteps of the game's greats were fully appreciated by Hall.

* * *

The first big match of the English season at Lord's saw Sir Pelham Warner's XI take on an Army XI over a Saturday and Monday. During matches at Lord's in 1942, both sides would change in the Middlesex dressing room, the pavilion's upper floor being out of bounds to members. Despite the rotten weather, 11,000 spectators watched the match and £180 was raised for war charities. During the rest day, the Army side, with the addition of Denis Compton, played a charity match at Beaconsfield, where £200 was raised for the Bucks Welfare Fund for Troops. Of the three branches of the services, it was usually the Royal Navy, for obvious reasons, who struggled to raise a team even remotely approaching their true strength. However, in Surgeon Lieutenant Ken Cranston they had discovered a batsman, tall, powerful, and orthodox, of whom it was hoped that more would be heard. A Royal Navy Air Station cricket team, 'somewhere in England', saw Major Lionel Tennyson top the batting averages. A Civil Defence Services team, including John Langridge, James Langridge, Leslie Compton and Frank Lee, easily overcame an RAF XI at Lord's on 4 July, whilst Major Leo Bennett scored a century for the Home Guard against the Eton Ramblers at Lord's on 7 July.

It was not possible to repeat the 1941 five-match series between the RAF and Army, as several service personnel had been transferred to the Middle East. However, in the two inter-service matches that were possible, the RAF trounced the Army at Lord's in June with a Cyril Washbrook century and five for 70 from Kent's Leslie Todd. The all-rounder was described by his county teammate Les Ames as 'a stroppy bugger but on his best days … a useful bugger'. In September, the return fixture took place as 14,000 spectators saw an exciting finish with the RAF finishing on 266 for nine (Ames 70) in reply to the Army's 291 for three. Nottinghamshire's whimsical Charlie Harris, after a meditative beginning, drove repeatedly through the covers in his 115. *The Cricketer* commented that 'Sergeant T.G. Evans, of the Army and Kent, showed very fine form as wicketkeeper. A discovery indeed.' However, Pelham Warner regretted that greater consideration had not been given to younger players in the selection of some of the representative service teams. He argued that Alec Bedser and Reg Simpson should have been in the RAF XI for this match rather than players well past their thirtieth birthdays.

Services cricket was frequently available to players of all standards. Pelham Warner's XI played Aldershot Command with Major General Roger Evans, commanding the district, present on the ground to spur his troops to victory. Playing for Southern Command against the RASC at Bristol on 25 July, 41-year-old Essex all-rounder Stan Nichols bowled unchanged for nearly three hours, sending down eighteen eight-ball overs and taking seven for 64. Despite also top scoring with 32, his team lost by 14 runs. Chelmsford hosted good class cricket on 4 and 5 July when Peter Smith's Army XI took on AA Command. There were good performances from Maurice Leyland, Frank Smailes, Brian

Sellers and Doug Wright for the Anti-Aircraft side, whilst Charles Palmer, who would later serve as president of MCC and chairman of the Test and County Cricket Board, scored 75 for Smith's team.

The Royal Australian Air Force XI was also making its mark with its enthusiasm and excellent fielding. In April 1943, a circular had been sent to every RAF station in the country asking all Australians who had played first-grade cricket at home to submit their names, clubs and past performances to selectors appointed to choose the representative RAAF team. The resultant team impressed one commentator in their victory over an RAF XI with their agility and 'comprehensive brio'. Although this early wartime iteration of the RAAF XI had yet to reach the heights of batting and bowling excellence it would attain in the second half of the war, their entertaining and exhilarating cricket provided a further boon to the British wartime cricket scene.

Cricket at Lord's abounded in tight finishes in 1942. On 30 May, the British Empire XI beat the Buccaneers, which included the Bedser twins, by 2 runs on the last ball of the match. Bertie Clarke bowled it to George Lambert, the Gloucestershire fast-medium bowler and often effective lower-order batsman. Lambert drove it high and far, into the off side. A boundary seemed certain but Les Thompson, running from the on side of the screen at the Nursery end, took a wonderful catch. Then, on 27 June, Cambridge beat Oxford in their university encounter on the seventh ball of the last over, when A.F.G. Austin, a slow leg-breaker, bowled out the Oxford captain, W.J.H. Butterfield. The year saw the best wartime attendance and charity fundraising at Lord's, with 89,299 spectators raising £1,397. MCC's 6,950 members decided collectively that the future of the English game would best be enhanced by providing a grant of £100 each to Oxford University, Cambridge University, Eton College and Harrow School.

The British Empire XI decided that all monies raised in 1942 were to go to Mrs Churchill's Aid to Russia fund. In doing so they became part of strenuous efforts to bring the previously demonised Red Empire into the collective conception of the Allied war effort. Desmond Donnelly wrote:

> It is a far cry from the sunny cricket grounds of England to the war-scarred road to Smolensk, but the writer is sure that all cricketers and cricket enthusiasts will join in an effort to send some small token of appreciation and admiration to a people whose service to humanity has been incalculable.

Donnelly, never one to leave an idea unfloated, also proposed a British Empire XI tour of England in the first post-war season, much in the manner of the AIF side of 1919. His ambitions even extended to the possibility of a British Empire XI touring India in the first winter after the war. He also suggested a regular R.P. Nelson Memorial Match and an end-of-season festival at a seaside resort:

> The aims of the British Empire Cricket Club will always be to try to bind still closer in peace the bonds that unite our great Empire in war, to play the

game in its happiest sense, free from the grim struggle for points and the cares of competitive cricket, and to carry on some of the good fellowship and camaraderie which characterises a nation at war, but was lost so soon after the last armistice.

Circumstances conspired that the British Empire XI would turn out to be a wartime-only enterprise. Donnelly himself would go on to serve as MP for Pembrokeshire from 1950 to 1970 and establish himself as a colourful character in politics and journalism before taking his life by his own hand in 1974. The make-up of the side began to change, with previously familiar faces missing due to the ever-increasing demands of the services. One new arrival would be Trevor Bailey, considered the best all-round public school cricketer of the war period. At the time, the man who would later earn the soubriquet 'The Barnacle' was considered an alert, attacking batsman with a splendid defence, a lively varied and judicious fast bowler and a beautiful slip or cover fielder. At Slough on 16–17 May, the hosts won a gripping match against the XI by 12 runs, with Frank Edwards' eight for 80 bowling them to victory. The Essex pair of Sonny Avery and Harry Crabtree each scored 116 as the XI demolished Wembley on 19 July, winning by an innings and 95 runs in one day. Ray Smith made a rare appearance against the British Empire XI for his eponymous Essex XI. He marked the occasion with twelve wickets in the match for just 35 runs as Essex won by nine wickets.

The XI played C.C. Goodway's XI at King's Heath, Birmingham, on 5 July, attracting a crowd of over 4,000. On 11–12 July, thoughts of the late Bob Nelson were in the minds of both sides as the Empire XI played Northamptonshire,

The British Empire XI take to the field at Lord's to play the RAF, 18 July 1942. (*Courtesy Peter Crabtree*)

winning by 89 runs. When close to full strength the British Empire XI was of strong county standard, attracting good crowds. They played thirty-four matches, winning twenty-three, losing five and drawing six. Bertie Clarke's leg breaks, delivered at a fast pace off a longish run, claimed 129 wickets at 10.17 each. He had the knack of unsettling the best and unhooking the weaker opponents, performing the hat-trick three times in a fortnight against Wembley, Harpenden and the Metropolitan Police. Ray Smith captained the team for most matches, with regulars including Sonny Avery, Harry Crabtree and Harry Halliday. Smith gave a wonderful display of hitting in a two-day match against Peterborough Town, amassing 138 in seventy minutes, including 32 in one over. By now the management committee included Pelham Warner and Stanley Rous, Secretary of the Football Association and prominent Red Cross fundraiser.

The British Empire XI's fellow wartime combination, the London Counties XI, again brought attractive and powerful cricket to districts not usually, even in times of peace, thus entertained. Many matches were won with something more than ease, with twenty-four wins and just one defeat in their thirty-seven matches, but the playing mattered far more than the manner of winning. Denis Compton headed the batting averages with 86.80, followed by Jack O'Connor's 64.25. The latter's tally included 100 not out at Abingdon on 6 June. Besides the familiar worthies of the Home Counties, the brothers Jack and Frank Lee of Somerset and 42-year-old Stuart Boyes of Hampshire – still a fine left-hand slow bowler and close fielder – gave their help. On one occasion, the Counties XI bowlers were put to the sword by Les Ames, who hit a two-hour century for Coventry and District at the city's Courtaulds Ground.

Jack Appleyard's Red Cross matches continued in the impressive setting of Leeds's Roundhay Park, bringing the total raised over the first three wartime summers to £2,500. This sum enabled the funding of two Red Cross Cricketers' beds at Leeds General Infirmary. Elsewhere in the city, The Leeds and District League was augmented for the 1942 season by the addition of a Royal Army Pay Corps team.

* * *

Hove staged a match every Sunday afternoon, to provide relaxation for the services, with no charge for admission. The majority of matches featured an RAF XI under the management of Pilot Officer H.P. Chaplin, captain of Sussex before the previous war. W.N. Riley, a former Leicestershire amateur, serving as Brighton's ARP Controller, arranged a 'Seven Services' tournament of twenty-two matches on Wednesdays and Saturdays between Navy, Army, RAF, Home Guard, Police, National Fire Service and Civil Defence. Matches were played on the time-limit system, and seldom did any team bat up to the full limit. Pleasant and keen as the cricket was, most of the scoring and wicket-taking was done by first-class players of tried ability, and, so far as Sussex were concerned, no new stars, let alone comets, whizzed across the sky. In one match the Police were dismissed in forty minutes for 13, Alec Bedser in devastating form with nine for 3. The tournament was won by the Royal Air Force, led by H.P. Chaplin. The Bedser twins were often prominent in bowling, batting, or both, and the bowling averages were headed by 18-year-old H.P.H. Kiddle. The youngster, a bomber navigator serving with 180 Squadron, would die on active service in April 1944. His plane crashed returning from a night flying exercise at Swanton Morley in Norfolk. Kiddle had been a fast-medium bowling contemporary of Trevor Bailey's at Dulwich College. The Royal Navy team, for whom Surgeon Lieutenant Ken Cranston batted very well, came second. Bottom place was taken by the Army team, led by the tireless Captain Maurice Tate. *Wisden's Notes of the Season* commented: 'The years cannot take away his length, but they have confiscated something of that wonderful "nip".'

Sussex were able to match the five fixtures they had arranged in 1941. One of these, billed as M.W. Tate's XI *v* A.R. Gover's XI at Bognor Regis, was a low-scoring affair, but £300 was raised for the Coast Regiment Fund as Denis Compton, Tom Pearce, Jim Parks, Arthur Gilligan and the Bedser twins appeared. Another match was against Denis Compton's XI, for whom Trevor Bailey took six for 29. Hove also hosted a match between a combined Navy and RAF side, for whom Eric Bedser scored 134 in a convincing win over the Army. The county also organised a Sussex League, giving a rare opportunity outside of the North and Midlands for truly competitive cricket. In the final match of the season at Hove, Southern Command played Western Command, with Eric Bedser taking four wickets in five balls, including the hat-trick and scoring 52 not out.

Derbyshire managed a solitary match, against Nottinghamshire. Gloucestershire's sole fixture was against an RAF XI. Surrey, unable to use their home ground of The Oval, organised a round of matches at the county's out grounds to give their Colts an opportunity to develop. Under the care and encouragement of Andrew Kempton, Surrey Colts drew from all classes of society. Kempton wrote: 'The lads who have comprised this side have come from Public Schools, Secondary Schools, and village clubs, and their enthusiasm for each other's success has made the experiment well worthwhile.'

Another splendid encounter took place between the combined Middlesex and Essex team against Kent and Surrey at Lord's during the Holidays at Home week. In front of a bumper August bank holiday crowd of 22,000, Trevor Bailey, announcing his presence in top-class cricket, took three wickets in his first over, ending with four for 36 as Sergeant Godfrey Evans led the opposition resistance with 55 out of a total of 193. Middlesex and Essex made 281, thanks to 51 from Stan Nichols. The Kent and Surrey second innings yielded 277 for six, setting Middlesex and Essex an improbable 190 in 100 minutes. Major Errol Holmes, returning to captain Kent and Surrey after a year's absence from all cricket, drove forcefully for his 39 and 114 not out. Denis Compton and Bill Edrich, in a foretaste of their sunshine batting of 1947, added 68 in thirty-five minutes, leaving 4 needed off the last ball to pull off an improbable victory. Compton advanced down the pitch ready to smite the ball over the boundary for six but missed completely and was stumped by Evans. Thousands left Lord's uplifted by such an enthralling and high-quality encounter and with the King George's War Fund several hundred pounds to the good.

Worcestershire and Warwickshire were in action at the Birmingham Cricket Festival at Edgbaston. The Lord Mayor of Birmingham had commissioned a cricket week as part of the Holidays at Home scheme to provide some relief for the city's munitions workers who had been hard at work in the workshop of Britain, whilst suffering particularly heavy hammering in the Blitz. An appeal was placed in *The Cricketer* for first-class players who might be available, promising that travelling expenses would be paid and hospitality arranged. Midlands cricket followers witnessed a Coventry District League XI beating a Birmingham District League XI. Warwickshire drew with an England Civil Defence XI with Bob Wyatt scoring 171 not out in three and a half hours. Harold Gimblett, Frank Lee, John and James Langridge and Leslie Compton appeared for the Civil Defence team. A Northern Command XI beat a combined Leicestershire and Warwickshire XI whilst a Birmingham League XI drew with a United Services XI. The festival underpinned a resilience in cricketing interest in the Shakespeare county, with Warwickshire CCC raising £705 through membership subscription, although ending the season with a deficit of £51, and being able to set aside £300 for repairs and maintenance. The festival week had raised £486 for the Lord Mayor of Birmingham's War Relief Fund.

The festival was the brainchild of Lieutenant Colonel Reginald 'Rusty' Scorer, a local councillor and a hard-working charity organiser. Scorer had played first-class cricket for Warwickshire in the 1930s and would organise successful festivals for four consecutive wartime summers. *Wisden* noted: 'his ambition to provide carefree cricket for the munition workers and citizens of Birmingham met with ready co-operation from the leading cricketers in the country, who provided grand entertainment in those four annual festivals for altogether nearly 140,000 people. Charity benefited to the extent of almost £10,000.' Scorer was an innovator. He employed loudspeakers to play music and broadcast announcements during interval breaks. This was a new way to ensure the crowd was being entertained and kept fully informed of all the action. A Holidays at Home month was organised by Worcester Council, which included twenty-eight cricket matches. A fourteen-overs per side knockout tournament was held at various grounds, with the final at the New Road county headquarters.

Kent's membership was holding firm, with 886 members paying all or part of their subscription, resulting in a profit of £172 1s 0d. An impressive 132 matches were played on the St Lawrence Ground in addition to three athletic sports meetings. The annual report paid tribute to the groundsman, without quite being able to acknowledge the hired hand with a Christian name or title: 'Great credit is due to Murrin for having prepared so many pitches.' Furthermore, it was made clear that MCC's 'kindly' offer to Kent CCC members to use the Lord's pavilion when visiting the famous ground 'does not extend to Lady or Junior members'. J.B. Murrin, who had been head groundsman for forty years, was to lose his home during an air raid and temporarily lived on the ground that he curated.

The ladies toilet was used as an explosives store. The Canterbury city authorities established a control room and air-raid shelter under the Concrete Stand, while the Iron Stand was used as a petrol store. The outfield hosted physical training by a local girls' school, cross-country practice by the Army motorcyclists, and Home Guard training. Across the war, an estimated 268 incendiaries fell on the ground's estate, 138 on the playing area, but damage was negligible. Kent CCC sought compensation for War Office 'dilapidations' and received £750. Despite these privations the Centenary of the Canterbury Week was celebrated with matches between Canterbury and District v Ashford and District Service XIs on the August bank holiday and fixtures involving Civil Defence and military sides. The start of the festival was marked by the laying of a wreath on behalf of Kent CCC at the Colin Blythe Memorial outside the ground.

Elsewhere in the county, the Angel Ground at Tonbridge hosted some cricket during the war, including a Frank Woolley XI v English Counties XI in August 1941. The ground's last-ever cricket match in 1942 was abandoned when enemy aircraft, returning from a raid in the London area, started to jettison bombs over the town. The military had also made use of the ground, causing damage. Heavy lorries motored over the playing area and the wickets were used as a dumping ground for stores, particularly prior to D-Day. Weeds flourished everywhere. Already in debt, the club had to put the ground up for sale and no further county matches would be played there. At Blackheath some limited cricket was possible despite eight bombs falling on the ground during the war.

Dover's ground served as the headquarters for a Royal Signals Unit and survived relatively unscathed. Maidstone's pavilion was requisitioned by the military, including the West Kent Yeomanry, New Zealand forces, and the Home Guard. The playing area was used by Maidstone Grammar School and the Royal West Kent Regiment. Tunbridge Wells' beautiful Nevill Ground served as a centre for the local Home Guard and was used for recreation and exercise by the XII Corps troops stationed in the area. Field Marshal Montgomery also used the ground for his strenuous pre-breakfast exercise.

The players and officials of Kempsey CC in Worcestershire sacrificed their club to the war effort. In February, its rented cricket field was ploughed over by orders of the War Agricultural Committee. The sale of the pavilion, shed, mower and sundry equipment raised £133, which the club forwarded to the Prime Ministers' office. Winston Churchill's secretary replied, expressing the PM's thanks. Cricket gear was stored, in order to start a new cricket club in Kempsey after the war.

* * *

As the first-class counties soldiered on providing what wartime playing fare circumstances would allow, thought was being given to the structure of the post-war domestic game. MCC called a meeting of the Advisory County Cricket Committee on 8 December, a group to which, opined R.C. Robertson-Glasgow, 'belongs the ripest knowledge of what kind of cricket is likely to prove convenient, entertaining, and, at the same time, cricket'. Committee members were asked to consult with their counties and return for a meeting the following summer. All first-class counties with the exception of Derbyshire were represented. The preponderance of those with military and aristocratic connections was notable. Bold innovation was unlikely to emanate from such a traditionalist collective:

MCC: S. Christopherson (President), Lt Col Sir Stanley Jackson, Lord Cobham, W. Findlay, Sir Pelham Warner, Col R.S. Rait Kerr
Essex: A.J. Spelling
Glamorgan: F.D. Pipe
Gloucestershire: Lt Col H.A. Henson, F.O. Wills
Hampshire: Col W.K. Pearce, W.H. Sprankling, W.R. Ponting
Kent: Lord Cornwallis, J.R. Mason
Lancashire: T.A. Higson, Maj R. Howard
Leicestershire: Sir Julian Cahn
Middlesex: R.H. Twining, Maj G.O. Allen
Northamptonshire: Lt Col T.E. Manning
Nottinghamshire: Sir Douglas McCraith
Somerset: Brig E.H. Lancaster
Surrey: B.A. Glanvill, H.D.G. Leveson Gower, A.F. Davey
Sussex: Sir Home Gordon, W.L. Knowles
Warwickshire: Dr H. Thwaite
Worcestershire: Lord Cobham
Yorkshire: E.F. Holdsworth
Minor counties: C.B.L. Prior

Plum Warner reckoned that keen competitiveness on display during the Essex and Middlesex *v* Surrey and Kent match 'gave a very clear indication that the general public will greatly welcome a return to county cricket after the war'. He floated the possibility of regional leagues running alongside the County Championship.

Another concern for some was the post-war provision of amateur county cricketers. It was recognised in the Notes and Comments section of *The Cricketer* that most of the cricketers emerging from the public school milieu 'will be so busy keeping the wolf from the door' that little time would be left for county cricket. This would be of particular concern to counties such as Middlesex, who had employed only forty-four professionals in 1878–1937 compared to Yorkshire's 128. Nottinghamshire had only featured thirty amateurs in the same period. Ric Sissons has calculated that between 1919 and 1939, the percentage of County Championship appearances by amateurs fell from 39 to 19. Home Gordon expressed sympathy for the plight of the professional county player who had missed out on his potential benefit match since the start of the war. Once the conflict was concluded, counties in a perilous financial situation might be reluctant to allocate a big match to a professional. Furthermore, that player's cricket powers and thus the amount of money he may have attracted could have waned in the interim.

This theme of the amateur/professional divide would be revisited in R.C. Robertson-Glasgow's *Wisden Notes on Season 1943*, in which he called for a more fundamental change in the class structure of cricket, suggesting the distinction should be abolished. For 'Crusoe', the cricket field was a place of 'good company among players of all ages and all walks of life' on which 'effortless and enduring friendships' could be fostered. The removal of the artificial construct of 'Players' and 'Gentlemen' meant 'the sweeping away of anachronisms and the exploding of humbug'. Practices such as amateurs and professionals using separate dressing rooms, and entering the field of play from different gates, were the more overt symbols of this disjoint. Furthermore, professionals were expected to address an amateur as 'Sir', 'Mister' or possibly 'Skipper'. However, some professionals did prefer having a distinct changing room in which they did not have to curb their language or moderate their behaviours and during the 1930s there had been few strident calls for reform or abolition of the divide. Cricketers and cricket followers tended to identify with club, county or even region rather than view the game through the prism of the British social class structure.

It was not just amongst the players that class divides were evident. Cricket was riddled with forms of exclusion. Differentiated access at most grounds to pavilions, grandstands and popular sides at county grounds emphasised the difference in social backgrounds of spectators. Socially exclusive clubs, often based on previous attendance at a particular public school, received extensive coverage in the cricket press. Yet in the context of the great slump of the 1930s, low pay, unemployment and slum housing were more pressing matters than cricketing structures and practices.

Nevertheless Robertson-Glasgow argued that even if an amateur were not paid directly for their playing contribution, the publicity their exploits attracted meant extra clients in their business lives. Thus, cricket was the indirect source of their livelihood. 'Crusoe' was not ignorant of the continuing existing of 'a very few' amateurs whose private means enabled them to play for expenses only: 'Long may cricket encourage and be encouraged by such men. Their unbiased leadership and natural generosity have served cricket honourably and long,' but they were 'survivors of an almost lost society, of an age that is nearly gone'. The absurdity of placing a professional's initials after his surname on the scorecard and having him enter the playing field by a different gate to his amateur teammates 'have long seemed vastly absurd'.

The interwar years had seen the professional cricketer reach new heights of respectability, with a handful moving on to county committees. Jack Hobbs, Patsy Hendren, Wally Hammond and Herbert Sutcliffe were, according to Ric Sissons, 'erudite, assured, polite, middle class and successful', acting as role models for other professional cricketers. Underpinning that respectability in the case of Hobbs, Sutcliffe and Hendren was a strain of religiosity. Hobbs was a regular churchgoer, Hendren a devout Roman Catholic and Sutcliffe a pillar of the Congregational Church. The quartet had risen from disadvantageous starts in life, Sutcliffe and Hendren having been orphaned at a young age and Hammond's father having been killed in the Great War.

By 1939, Len Hutton was emerging as the standout representative of the new generation of the respectable professional and would eventually be appointed as England's first full-time professional captain in 1952. Whilst the war would not directly lead to a change of heart on the amateur/professional issue amongst MCC and county committees, the general wave of egalitarianism that swept through post-war Britain would eventually make such anachronistic attitudes increasingly marginalised. The officer commissions and distinguished war records of professional cricketers such as Les Ames, Bill Edrich, Bill Bowes, Herbert Sutcliffe, Alf Gover and Hedley Verity made it difficult to argue that only men of independent means would make great leaders.

* * *

The Bradford League had provided the most successful league cricket in Britain during 1940 and 1941. Big money spent on professional fees had come pouring back through the gates. Windhill announced a profit of over £400, both Undercliffe and Bingley around £300. For 1942, Windhill would have to manage without Learie Constantine but had poached Bill Copson and Alf Pope from newly promoted Saltaire. The latter recruited George Pope from Lidget Green. By the beginning of the season, the league could boast that forty-one Test players had graced its grounds over the course of both world wars. Maurice Leyland and Paul Gibb had joined Undercliffe and Lidget Green respectively. Only three clubs had no professionals – Bankfoot, East Bierley and Great Horton. Signing top-class talent from around the world was not an automatic passport to success, as Great Horton surprisingly beat Windhill, with their five county players, by six runs.

Eddie Paynter began the season reeling off runs like a machine for Keighley, with his six consecutive scores of over 50 setting a new league record. Captain R.T. Bryan, formerly skipper of Kent, was a popular addition to the Bingley side – 'the most cultured amateur batsman in the league', according to *The Cricketer.*

One of the notable features of the Bradford League was that, with so many of the younger players having been called up, many of the clubs were glad of the help of men who normally might have been considered too old for the game. Many veterans who figured in the league thoroughly justified their comebacks. 'Charlie' Lee, aged 52, was still good enough to open the batting for Saltaire having made his league debut back in 1911. T.A. 'Sandy' Jacques, the former Yorkshire fast bowler whose first-class career was blighted by injury, passed 500 league wickets in his seventh season. The only bowler to date who had finished as premier bowler in the league more than Jacques' four occasions was Sydney Barnes, nine times.

On 18 and 25 July, Tommy Mitchell, the Derbyshire spinner and former coalminer, representing Lidget Green, took eight for 33 and nine for 48 against Windhill and Great Horton respectively. These performances nudged his team towards success in a very tightly contested Bradford League. In the final match of the season Mitchell and his partner A. Bastow established a remarkable record by claiming all 144 wickets their team took that season. Taking three points from Idle was enough for Lidget Green to be crowned champions. Eddie Paynter topped the league averages with 970 runs at 138.55. His fellow Keighley professional Manny Martindale provided the bowling complement to Paynter's batting, ensuring promotion to Division A for their club. *Wisden* praised the standard and style of play in the Bradford League: 'specimens were provided of a type of play, intense, competitive, and enjoyable, which may yet become the standard first-class game of future years.'

A special match to mark the seventieth birthday of Ernest Holdsworth, Chairman of the Cricket Committee at Yorkshire CCC, was arranged by Bowling Old Lane, the club of which he had been a member for sixty years, twenty-seven of them as captain. He bowled one of the best overs of the game and smote a mighty six. The Bradford League secretary F. Milton Watmough alliterated, 'Few men have such a passion for the game as this very virile veteran.'

The Huddersfield and District League saw new players stepping up to replace those such as Holdsworth, the Huddersfield all-rounder who had been reported missing in Malaya. Bill Andrews, the Somerset all-rounder, joined Slaithwaite whilst a call went out for more umpires to preside over matches. On 1 August, the final of the league's Sykes Cup took place at Fartown. Thongsbridge could only muster 63 runs, making for a straightforward win for Linthwaite, disappointing the neutrals in a 5,180-strong crowd, who paid £158 1s 10d at the turnstiles. Fenton Brook of Almondbury scored 200 runs in two hours against Lockwood, out of a total of 270 for seven. This was only the third ever double-century in the league. Another notable performer in the league in 1942 was 14-year-old Eddie Leadbeater, a future Yorkshire and England leg-spinner. One of seven regulars aged 18 or under put into the field by Almondbury, Leadbeater had already come to the notice of George Hirst.

In the Birmingham League, West Bromwich Dartmouth won the championship for the second year in succession, largely due to the skill of Eric Hollies, the England and Warwickshire leg-break bowler. Once more, 48-year-old Harold Kirton (Mitchells and Butlers), who had played two matches for Warwickshire in the 1920s, showed fine form as a batsman, heading the league averages with 68.40 for ten innings. Most clubs still engaged professionals, but Aston Unity continued their wartime nomadic existence due to the unavailability of their ground. In the Durham League of ten teams, Sunderland Police made a welcome appearance and finished third. South Shields won the tournament for the fourth time.

The North Staffordshire and District League was forced to cut the number of competing clubs from sixteen to ten, with Leek being included on the proviso that they would not have to travel to away matches at Bignall End and Silverdale. Nantwich were unable to continue due to excessive travelling demands whilst Caverswell had lost their ground, and Porthill and Fenton had lost too many players to continue. Crewe Rolls Royce applied to join but were rejected due to the travelling commitments this would have meant for many clubs.

One Central Lancashire League case demonstrated the emotional and psychological strain under which many players turned out in front of large and demanding Saturday crowds. Lionel Montague 'Monty' Cranfield, a Gloucestershire leg and off-break bowler, experienced a nervous breakdown during service with the Manchester AFS and was put onto farming duties. Cranfield had been playing for Castleton Moor in the Central Lancashire League in 1941. The *Rochdale Observer* noted that he had 'badly damaged a hand at work' and was not 'thoroughly fit for several games'. The same newspaper on 18 April 1942 hoped that Monty would be able to join his father, Lionel, in playing for Castleton Moor 'as the warmer weather arrives … during the past winter he has been down with pneumonia'.

* * *

The Club Cricket Conference sustained itself for a third wartime season. Highgate CC managed to run two Saturday and one Sunday sides whilst Ealing Dean CC succeeded in surpassing 100 completed fixtures, which allowed R.D. Gardiner to set a new club record of 165 wickets. A.W.T. Langford reported that club cricket, despite so many familiar faces being absent on war service, was 'generally in a surprisingly flourishing condition', with some clubs playing on until October. One of these was Gedling Colliery in Nottinghamshire, who once again could proudly boast matches across seven months of the year. H. Bettison, well into his sixties, took over 150 wickets in the season. In London cricket, the prolific Len Newman extended his career tally of centuries to 211 whilst Trayton Grinter, the former Essex amateur and Frinton CC captain, reached the 200-century landmark. Grinter's achievement was all the more remarkable given a handicapped left arm caused by a severe wound he sustained at the Battle of Loos in 1915 while serving with the Artists Rifles.

The club game would provide players with memories to treasure and pass on to their grandchildren. On 29 August, the match between Hornsey and Southgate produced a remarkable last wicket stand. T. Plant and R.W. Somerville of Hornsey stayed together for the last hour and thirty-five minutes, added 79 runs, and saved the match. Although an astonishing number of clubs were able to keep going despite the war, the wandering sides almost entirely disappeared. A few decided to continue by arranging one or two matches a year. For example, the Buccaneers played the British Empire XI and the Stoics managed to play an annual game with Sutton.

In a match played at Leamington on 13 September, Captain G.A. Palmer, briefly of Warwickshire CCC, took a hat-trick in unusual, possibly unique circumstances. Playing for an Army XI v Lockheads Hydraulic Brakes Engineering Co., he bowled three balls of identical flight and pitch, to which each batsman played the same sort of stroke, the ball ending up in the hands of Sergeant Antrobus in the gully on every occasion. Brighton Electricity played their annual Christmas Day morning match in Preston Par against St Mary's and St Anne's CC, with the former winning by one run. One 14-year-old making a mark was R.J. Attawell, who made 119 out of East Molesey's 190 for seven against Cheam in June. Attawell would play for Surrey 2nd XI after the war. Trevor Bailey turned out for Beckenham on four occasions, scoring 101 against the Metropolitan Police.

Inevitably for others the season was far from smooth. On 27 August a formation of a dozen FW190s flew over Folkestone. On the county ground adjoining Cheriton Road a match was taking place between an RAMC Field Ambulance XI and the Folkestone Police XI. A 500kg bomb screamed towards the pitch, exploded near the wicket and killed Lance Corporal H.J. Harris, who was fielding at square leg. His comrade, Private C.D. Sincock, was seriously injured and Police Sergeant Alfred Gray, watching from the boundary, was hit by shrapnel. Chief Constable R.C.M. Jenkins was trapped when the stand collapsed.

Lætitia Stapleton, a lifelong Sussex CCC devotee, recalled a dramatic event at Hove in her cricketing memoirs:

One Saturday afternoon there was a tip-and-run raid on Brighton and a bomb fell in the south-east corner of the County Ground. The Secretary called out, 'Lie down!' as the plane zoomed towards the pavilion. Fortunately, the bomb failed to explode, and the ground was quickly cleared. Arthur Gilligan, who was playing in the match, records that Maurice Tate, his hand in his mouth in that characteristic gesture of his, said, 'What a nerve! Fancy them doing that to US!'

To support the Holidays at Home campaign the Public Schools Wanderers Club arranged an extensive programme of fixtures across the first fortnight of August. Restricted to those boys whose parents had bought them a place at such a school, the event was permitted to use the grounds of Guy's Hospital, Honor Oak CC and Dulwich CC. Prospective public school players were invited to submit their particulars to the organisers to ensure only the accepted classes of people were involved. More meritocratically, George Hirst continued to comb the county of Yorkshire for youthful talent, watching over 1,000 youths across the three ridings through the summer months.

It was reported that Roman Catholic schools were continuing to play cricket on a Sunday, as the practice of Sabbath play became more widespread. Home Gordon described how Sunday cricket was played at Hove for the first time, provoking but one letter of objection, from the Lord's Day Observance Society. Down in the far south-west of England, S. Canynge Caple, who had written *The Cricketers' Who's Who* in 1934, was serving as an assistant master at Pendragon School in Tintagel. One of his duties was cricket coaching, with many of the pupils being evacuees from the bombed areas. Fired with enthusiasm at their willingness to learn, and excitement at three talented 'finds', Caple appealed in *The Cricketer* for donations as the boys' parents could not afford cricket gear.

* * *

Women's cricket continued. Netta Rheinberg ensured a group of West London women could continue playing by combining members of different clubs, but the annual WCA week at Colwall was once again deemed out of the question. During one match at Finchley, women had to dive for cover in the face of aerial machine-gunning. The British Empire XI took on an All-Star Women's XI at Harrow's Headstone Lane ground. Future England bowler Megan Lowe was recounted to have 'bowled a West Indian first ball, something which still rankled twenty years later'. Myrtle Maclagan described herself as 'being exhibit "A" in a match between Officers and Sergeants. On the basis of her performance she was asked to play for the Royal Artillery by Captain James Macdonald, who had played first-class cricket for Ireland before the war.

* * *

The 1942 *Wisden Cricketers' Almanack* appeared on a restricted print run of 900 hardback editions and 4,100 softback. The space given over to obituaries of young players cut down in their prime increased, while further grim stories mounted up ready for inclusion in the 1943 edition. Newspaper pages devoted a depressingly rising number of column inches to eulogies for the dead. Cricketers around the world laid down their lives in the cause of freedom. A.B.C. 'Chud' Langton had played fifteen tests for South Africa in 1935–39. In the 1938/39 'Timeless Test' Langton had bowled ninety-one eight-

Chud Langton.

ball overs, the fifth highest workload in Test history. He had made valuable contributions to South Africa's first-ever Test victory in England, taking two for 58 and four for 31, and making 44 batting at No. 8 in the second innings at Lord's in 1935. In November 1942, while serving as a flight lieutenant in the South African Air Force, his Lockheed B34 Ventura bomber spun and crashed on landing. The young sportsman rests in the Maiduguri Cemetery in Northern Nigeria.

Although not directly related to the prosecution of the war, the death of the popular dual international and FA Cup winner Andy Ducat brought sadness across the cricket world. Playing for Surrey Home Guard against Sussex Home Guard at Lord's on 23 July, 56-year-old Ducat collapsed at the crease and died suddenly of a heart attack. Cecil Somerset, a member of the Sussex General Committee who had been fielding close by, told Home Gordon:

> Oddly enough, as Ducat came in I thought that though the oldest, he looked by far the fittest man in the match. He ran a very short run and before he had quite recovered his breath played the next ball. It was a yorker and he jabbed it hard with the bottom of his bat. Then he fell down, collapsing, and though his pulse just flickered for half a minute, he was completely unconscious and death was virtually instantaneous.

Bob Attwell, a chemist from Cranleigh, was batting at the other end at that fateful moment. He recalled several decades later:

> Andy hit the ball past me to mid on … I was returning to the crease after backing up and I heard a gasp … I turned round and saw Andy on his back. All I could do was remove his false teeth, give his heart a thump, and give some massage and artificial respiration but it was all to no avail.

It was Attwell's final match before joining the Army, 'not the most pleasant of send-offs', he reflected.

On 17 December, Charlie Walker, who had toured England as a reserve wicketkeeper on the 1930 and 1938 Ashes tours, was serving as an air gunner on an Avro Lancaster in 14 Operational Training Unit. In a mission over Saxony his plane was shot down, killing the whole crew. Flying Officer F.S. Haden, RNZAF, was killed on active service. He was one of New Zealand's most promising cricketers, having played for Auckland. The previous year Haden had formed and captained the first RNZAF cricket team to play in England. In July 1942, the announcement of the tragic death of D.A.R. 'Sonny' Moloney reached his NZEF comrades back at Maadi Camp. Second Lieutenant Moloney had died of wounds on 15 July, after being taken prisoner at the First Battle of El Alamein. The bespectacled Moloney was a hugely popular figure who had played three Tests for New Zealand on the 1937 tour of England.

Sonny Moloney.

South Hampstead CC were due to host a RNZAF XI on Sunday, 3 August. Sadly, the eleven became nine as Clarrie Lund of the YMCA Club in Auckland and Reg Lees had been killed a few days beforehand. The home side provided two extra players for the Kiwis. A further RNZAF player, Hurricane fighter pilot J.S. Jones, was killed in action eleven days before he was due to play at Lord's.

Outwardly Horsham CC's ground remained unchanged after nearly three years of war, but in the somewhat old-fashioned pavilion there had been erected a tragic reminder of the ravages of war – a wooden memorial tablet commemorating brothers Pilot Officer Peter Guy Campbell Wood, RAFVR, killed over Cologne on 31 August 1941, aged 20, and Sergeant Navigator Eric Ian Campbell Wood, RAFVR, killed over Essen on 9 March 1942, aged 22.

Lieutenant Colonel F.G.B. Arkwright, killed in action in Egypt on 1 July, had played for Hampshire and The Army, as well as in many service matches in Cairo and Tidworth. He had won the MC during the Battle of France serving with the 12th Lancers. Captain Richard Tindall, King's Royal Rifle Corps, was killed in Libya. He had won his blue at Oxford in the early 1930s and played Minor Counties cricket for Dorset up to 1939. On 22 January 1942 Tindall was killed in an air raid. H.S. Altham wrote: 'He made friends as naturally as the sunshine scatters the mists of morning, and there was never a friend but was the happier and better for his friendship.' Sub Lieutenant G.J. Adams was killed while on active service with the RNVR only a week after his marriage. He was a cricketer of outstanding promise, being in the Bishop's Stortford side from 1934 to 1938. In 1937 he scored three centuries in four matches, including 100 not out against a powerful MCC side. He was serving on HMS *Argus*.

Pilot Officer Claude Ashton lost his life on 31 October. A well-known cricketer, association footballer, hockey, rackets and fives player, Ashton was one of a trio of brothers who represented Cambridge University and the Corinthians at football and their university at cricket. Aged 41 at the time of his death, Ashton was far above the accepted age for admission to combatant duties in the RAF, but he would not rest content until he found himself in the air, commencing operational duties in 1941.

Claude Ashton.

Serving with 256 Squadron, Ashton was the observer in a Bristol Beaufighter piloted by Roger Winlaw which collided with a Vickers Wellington near Caernarfon. Thirty-year-old Winlaw had played fifty-two matches for Cambridge University and Surrey before taking a post as a master at Harrow School, turning out for Bedfordshire in Minor Counties cricket during the summer holidays. 'Two very gallant gentlemen,' mourned *The Cricketer* at this double loss to the game and the country.

Roger Human, a softly spoken history master at Bromsgrove School, had been a surprise selection for MCC's abandoned 1939/40 tour of India. During the war he had played for British Empire XI *v* London Counties XI at Reading on 21 June 1941. A solidly unspectacular performer but amiable team man, Human did eventually reach India, serving as adjutant in the

Roger Human. (*Worcestershire CCC Heritage Collection*)

6th Oxford and Bucks Light Infantry. Sadly, Captain Human died of a brain haemorrhage on active service on 21 November 1942. Private John Robertson of 5/7th Battalion Gordon Highlanders, a stylish batsman and one of the finest fieldsmen in Scotland, was killed in action at El Alamein. Robertson was captain of Aberdeenshire and had represented Scotland. Robertson had been

Stan and Elma Sismey.

something of a prodigy, selected to play for his county aged 15, and possessed, to an admirer, a mind 'at once original, well balanced, fertile and profound'.

Hubert 'Trilby' Freakes had played ten Currie Cup matches for Eastern Province from the age of 17, scoring 122 not out against Natal aged 17 years and 10 months. He gained a Rhodes scholarship to Magdalen College, Oxford, and played Rugby Union for England. Having joined the RAFVR, Flying Officer Freakes was attached to the Royal Air Force Ferry Command, delivering new aircraft from factories in Canada and the United States to British air bases. The sporting all-rounder was killed on 10 March 1942 when a bomber he was piloting crashed at Honeybourne Airfield, Worcestershire. His grieving parents donated a magnificent memorial shield to be awarded as a trophy for the annual house cricket competition at Maritzburg College. It is still awarded today.

One who narrowly escaped being added to the roll of honour was New South Wales wicketkeeper Stan Sismey. On 18 May he was the co-pilot of a Consolidated Catalina flying boat journeying over the Mediterranean off Oran, French Algeria. The Catalina, assigned to No. 202 Squadron, RAF, based at Gibraltar, was attacked by three Dewoitine D.520 fighters belonging to the Vichy French Air Force. Sismey received multiple shrapnel wounds in his back as the crew made a forced landing in the sea. Sismey and his comrades spent eight hours in the Mediterranean as their aircraft sank and dogfights took place above them. The unconscious Sismey and the rest of the crew were eventually picked up by the British destroyer HMS *Ithuriel*. Sismey retained many metal fragments in his body, joking that there was so much shrapnel in his back that the compasses of the aircraft he flew were affected. Sismey did not return to operational duty for two years, then was offered a posting to the RAF as a test pilot.

* * *

No matter in what outpost British and Commonwealth forces found themselves, cricket was organised. In the Pacific Ocean, men of the NZ Forces took on a Fijian side evenly balanced between native players and those of Western extraction. The Kiwis played the match at the beach-lined Lautoka Ground dressed in khaki. The NZ team, including Ces Burke, who would play in the first post-war Test match, were heavily defeated by a Fiji Representative Team. For the first time, an Indian took part in top-level Fijian cricket, Amenayasi Turanga, taking six for 15 as the visitors were bowled out for 22. A gold miner, he was killed by electrocution a fortnight later. One of the half-dozen best Fijians of all time, he was a ferocious hitter, once scoring 106 in twenty-eight minutes on a concrete pitch. Doug Freeman, who had made his Test debut for New Zealand in 1933 aged 18, bowled well for the Fijian side in the second innings. An Australian correspondent reported that league matches were in full swing in the area around the Port Moresby Airfield Complex on Papua New Guinea, an RAF side being the prospective champions. He was much impressed by the enthusiasm of the natives who had been taught to play cricket by Christian missionaries. They could give 100 runs and a beating to the best British and Australian service sides.

The Argentine cricket season concluded with a charity match between the City and Suburbs, the receipts for which were shared between the British Hospital and the British and American Benevolent Society. Fifteen teams competed in the various championships. Organised league and cup cricket continued in Ireland, with N.H. 'Ham' Lambert scoring 149 not out for Leinster against Dublin University, despite ending on the losing side. Lambert was a pioneering veterinary surgeon whose grave simply reads 'a lovely man'. Lambert played nine first-class matches for Ireland from 1933 to 1947, also representing his country at rugby union. In Gibraltar the Royal Engineers constructed a matting wicket, a pavilion and a scoreboard. The playing season ran from May to October, and a league was set up with daily matches. Scotland could boast that the playing standard in the Western Union competitions had been maintained. Prominent participants included Bryan Valentine of Kent and England, Mark Tindall, the former Cambridge University captain, Ken Scott of Oxford and Sussex, and Bert Tobin, the South Australian cricketer. Scott, of the 6th Battalion Queen's Own Royal West Kent Regiment, would die in action in Sicily in August 1943, having been awarded the Military Cross. His gravestone contains the popular epitaph from John 15:13: *Greater Love Hath No Man Than This, That A Man Lay Down His Life For His Friends.*

Winnetka Cricket Club were crowned champion of the Chicago League for the third successive year, with the competition being reduced from seven to six clubs due to the demands on players' time from civilian war work and armed forces call-ups. For the following season the champions were forced to amalgamate with Oak Park CC in order to field a team. In Philadelphia, the Inter-Collegiate League Championship was revived for the first time since 1923. Over ninety matches were played, with Philadelphia General Electric winning the New York and Metropolitan League Cup. Elsewhere in America, what was believed to have been the first cricket match ever played in Arizona took place between teams of RAF cadets representing England and Scotland. The action was held on a baseball ground and was played at night under artificial light. The local paper reported: 'American spectators were politely restrained. They followed the multiplying score in a puzzled manner until a booming drive over the fence brought them to their feet with shouts of "a homer!" They returned to their seats when the announcer advised that the batsman had just knocked a full boundary.'

* * *

The cricketing year drew to a close with matches in South Africa and Australia. On 26 and 27 December, a first-class match took place at Johannesburg's Wanderers Ground between A Combined Air Force XI and The Rest of South Africa. Walter Hammond captained the flyers' XI, thus becoming one of the few English players to appear in a first-class match during wartime. The great man was 'very much out of practice' but later made some fine strokes including two powerful sixes. His sporting declaration on the second day allowed the Springboks to win the match in the final over, *The Cricketer* reporting, 'a fine game with a fine climax and for a fine cause', with £1,000 being raised for war charities. At noon on the second day, spectators and players observed two minutes' silence in honour of the sportsmen of the allied nations who had fallen in the conflict.

C. V. GRIMMETT
SOUTH AUSTRALIA

Across the Pacific Ocean, two-day matches took place in Sydney, Melbourne and Adelaide over Christmas. Jack Fingleton and Don Tallon were given leave by the Army to play, but Lindsay Hassett had to remain at his anti-aircraft post in New Guinea. A convalescing Don Bradman had been playing golf and tennis but turned down an invitation to play due to continuing pain from the fibrositis which saw him discharged from the Army in 1941. However, Flight Lieutenant Bill Brown flew 300 miles from his base in the Far East theatre of war to captain the Services XI *v* New South Wales at Sydney. At Melbourne, 48-year-old Captain Bert Oldfield, who had served on the Ypres Salient in the previous war, led The Army against Other Services. Meanwhile his fellow past master, 50-year-old Clarrie Grimmett, took five for 98 in twenty-one eight-ball overs for South Australia against a Services XI.

Clarrie Grimmett.

Australian cricket had a melancholy air as it mourned the loss of the country's only Test player to die in action during the war. The fifth Test of the 1936/37 Ashes series at the MCG saw the Australian first innings scorecard include the line 'R.G. Gregory c Verity b Farnes 80'. In 1942, Pilot Officer Ross Gregory wrote to his family that should he die, they should 'derive a certain amount of comfort from the knowledge that I went down doing my duty'. The young hero's bomber duly went down near the town of Gaffargaon in East Bengal on 10 June, crashing on an action to disrupt Japanese operations in Burma. Like so many airmen, his body was never found and his name appears alongside 24,000 others on the Kranji Memorial in Singapore. Had he lived, Gregory would have been in his early thirties on the resumption of Test cricket and a contender for a place in Don Bradman's 1948 Invincibles. Rather than this unrealised cricketing legacy, Gregory's gripping personal diary, edited and published by David Frith, remains as a tribute to a remarkable young man. His farewell letter, written on 16 November 1941 for his parents to read in the event of his death, showed a resolute character with noble values. An alumnus of Wesley College in Melbourne, Gregory's testament was imbued with quasi-Christian notions of sacrifice, a higher power and an afterlife:

> As you both know, I together with thousands of other men, believe that the freedom we all cherish and enjoy is worthy of a fight, in order that it may be preserved. Therefore, it is undoubtedly one's duty to do everything possible to preserve such freedom. In laying down his life, no man can do more, and no one calling himself a man would do less. …
>
> I thank God that I was fit and able to understand the more important duty of helping thousands of other freedom loving people in the cause of justice.

Having acknowledged the sacrifice of parents losing sons and daughters in these righteous causes, Gregory signed off his thoughts in this world with the prospect of joy in the next:

> Although it was my wish to be with you both in your latter years of life, I look forward to seeing you both in a more peaceful and beautiful life of the future.
>
> Your loving son
Ross

The year 1942 had proved a desperately sad one, involving the death and imprisonment of many prominent cricketers. The game had soldiered on. It was, regrettably, only halfway through the Grim Test match of war.

Chapter 5

1943: Old Friends Unexpectedly Met

'Always remember to do what's right and to fight for what's right if necessary.'
Hedley Verity

The year 1943 dawned in New Zealand's 45th parallel with a drawn match between Wellington and a Services XI. Meanwhile, Otago played Canterbury, both matches filling two days. The latter match ended with Canterbury needing 25 runs for victory with three wickets in hand. The country's National Patriotic Fun Board issued 103 sets of cricket gear, with a total value of £2,690, to men stationed in Egypt. The Maadi Camp inter-unit competition extended to thirty-six teams, including one from the Maori Battalion. A match between the Army and Air Force took place at Lancaster Park, Christchurch, on the first three days of April, with the soldiers crushing the airmen by 203 runs.

In Australia, all the state associations bar one managed to keep inter-district cricket going. The South Australian Government had decided to close all racecourses for the duration, so the cricket association had seen fit to reorganise cricket on a wartime basis to pre-empt similar restrictions. In Adelaide, a pool of club players was formed, from which half a dozen teams were chosen, each taking the names of the captains; e.g. Grimmett's XI and Hamence's XI. Army and Air Force teams were added to the mix.

In New South Wales, Bill O'Reilly topped the Sydney Grade bowling averages for the tenth time whilst Sid Barnes set a new record of 1,333 runs in a Sydney season. He was rated by many judges to be second only to Bradman. Australia's most eminent sportsman endured a second cricketless season, but advanced his business career by purchasing a seat on the Adelaide Stock Exchange. In Perth, 20-year-old Wally Driver smashed 221 not out in 115 minutes, all except three of his runs coming in boundaries. The final 100 runs were scored in thirty-five minutes. Driver's hitting ability was transferred from the game of baseball, having shone in matches against the United States Army teams before his transfer from Victoria to Western Australia.

At the Old Wanderers Ground in Johannesburg, the First Division (Union Defence Force) took on the Rest of South Africa over two days, reintroducing Johannesburg cricket enthusiasts to players they had not seen for over two years. The match ended in a thrilling draw. Dudley Nourse celebrated the occasion

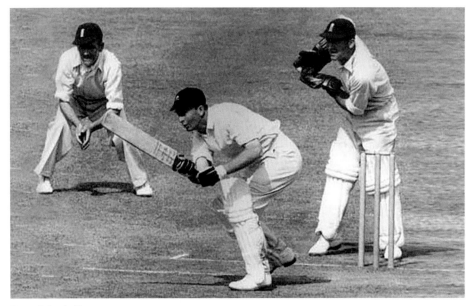

Bruce Mitchell.

with 141 not out. Later in the year, on the occasion of the Balfour Park Cricket Club's first essay at staging representative cricket, two strong sides were selected by the Transvaal Cricket Union to play in aid of a Military Hospital Fund. Situated on the outskirts of Johannesburg, the ground benefitted from a matting wicket, meaning the match was the first to be played in South Africa on such a surface for many years. Bruce Mitchell led his side to a six-wicket victory with his 105.

A January of storm and rain had given way to a February of brilliant weather in Trinidad. In the first of two matches between the hosts and Barbados, Patsy Hendren's ground record of 205 not out was broken in remarkable circumstances. Gerry Gomez, having been dropped before scoring, nearly run out on the same over and suffering from malaria, drove and pulled his way to 216 not out. Gomez's new record was under threat during the second of the two matches, as the ever-improving Frank Worrell achieved the highest score by a visiting batsman at the St Clair Oval. The appreciative crowds across the pair of four-day fixtures were augmented by service personnel, P.L. Thomson describing 'the English sailor, bronzed and happy, men in the sky-blue of the RAF, young naval officers sitting on the grass and enjoying the sun, and … the American soldier having a really good time and wondering what it was all about'.

* * *

Aside from the wartime relief to be experienced at such encounters, the bleak toll of death continued to mount. Ken Ridings, a promising player with a highest first-class score of 151 for South Australia, met his end in May. Serving as first pilot on a Short Sunderland which took off from RAF Mount Batten, detailed to conduct an anti-submarine sweep over the North Atlantic, Ridings and his comrades were shot out of the sky by a Junkers Ju 88, killing the entire crew. Lance Sergeant Frank Sides of the AIF had played twenty-two Sheffield Shield matches for Queensland and Victoria, having become Queensland's youngest debutant aged 17 in October 1930. The dashing left-handed batsman had been serving with 2/3 Independent Company (2/3 Commando Unit) Australian Infantry. Tasked with launching a guerrilla campaign against the

Frank Sides.

Japanese around Salamaua, Sides and his comrades patrolled deep into enemy territory, setting ambushes and gathering intelligence. Having captured the strategically important Ambush Knoll, fifty-two men of the unit managed to hold it against a Japanese counter-attack but suffered heavy casualties as a result. One of the fatalities was Frank Sides. Queensland's *Cairns Post* recalled, 'Frank died as he lived – gentle, determined and courageous.' His gravestone in Lae War Cemetery, Papua New Guinea, pays tribute to the cricketing fallen hero: 'THE CLOSE OF A NOBLE INNINGS. HIS DUTY WELL DONE.'

Flight Lieutenant Lancelot Hingley was reported missing, his remains never to be found. He had played for MCC in the Tom Brown Centenary Match in 1941, arriving on the ground a few hours after taking part in night operations over Germany. His late arrival had led to an upbraiding by Pelham Warner who, learning later of the young man's circumstances, apologised and the two became friends. Warner wrote: 'no keener cricketer ever lived.'

This year also brought the death of the war's most eminent cricketing fatality, Captain Hedley Verity. Before the invasion of Sicily, Lieutenant Colonel Shaw, commanding officer of 1st Battalion Green Howards, arranged one final cricket match for his men in the sealed area at El Shatt camp. The opponents included General Sir Miles Dempsey, commander of XIII Corps. A railway sleeper was found and attached to a chain at the rear of a truck and dragged round a flat area of salt and sand to create a cricket pitch. Some matting was placed over concrete and a wicket established. Hedley Verity took six for 37 'bowling imperturbably and as near perfectly as made no difference'. It was to be the great man's final performance. On 20 July, the Green Howards launched their attack on the blazing plain of Catania. Captain Verity was hit in the chest.

Lying in a cornfield, he urged his men forwards, but they were forced to retreat. They last saw their leader with his head being cradled by his batman, Thomas Reynoldson. Verity died eleven days later at Caserta Military Hospital, despite the care of Italian medical orderlies and captured RAMC men. He had written to his sons, Wilfred and Douglas: 'Always remember to do what's right and to fight for what's right if necessary.' This was a creed Verity had followed through, even to the end of his world. Verity's family, his comrades and the post-war cricketing scene would be denied his gracious and noble presence.

News spread far and wide of Verity's death. Corporal L.W. Hall, a Leyton club cricketer serving with the RAF in Ceylon, recorded in a letter to a friend:

> I feel I must pause to pay tribute to the memory of Verity. Some weeks ago I commented on the fact that he was 'Missing'. Later it was announced that he might be wounded and a Prisoner of War. Now comes the news that he has died of wounds whilst a POW. I was very sorry indeed to read this. His death will be a big loss to Yorkshire and England. I wonder whether Yorkshire will be able to produce a left-hand slow bowler to succeed him as he succeeded Rhodes.

Hall had seen Verity in action five years previously, recalling him bowling Don Bradman for 18 in the Lord's test.

Kent CCC's annual report bleakly stated: 'Flight Lieutenant F.G.H. Chalk is missing.' The popular and gregarious club captain, a former schoolmaster at Malvern College, had been awarded the DFC in 1941 while serving as a rear gunner in 218 Squadron in an attack on Hanover. On the return journey over Amsterdam the aircraft was attacked by a Messerschmitt 110 and P/O Chalk fired two steady bursts which entered the enemy aircraft, causing it to break away with flames coming from the starboard side. On 17 February 1943, having been promoted to flight lieutenant, he was shot down over Louches in northern France. Chalk remained on the missing list for almost a year before being presumed dead the following January, another former cricketing schoolmaster to be taken so early from the world.

On 4 December, Major Tristan Ballance became the fourth Oxford blue of 1937 to perish in the war. Ballance, a major in the Durham Light Infantry, had appeared regularly for Norfolk. Like Ken Farnes, Gerry Chalk and Roger Human, Ballance was a schoolmaster, serving at Brighton College. He had previously won an MC at the Battle of Sedjenane on 2 March 1943, leading twenty men during a ferocious three-hour battle.

Gerry Chalk.

Other renowned cricketers were fortunate to escape with their lives, with their honour greatly enhanced. Acting Flight Lieutenant Alec MacKenzie, the Hampshire all-rounder, became the first professional cricketer to be awarded the DSO. He had already won a DFC the previous year. He brought home a disabled Lancaster from a raid on Berlin. His aircraft was subjected to heavy and accurate anti-aircraft fire. Two of its engines were rendered unserviceable. Height was lost but, although faced with a 300-mile flight across the North Sea, MacKenzie continued his journey. Halfway across the water a third engine overheated. It was now down to 600 feet and the situation appeared hopeless. MacKenzie, displaying grim determination, flew on and eventually reached England, landing his damaged aircraft, saving his own life and those of his crew. The modest MacKenzie, who had previously played for Kent, was made the guest of honour at Canterbury's 1943 Wings for Victory week.

Bryan Valentine, the Kent and England batsman, was awarded the Military Cross while serving with the Royal West Kent Regiment 'in recognition of gallant and distinguished services in North Africa'. Valentine would return to captain his county for the first three post-war seasons despite being badly wounded during the hostilities. New Zealander Bill Carson was also awarded the MC for quickly positioning his guns to fire accurately against two well-equipped Italian battalions at the Battle of Mareth in March 1943. Another gallant cricketing comrade was Leicestershire's John Sharp, who earned a bar to his MC. Sharp would become Personal Liaison Officer to Field Marshal Montgomery in 1945 and eventually rise to the rank of Commander-in-Chief of Allied Forces in Northern Europe in the 1970s.

Continuing Luftwaffe assaults on the home front took its toll of cricketing life. May saw the worst raid of the war on the picturesque Suffolk coastal town of Southwold. Seven fighter-bombers targeting Lowestoft spotted barrage balloons over the port, turned south and flew at 100 feet above Southwold. One bomb destroyed a building in the grounds of St Felix School. Four more hit the town, blowing out the windows of St Edmund's Church and destroying nearby houses in Hollyhock Square, killing six people. Amongst those killed was 69-year-old George Katinakis. A right-handed batsman, Katinakis had made his first-class debut for Hampshire in 1904, playing a handful of matches for the county.

* * *

Whatever the challenges, the cricketing show had to go on. The British Empire XI entered their fourth wartime season with an admixture of established stalwarts such as Ray Smith, Harry Crabtree and Bertie Clarke, and the usual rotation players of eminent and modest reputation. Crabtree weighed in with a new club aggregate record of 987 runs, appearing in thirty-one of their thirty-three matches. In one rich vein of form in early July, the Essex man took 112 off the Metropolitan Police XI at Sutton, before travelling up to Spinney Hill the following day to put Northamptonshire to the sword to the tune of 102 not out. Yorkshire's Harry Halliday scored 105 for the XI against Highams Park at Chingford. Stewie Dempster led his own XI against the British Empire XI at Epsom on 15 August, weighing in with a half-century. Despite some stout lower-order resistance from Stan Nichols and Roly Jenkins, the Kiwi side's 252 was not enough to vanquish the Empire XI, for whom Leslie Todd top scored with 122.

A showcase Lord's match was played on 24 June against London Counties XI. Taking advantage of six dropped chances, Harry Crabtree, Laurie Fishlock and Harry Halliday all made useful

Harry Crabtree and Jim Parks open the batting for the British Empire XI. *(Courtesy Peter Crabtree)*

contributions for the Empire XI's 253 for seven. Eight thousand spectators were then treated to yet another fine Lord's innings by Denis Compton, this time in tandem with his brother Leslie. Their 131-run partnership came in seventy minutes before the contrasting styles of the speed of Trevor Bailey and the guile of Bertie Clarke bundled out the rest of the London Counties batting to claim a 52-run victory. A late August two-day encounter took place between Coventry and District and the British Empire XI, with Arthur Fagg's 101 setting up a victory for the Midland team. The Kentish man was joined in the Coventry team by Essex's Jack O' Connor.

For London Counties XI's fourth wartime fixture programme, professional players would be paid 30/- per match plus expenses, a similar amount to that which other sportsmen and ENSA entertainers were due. The XI raised over £2,000 for charity in their thirty-four matches. Whilst some voices had been raised in objection to the fielding of over-40 veterans in big matches at Lord's and elsewhere, arguing it was restricting the throughflow of younger talent, W.M.F Bebbington argued that the London Counties XI's tendency to 'retain before the public eye those idols who have contributed so much to the game' allowed such masters to give their side a balanced blend of youth and experience. Leslie Compton made 120 for London Counties XI at Southall whilst Coventry and District XI, which included Bob Wyatt, Roly Jenkins and 'Lofty' Herman, drew with London Counties in a two-innings, two-day match.

The contribution of some members of the XI to the game extended beyond the playing of fixtures around the country. The grand old man of Yorkshire and England cricket, George Hirst, approaching his seventy-second birthday, began a seven-week tour which took him to many corners of Yorkshire. He coached elementary schoolboys and specially selected young players. 'Even in wartime, Yorkshire leave nothing to chance in the way of unearthing talent,' noted *The Cricketer*. Unfortunately, for the second year in succession, Hirst was unable to make it to Hull. In a city that has always been somewhat of a cricketing outpost as far as Yorkshire CCC is concerned, the secretary of Hull CC, Norman Pogson, paid London Counties umpires Frank Chester and Harry Lee to remain in the city for two days following their London Counties fixture to coach the city's cricketing youth.

Consideration was also given to the fact that many county players were receiving multiple requests to play on the same day for various services and invitational XIs, causing anxiety and confusion as to which to prioritise. Pelham Warner convened cricketing representatives from each of the armed services, civil defence services, the British Empire XI and London Counties XI. It was decided which fixtures should take precedence and after the teams for those matches had been chosen then lists of players available for other fixtures would be circulated. It was also agreed to broaden the spread of players invited to appear in the major matches. Thus, it was after three wartime seasons had already been played that central co-ordination of the fixture list was arranged. Despite this careful planning, Both Denis Compton and Leslie Todd found themselves double-booked in May.

* * *

MCC decided to discontinue the practice of allowing free entry to Lord's for members of the armed forces. Following representations from the service chiefs, it was recognised that in an era of total war, every citizen was playing their part, 'and it is invidious to discriminate'. Furthermore, the gate money was distributed to charities and many of those in uniform would wish to pay admission. This spirit of egalitarianism did not extend to admission to the pavilion, which 'officers in uniform' were entitled to, but not other ranks. Another indication of wartime cricketing spirit was noted by Home Gordon, the 'prompt and ungrumbling acceptance of the umpire's verdict. I have seen a few shocking verdicts, but none of the pre-war disgruntlement on returning to the pavilion.'

Gordon had conversations with prominent officers across the three services:

> Unanimously they all laid stress of the importance of carrying on cricket until the national exigencies rendered it impossible, one even volunteering to fill up places in any eleven from men under his own command. Another told me it was far better that public interest should be healthily distracted than that there should be incessant attention concentrated on what was happening overseas. Definitely Sussex will carry on, for patriotic reasons, regarding relaxation as invaluable.

The Yorkshire Cricket Federation, founded in 1929 to represent the interests of clubs in the Bradford, Huddersfield, North Yorkshire and South Durham, Leeds and Yorkshire Council Leagues, ended the season representing thirty-seven organisations comprising 600 clubs. The chief activity of the federation during the early part of the year had been a struggle with the Board of Trade to obtain recognition of the claims of non-priority clubs for permits to enable them to receive supplies of equipment. This was successful in enabling most clubs to fulfil all their fixtures. The federation had also saved some grounds from going under the plough following orders from local War Agricultural Committees. A further impediment to playing cricket, the availability of willow to manufacture cricket bats, was raised in the House of Commons by Captain Leonard Plugge, the Unionist Member for Chatham. Plugge enquired of the Minister of Agriculture on a set of revised by-laws of the Essex Rivers Catchment Board which might affect the cultivation of the willow tree. The Minister, R.S. Hudson, replied that he would carefully consider the objections he had already received, and any subsequent ones.

Aside from the threat of being turned over to agriculture, many cricket grounds were left untended during the war. Several club enthusiasts sought to maintain squares in some kind of order. Some had carved up outfields in allotments as the nation sought to Dig for Victory. *The Cricketer* averred that this would be beneficial in keeping down weeds, and the manures and fertilisers would add to the richness of the soil, resulting in a better post-war outfield. The preservation of cricket grounds from post-war development was a stark problem facing clubs in the southern Club Cricket Conference as well as the Yorkshire Cricket Federation. The pressure on land use in London and the great industrial cities of the North meant that clubs there were under particular threat. Representations were made by the CCC to the London County Council and the Ministry of Works and Planning. The LCC's proposals of allotting 4 acres of open space per 1,000 of population meant that little space would be left for sports clubs.

* * *

By 1943 it could be fairly argued that the Bradford League had mutated from a peacetime parochial competition to one of a national and international flavour. During the previous seasons representatives of fourteen of the seventeen first-class counties had taken part, in addition to the prominent West Indian cricketers. Clubs had reaped a handsome financial whirlwind, which enabled them to reinforce their professional engagements for 1943. It was anticipated that Len Hutton's left arm would be sufficiently recovered to enable him to play for Pudsey whilst Saltaire were able to secure the left-arm venom of Bill Voce. Gloucestershire and England off-spinner Tom Goddard made a fine Bradford League debut for Saltaire against Brighouse, taking nine for 19, receiving

5 guineas in collection money for his efforts, whilst Eddie Paynter scooped £11 for his 109 not out. Other professionals joining the league included Emrys Davies of Glamorgan and Jim Cutmore of Essex.

Rules on collections had been altered to restrict them to a batsman making 50 runs, a bowler performing a hat-trick or a bowler taking six or more wickets at an average of 6 runs or less. In Hutton's first match back after his long sojourn, on 24 April, he was bowled by a local player named Deadman for a duck. Meanwhile, his Yorkshire teammate Ellis Robinson took four wickets in four balls, emulating the league feat of S.F. Barnes, C.F. Grimshaw and Learie Constantine.

On 29 May, more than 3,000 spectators descended on Lidget Green's ground to see the previous year's Bradford League champions defeated by a strong Windhill XI including Denis Smith, Alf Pope and Bill Copson. Smith made exactly 100. A keenly fought Priestley Cup tie between Keighley and Bingley saw Eddie Paynter score 101 in a total of 197, with Somerset's mercurial fast-medium bowler Bill Andrews taking nine for 79 for the opposition. The diminutive Lancastrian's efforts were not enough to prevent a seven-wicket Bingley victory, with Nottinghamshire's Walter Keeton also reaching three figures; 5,000 spectators paying 7d per head ensured match receipts of £103. Pudsey St Lawrence also reached the semi-finals thanks to a second-wicket partnership of 106 between the Hutton brothers, Len and George. Cup matches took place with unusual rules, with the team batting first having to suspend their innings on reaching 150. If the other team then reached the same mark it was up to the fielding captain to decide whether to resume their innings or allow the batting side to play on. 'This rule is declared to be the most popular rule the League has ever made,' wrote the Bradford League secretary, F. Milton Watmough.

One Bradford League match showed that club amateurs could raise their game against cricketing greats. Windhill, whose line-up included a quintet of county and Test players – Alf Pope, Denis Smith, Bill Copson, Les Ames and Jim Cutmore – were laid low by bottom of the table Idle, for whom Robert Rae, whose first-class career would amount to a mere one match in 1945, took eight for 86. Not content with the steamrollering bowling attack of Copson and Alf Pope, Windhill also managed to secure the correct, classical and fluent batting services of Les Ames for their match against Eccleshill, the Kent and England great making 75 not out. Promisingly for the future of Yorkshire and England cricket, Len Hutton had rediscovered some form, scoring 105 for Pudsey against Bankfoot. In addition to his 417 aggregate by the end of June, he had also claimed thirty-three wickets for 262 runs.

The semi-finals of the Priestley Cup saw Len Hutton rewarded with a collection for his 69 and five for 63 for Pudsey St Lawrence. A crowd of 6,000 thronged Bradford Park Avenue for the first day of the Priestley Cup Final, shelling out

£320 for admission, £31 for a collection for the Red Cross and over £16 for Len Hutton's 64. The match was not concluded until a few weeks later, with a further 4,000 spectators watching Hutton and his teammates claim the honours. Over £538 was raised for charity. Seventy-five first-class players, including fourteen Test cricketers, had taken part in the league's 1943 season.

Les Ames.

The conclusion of the league's A Division was a nail-biting one. Both Windhill and Saltaire were in with a chance of being crowned champions, with the former having the seemingly easier task of beating already relegated Yeadon. Windhill fielded their big guns: Cutmore, Smith, Copson, Pope, Ames and Constantine. A teenage Yeadon bowler, Hambleton, took six for 30 including Cutmore, Ames, Smith and Pope before Charlie Harris's 85 not out steered Yeadon to victory. This allowed Saltaire to slide past Windhill to end up as champions by five points.

Whilst Yorkshire crowds enjoyed fine and keenly contested matches featuring some of the greatest names on the cricketing circuit, future *Wisden* editor Norman Preston examined the underlying factors behind northern counties' dominance. Preston stated that northern counties won the championship far more frequently than their southern rivals, and that the talent ground of league cricket was a significant contributor to this success. Other reasons suggested were larger population centres from which to draw on and a natural doggedness of character. It was pointed out that Australia, with a population seven times smaller than that of England, had a superior record over their Ashes rivals. The success of the Dominions at Test level was ascribed to the organisation of their grassroots cricket into leagues.

Meanwhile, controversy surrounded Almondbury's tie against Paddock in the Huddersfield and District League's Sykes Cup. One of the Paddock XI, F. Gawthorpe, was ineligible and the league committee ordered the match to be replayed. However, according to league rules Almondbury should have been awarded the match outright. Justice was served as 15-year-old Eddie Leadbeater took six for 16 with his 16-year-old teammate F. Pickering taking four for 14 to secure a 50-run win.

An exciting finish in the first round of the Sykes Cup saw Kirkburton claim their first victory of the season, inching home by 3 runs mainly thanks to veteran bowler Bob Blackburn's nine for 43. Dr H.A. Fraser, a former captain of British Guiana who would become that nation's Chief Veterinary Officer after the war, scored 33 not out for Slaithwaite supporting Tommy Lodge (86 not out) as the pair steered their team to victory over Broad Oak. One of the largest crowds ever assembled for the Sykes Cup Final paid £198 gate money to see Slaithwaite take on Elland. Horace Walker earned £34 10s for his painstaking 64 for Elland, a record collection for the league. Tommy Lodge's 56 not out guided Slaithwaite to victory, although he had to settle for a whip-round of £13. Hall Bower had claimed the league honours by the end of the season. Aside from on-the-field pursuits, Slaithwaite were pleased to report that across the first four wartime summers the club's Comforts Committee had raised £411 to support their serving members.

In the Birmingham League, George Paine, the Warwickshire professional who had appeared in four Test matches, made 131 for Kidderminster v Moseley in a club record opening stand of 215 in just 105 minutes, R.E. McKinlay being his batting partner. West Bromwich Dartmouth carried off the league championship for the third successive year, largely thanks to the bowling of Eric Hollies. An extraordinary match took place involving Burslem at Bignall End in the North Staffordshire League. Burslem's previously unblemished record ended as they were dismissed for just 24. In reply the hosts had reached 7 before rain stopped play. The umpires deemed conditions fit for the resumption of play at 7.45, leaving just fifteen minutes for Bignall End to score the additional 18 runs needed for victory. They lost four wickets trying to force the pace and still required 13 off the final over; 12 were scored from five balls and the field closed in to prevent a single. A. Lockett forced the ball through the fielders for the winning run. In another remarkable match, Leek dismissed Norton for just 5, with their captain, W.S. Hutchinson, taking the last six wickets in eleven balls for no runs, including the hat-trick. Bignall End finished the season as league champions.

The Lancashire League maintained its decision to forego professionals. The Central Lancashire League had more stars, including Charlie Hallows, Jack Iddon and Edwin St Hill. Norman Oldfield, who had made his Test debut against the West Indies in 1939, was playing for Dukenfield in the Lancashire and Cheshire League. Blackpool Services were hoping to complete a hat-trick of wins in the Ribblesdale League. By the end of June, Jack Crapp, who would later become the first Cornishman to play for England, extended his season's batting average for 348, having only been dismissed once. A strong Ribblesdale League side vanquished Blackpool. As well as Crapp, the league side could boast the talents of George Cox and Tich Cornford of Sussex, Ellis Robinson of Yorkshire, Bill Andrews of Somerset, and Dennis Watkin and Jack Blood of Nottinghamshire.

Lancashire's Winston Place was in fine form in the Bolton League in July, with successive innings of 100 and 80, both not out, for Horwich RMI. Veteran Charlie Hallows continued to accrue runs in the Central Lancashire League, it being reported that 'some of the old power has gone from Hallows' batting, but the accuracy of his placing is an object lesson to younger players'. Enfield were victorious in the Lancashire League whilst Castleton Moor's bowling won them the Central Lancashire League.

* * *

On a high July summer's day, Northamptonshire, with 96 from the cultured Dennis Brookes, drew with the London Counties XI. Brookes, a loyal servant of the county, would go on to become Northamptonshire's leading first-class run-scorer and first professional captain. Such was the demand for famous players to make up teams, the following weekend Brookes turned out for Gloucestershire against the RAF, making 69. The following day, the Kippax-born batsman continued his purple patch with 62 for a strong Tom Goddard's XI. An attempt to provide an even contest by allowing a Local War Industries team to field sixteen players failed as the respective scores were 279 for four and 74 all out. At the end of the

Dennis Brookes.

month, the Gloucester ground clearly being to Brookes's liking, he took apart the county's bowling for The Rest to the tune of 159 runs. Northamptonshire appointed a new captain in Peter Murray-Willis, who had been discharged from the RAF on medical grounds and established a special subcommittee to further the county's post-war interests. A decent programme of fifteen matches took place that season, including fixtures against the British Empire XI, Eastern Command, London Counties, The Buccaneers, Leicestershire and an Army XI, all at the Spinney Hill ground. Frequent candidates for elimination from the County Championship during pre-war discussions about streamlining the first-class game in England, Northamptonshire remained a vibrant force in wartime cricket. Crowds of over 2,000 enjoyed their matches against the British Empire XI, Leicestershire and the West Indies.

Despite the strong Northamptonshire showing in the wartime game, at the 1943 Middlesex CCC AGM, Pelham Warner spoke of there being 'too many counties' holding back the game. He also dug in his heels once more against the prospect of any change from the traditional County Championship format:

Do not be led away by the call for bright cricket. It is a leisurely, intricate game of skill. We live in an age of speed and people are apt to think that cricket must be speeded up, but my experience is that it is not necessary to have fast scoring to have interesting cricket. I do not wish to see anything better than two fine batsmen opposed to two first-class bowlers, backed up by good fielding, then the number of runs scored in an hour is unimportant.

Northamptonshire, Sussex, Hampshire, Leicestershire and Glamorgan managed to raise teams for the Holidays at Home week whilst Headingley saw Herbert Sutcliffe's XI take on Northern Command. County affiliations continued to be fluid, with Essex all-rounder Stan Nichols playing for a Notts and Derby XI, and Leicestershire including schoolboy Billy Sutcliffe (son of the eminent Herbert) and Learie Constantine. Sussex brothers James and John Langridge played for both the National Police XI and the National Fire Service in the same week.

Sergeant V.D. Guthrie of the RAAF appeared for Gloucestershire *v* RAF, sporting a white England Association Football shirt, complete with the three lions. Hampshire's Ted Drake, the famous Arsenal footballer, who also played in the ersatz Gloucestershire team, commented that he wondered what size ball would be used. Incidentally, Guthrie was originally left out of the match as the RAF were unwilling to play against twelve men. Sportingly, they relented and the Australian was allowed to bowl. The paucity of cricket equipment was evident as the RAF used a ball of inferior quality and the bat belonging to Les Berry, with which he had already scored 1,500 runs, was pitted and discoloured after making 83, there being pieces of the ball left sticking to the blade.

Worcester's leading citizens extended the previous year's four-week Holidays at Home extravaganza to six weeks. The New Road Ground, overlooked by the city's magnificent cathedral, was in heavy demand. One curiosity was a baseball match between two teams from the US Army, styled Yanks *v* Rebels. The latter won 3-2, with the commentator Lieutenant Hoskins declaring, 'This has been a very good game and this is a beautiful place for it.' A fourteen-over competition took place for the Eltex Cup, with the combination of workplace and service teams, including Archdales, National Fire Service, Civil

Advertisement for a cricket ball renovation service that appeared in *The Cricketer* magazine.

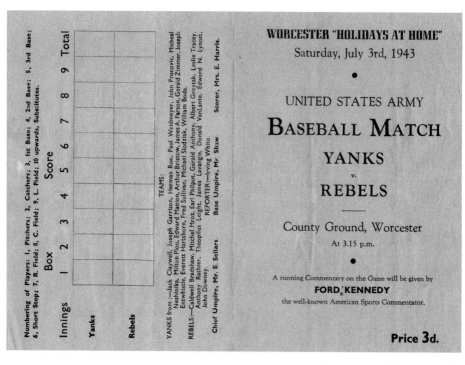

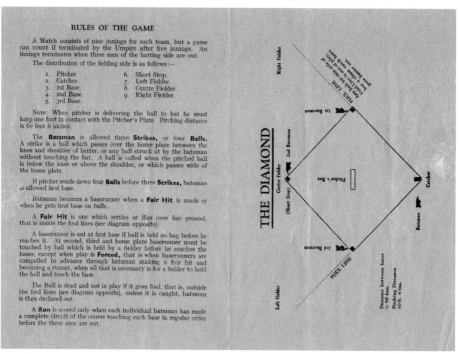

Match programme from a US Army baseball match at Worcester. *(Courtesy Worcestershire CCC Heritage Collection)*

Defence, Heenan & Froudes, Sentinel, Sheet Metal, Great Western Railways & London Midland Scottish, 1st Battalion Home Guard, Metal Castings, Seamless Tubings, Gas Company and Electricity Works. The ground was also put to more pious use on 3 September as that devout member of the Plymouth Brethren, General Sir William Dobbie, Governor of Malta during the siege, stood on the pavilion balcony to address a crowd gathered to observe a National Day of Prayer.

Nottinghamshire played their customary wartime matches against Derbyshire and Leicestershire at Trent Bridge, although all sides were depleted compared to their previous wartime iterations due to the demands of overseas military service. Reg Simpson was on the far side of the Atlantic training to be an aircraft pilot whilst Joe Hardstaff and Charlie Harris were stationed in India. Aircraftman Roy Genders, later to write two cricket books, *League Cricket in England* and a history of Worcestershire CCC, as well as numerous books on gardening and cigarette card collecting, top scored for Derbyshire.

Sadly another Nottinghamshire cricketer, Harold Larwood, had brought his eminent but contentious cricket career to a close. *The Cricketer* noted that the 38-year-old had 'apparently given up cricket and now devotes all his time to poultry farming and market gardening at Annesley Woodhouse'. Elsewhere in the county, P.A. Morley, a young club cricketer, was put on as the fourth change bowler against Caythorpe. Morley claimed a wicket with each of his first four balls. The fifth ball was hit for three, before three more wickets fell in the final three balls of the over, leaving him with the remarkable figures of 1-0-3-7.

Essex CCC had turned in a profit of £292 during the previous year, which enabled them to continue to provide coaching for young members and members' sons at the Crompton Parkinson Sports Ground in Chelmsford. The coaching was conducted under the supervision of experienced professional Jack O'Connor. Meanwhile, Surrey managed a significant surplus of £1,359 9s 7d. Much of this amount was being set aside to cover 'the very heavy cost of reconditioning The Oval after the war'. Kent CCC's profit was £234 5s 8d from the subscriptions of 840 members. A remarkable 133 matches were played on the St Lawrence Ground in addition to three athletic sports meetings, and a baseball match for Red Cross funds. 'These games are much appreciated by all ranks stationed in the neighbourhood,' stated the club's annual report. When necessary,

Harold Larwood.

two matches had been played simultaneously, hence the total coming to more than one a day for the four summer months.

Lancashire took on the Rest of England at Bolton on 1 July, with the 56-year-old Percy Holmes opening for the rest. Unfortunately, given the strength of the Lancashire team, which included Paynter, Place, Oldfield, Iddon, Hallows, Farrimond, Parkin and Duckworth, the match petered out into a tame draw. Yorkshire and Lancashire set aside their traditional Roses rivalry to take on the RAF at Sheffield on 14 and 15 August. The drawn match was notable for centuries from Lancastrian duo Cyril Washbrook and Albert Nutter. An emergent wartime talent who would make the transition to a successful post-war first-class career was David Fletcher. He made Surrey Colts' first century, having begun his club career aged 13 for Blackheath Wanderers 2nd XI.

Sussex came close to emulating Northamptonshire's fixture programme with thirteen matches, mainly at Hove but also Horsham and Chichester. The county ground was also extensively used as a multiple sports venue. On one June day there could be seen lawn tennis being played in the enclosure and a military football game elsewhere. Canadians were playing baseball on the outfield and the RAF were having a trial cricket match. Four Canadians placed themselves 20 yards behind the bowler 'to watch his pitching'. On 3 July, playing for the Royal Navy against the county, Trevor Bailey enhanced his growing reputation with a faultless and splendid century, which led one observer to imbue his strokeplay with nautical characteristics: 'His cool judgement in placing the ball emphasised he has command of every stroke, putting plenty of strength behind each, one drive being impelled as fast as a torpedo-charge.' With an eye to the future of the game, a Sussex Cricket Association was formed, which operated independently of the county club. The vision of the association was to act as a feeder of younger talent from the clubs through to the county team. A note of discord was struck as the association proposed to promote league cricket amongst clubs that wished to take part, bringing it into conflict with clubs that were already members of the Club Cricket Conference.

The customary big match between Middlesex and Essex and Kent and Surrey on 28 August was ruined as a spectacle by an admixture of avoidable and unavoidable circumstances. Rain meant no play was possible until 2.35 pm, by which time Sonny Avery had pulled out due to an accident.

Trevor Bailey.

Arthur Fagg had lost his cricket bag on a train and did not show up. Then a telephone call at 1.30 pm from Arsenal Football Club removed Leslie and Denis Compton for a match against Charlton Athletic. Bereft of the brothers, Middlesex and Essex slid to a heavy defeat.

The Cricketer speculated on the future feasibility of English county *v* Australian state matches given 'the amazing development of the aeroplane during the war'. Although matches such as Yorkshire *v* New South Wales would never come to pass, the further suggestion that a replacement player could be flown out during an overseas tour 'if a key man is crocked' was certainly one that would be implemented after the war. Seven decades later, it would be the individual cricketer who could jet their way around the world playing for various teams in a range of tournaments, with ties of loyalty to one particular team being weakened to the point of near elimination.

* * *

It was reported that Molly Hide, pre-war captain of the England Women's cricket team, was managing her father's 122-acre farm at Roundhurst near Haslemere. Hide had completed a Diploma in Agriculture in 1937 and rapidly expanded the amount of family land under plough at the start of the war, dramatically increasing yields of wheat and oats. The renowned agricultural writer E. Walford Lloyd noted:

> How good it is to know that even in the midst of all the hard work she is called upon to do in food production during this war, Miss Hide is full of confidence that, when Peace reigns once more, women's cricket will again flourish, and may even become more popular than ever.

Molly Hide.

Hide's erstwhile England teammate Myrtle Maclagan recorded that, given the more limited opportunities for play and travel during the war, even a rained-off match was a pleasure because the players could enjoy a trip to London and could dine out. In 1943, Maclagan led the ATS to victory over WAAF by 141 runs (Maclagan 96) and the WRNS by 210 runs (Maclagan 148 not out). She would go on to serve as a senior ATS officer in the Anti-Aircraft Regiment in Dover in 1944 during the flying bomb raids.

* * *

Several high-profile matches took place between different branches of the armed and civilian services. A strong gathering of players arrived at Lord's on 3 July for an RAF *v* Civil Defence match. The RAF compiled one of the highest totals in English wartime cricket, 319 for 4, with Cyril Washbrook and Les Ames making centuries, adding 150 runs in eighty minutes. Spectators, who numbered 14,000, enjoyed stout resistance by the Civil Defence before Alec Bedser's four for 59 brought the flyers the victory. An eclectic Coventry and District XI took on the RAF on 11 July. The Midland XI included Sussex's Jim Parks and James Langridge, Kiwi Stewie Dempster, Worcestershire's Roly Jenkins and Surrey's Jack Parker, who had been one of the unfortunate band who had missed out on the 1939/40 MCC tour of India. A keenly fought match ended in a five-run victory for Coventry, despite a fighting 77 by Surrey's Bob Gregory for the airmen.

For the showcase Army *v* Royal Navy match at Lord's in July, whilst the former had the advantage of several well-known names who had been playing regular top-class cricket during the war, the RN selectors had to sift the merits of 130 players who were recommended for inclusion by their commanding officers. This was a perennial problem for the Navy, whose cricketers would often experience extended periods at sea, with no opportunities for playing and practice, thus making it difficult for selectors to know who had the talent and who was in form.

One brilliant adornment to the second half of the 1943 season was the presence of players of the Royal Australian Air Force, the most dazzling of whom was Keith Miller. In a match for the United Services against Sussex, Miller announced his arrival in high standard cricket in no uncertain terms, hitting 134 not out in 120 minutes, including twelve fours and three sixes. Home Gordon recorded: 'The new star from the Antipodes puts tremendous power behind his bat. At one period in consecutive balls he lifted a ball into the tennis courts, drove the next hard past the screen and the third onto the roof of the pavilion.' The dashing young Australian then ripped through the Sussex batting with seven for 36, securing a victory by 225 runs. The quirks of wartime availability and selection meant that he then played a match for the county whom he had recently tormented, against the RAF, scoring 11 opening the batting and taking three for 41. The vigorous 23-year-old Australian made a marked contrast to his opening partner, the former Middlesex batsman Norman Moffat, who was approaching his sixtieth birthday. Herbert Chaplin, who had captained Sussex in the five pre-First World War seasons, turned out for the RAF against his old county having recently entered his seventh decade.

Miller had arrived in the UK in March 1943 and was dispatched to Bournemouth. He was quickly into cricketing action. Leo Bennett, captain of the BBC cricket team and occasional invitee of the British Empire XI, recalled a match played at Bournemouth CC's ground on 16 March against a RNZAF XI:

Keith Carmody, captain of the RAAF XI, and Walter Robins at Lord's, 1943. (*Australian War Memorial*)

'The weather was fine and warm, and spectators lounged in deck-chairs. The match took place on turf, began at 1.30 pm and finished at 4 pm, the Aussies winning by 76 runs. Playing were K. Carmody and Keith Miller.' Whilst Miller enjoyed his first trip to London, the Carlton Hotel in Bournemouth, where Miller regularly drank with his mates, suffered damage in an air raid, killing eight of his pals. His selection for the RAAF cricket team to play at Lord's had saved him.

On 5 June, the recently revamped RAAF team led by Keith Carmody appeared at Lord's for the first time. Their opponents were a Pelham Warner XI, which included England stars past and future in Bob Wyatt, Gubby Allen, Alec Bedser and Trevor Bailey. No respecter of niceties, Miller pushed a person who had entered the dressing room out of his way before the match started, unaware that it was Warner himself. He acquitted himself with more elan on the field, claiming two for 20 in ten eight-ball overs and top scoring with 45 out of the RAAF's total of 100. The only other player to make double figures, leg-spinning all-rounder Alex Barras, might have scarcely believed his luck at being able to walk through the Long Room and out onto the historic field. In July 1942, his Wellington bomber was shot down over Tobruk, Barras being the sole survivor of the five-man crew. Finding himself with 500 miles of desert between him and the British lines, the intrepid Western Australian decided to walk directly south into the desert. There he came across a group of Bedouins and produced his lifeline letter – a promise to any Arab helping a stranded Commonwealth serviceman a handsome reward from the British Government. They gave him native costume and escorted him 500 miles to freedom. Barras was awarded the Military Medal for this feat. Later in June, Keith Carmody executed a superb century for the RAAF against the South of England at Hove, as the Antipodean airmen served notice of their cricketing strength by defeating the southerners by ten wickets in a two-innings match.

Cheetham, Sismey (crouching in cap) and Papayanni in the nets at Lord's, 18 May 1945. (*Australian War Memorial*)

Another RAAF player, Stan Sismey, who had been badly wounded in combat the previous year, kept wicket with three or four pieces of shrapnel in his back. 'They do not worry me at the moment,' commented the stoic New South Welshman. He wore his state cap at Lord's, declaring: 'directly I heard I was coming this way and there was a possibility of getting some cricket I sent a message home asking for it.' Of lesser playing ability, but of inestimable spiritual and administrative value to RAAF cricketers, was their chaplain, the Reverend Dave Beyer. He opened Sussex's innings against Denis Compton's XI on 12 August at Chichester's Priory Park. Although unsuccessful on this occasion, being bowled by Alec Bedser for a duck, Beyer served nobly in the war. Joining the Royal Australian Air Force as a chaplain, 4th class, on 11 November 1940, he embarked for England in January 1943, travelling on escort duty via North America, and served for the remainder of the war at No. 11 Personnel Dispatch and Reception Centre, firstly at Bournemouth and later at Brighton.

As sole unit chaplain, Beyer would write hundreds of letters home to families of the airmen, conduct funerals, and produce a fortnightly magazine with a circulation of 300. Beyer's approach reflected the less class-ridden approach endemic in the Australian armed service. In his office, the motto 'Abandon rank all who enter' held sway, and men could talk over problems, read or write and receive comfort parcels from home. A keen sportsman, Beyer ministered to his men's physical as well as spiritual and pastoral needs, arranging regular cricket and other sporting fixtures against local teams. The *Australian Dictionary of National Biography* averred that 'Dave Beyer's approach coupled a robust, practical Christianity with a rich sense of humour'. After VE Day, Beyer worked with former prisoners of war and arrived home in June 1946.

The appreciation from English cricket crowds of the enterprise and excitement of the RAAF players was reciprocated by one of their number, Flight Lieutenant Bruce Andrew. Andrew, better known as an Australian Rules footballer, played several times in 1943. He penned an eloquent appreciation of the English game for *Wisden*, highlighting how cricket had fostered good fellowships between Australians and Englishmen during the 1943 season. Writing on behalf of his fellow Australians, Andrew declared:

> In England, cricket has been more than a game for them. Only those who have played with or against English clubs can appreciate the great difference between club cricket here and at home. We Australians love our cricket and thoroughly enjoy the way we play it, but we had to travel 12,000 miles to appreciate the real atmosphere of the great game which has contributed so much to war-time recreation. This may sound strange to English people who have seen Australian Test teams in action, but I am not thinking of big cricket. I refer to the club cricketers – the thousands of flannelled fools – who keep the game alive without receiving any limelight.

Andrew found solace in the:

> atmosphere of your smaller, friendly-looking grounds, where the spectators sit in deck chairs or on the grass around the boundary! These surroundings give the player confidence and make him feel at home. When stumps are drawn he is one of a happy family fraternising in the club room over a mild-and-bitter or a pale ale. Licensing laws in Australia do not encourage this after-the-game social spirit. Is it any wonder, then, that we park and club cricketers considered it a privilege to play in this country? … we Australians are glad we have had the opportunity of visiting the cradle of cricket. We greatly admire the game as it is played over here as well as your cricketers, and we appreciate all the hospitality we have received from everyone connected with it.

In all, the RAAF team played eight matches in 1943, with an equal share of victories and defeats. Against a Public School Wanderers XI at Hove, Keith Miller scored 141 in faster-than-even time. Although his reputation was being burnished on the field off play, away from the thrill of the sport, Miller continued to fail to see eye to eye with those tasked with channelling his mercurial talent. One night in late 1943, at RAF South Cerney in Gloucestershire, he was pulled over by his commanding officer for failing to wear a cap. In the ensuing altercation Miller squared up to the man, as if to punch him. His punishment for being found guilty of insubordination was a three-week disciplinary course with hard labour.

The final RAAF XI match of 1943 was against the RAF at Lord's, with Miller taking three for 23 and scoring 91. Miller also played for a Dominions XI against an England XI at Lord's, scoring 32. This was the first instance in which Miller and his future friend and sparring partner Denis Compton appeared in the same match. The occasion was marked by Miller bowling a bumper which flew over Compton's shoulder for four byes.

Although somewhat overshadowed by the glamorous Miller and his RAAF comrades, the contribution of the New Zealand Services XI added spice to English wartime cricketing fare. The outfit was formed at the beginning of 1943, with Pilot Officer Eric Grant acting as honorary secretary. Grant had navigated several raids with the New Zealand bomber squadron before taking on the role of sport officer, attached to the New Zealand Air Liaison Office. The National Patriotic Fund furnished playing kit and accessories. Players would be expected to stand their own rail fare, but usually found that off-duty leave would be granted to participate in morale-boosting sporting fixtures. The XI beat South Hampstead CC by 91 runs on 1 August, with Stewie Dempster scoring 64 and Reg Carter 84 not out. At Mote Park, Maidstone, on 14 August, they won bragging rights as they defeated an RAAF XI by 79 runs, with Geoff Rabone scoring 70 and taking three for 17.

Adversaries become comrades at Blackpool's Stanley Park Ground, which had been commandeered by the RAF for training purposes. A two-day match took place between a strong RAF XI against the Dominions on 21–22 August 1943. Six Kiwis took part alongside Keith Carmody, Mick Roper and Keith Miller. Due to the first day being ruined by rain, Miller led some players towards alternative entertainment in the local greyhound races.

North West cricket fans could feast on an array of entertainment during the

New Zealander Bob Metcalf's annotated match programme from RAF XI *v* Dominions at Blackpool. Metcalf recorded the crowd as 10–12,000, the scores of fellow Kiwis Stewie Dempster and Ken James, and that he claimed the wicket of Bob Wyatt for 37. (*Courtesy the Metcalf family*)

summer of 1943. A crowd of 10,000 thronged the ground at Fazakerley to watch a West Indies XI play a match for the Lord Mayor of Liverpool's Charity Fund. A fixture on 11 July at Colwyn Bay CC's delightful Rhos-on-Sea ground between North Wales and an Empire XI raised £3,664 for the Red Cross Prisoner of War Fund. Despite the match ending in a tame draw, the crowd was enchanted by a typically swashbuckling 57 by Learie Constantine, coming in at No. 6 for the Empire XI. Contributions from Lancashire quadragenarians Eddie Paynter and Charlie Hallows helped raise the final total to 217 for nine. The highest contribution for North Wales, who included Len Hutton amongst their number, was from 23-year-old Willie Watson, with 53. After the war, Watson would become the penultimate man to play both cricket and football for England. By the end of the season Colwyn Bay CC had generated £5,965 for various funds and charities. The £3,664 donated to the Red Cross was, according to the recipient of the cheque, Stanley Rous, a record for a cricket club.

Lancashire cricket followers could frequently watch a collection of players put together by the Ministry of Labour, irreverently called the 'Lancashire Circus', to assist in Wings for Victory and Holidays at Home weeks. At Didsbury, an England and Counties XII drew with a West Indies XII. Locals were treated to the Caribbean talents of Edwin St Hill, Learie Constantine and Clifford Roach against an English side packed with country stalwarts and the stardust of George Duckworth and Charlie Hallows. Broadly the same set of players, minus Duckworth, entertained the crowds at Longsight, Manchester, on 14 June in a low-scoring encounter. At Warrington, an England & Counties XI played a West Indies XII on 4 July, with the Caribbean team slumping to 87 all out in reply to England's 153 for six. The 42-year-old George Duckworth had also thrown himself wholeheartedly into the task of keeping the nation's larders well stocked. Rearing cattle and pigs on his 120-acre farm near Warrington, it was a commonplace sight to see the Lancashire and England gloveman driving his swine through the town's streets.

A charity match at Ealing between the home club and a Combined Services XI raised about £400 for the Merchant Navy Comforts Fund. The final big game of the 1943 season at Chichester generated £200 for the Royal Sussex Regiment PoW Fund. Parcels of cigarettes to the value of £979 and books to the value of £48 had been sent during the past year to camps in

George Duckworth.

Italy and Germany. Whit Monday, 14 June, saw the raising of what was thought to be the largest sum of money from one match in aid of the Red Cross, as the spectators enjoying the encounter between Cheam CC and Surrey Colts donated £500 to the noble cause. Several thousand people attended a match on 15 August between Finchley and A.J.B. Fowler's XII, with £150 being donated to the Merchant Navy Comforts Fund as a result. Fowler's team won on the final ball of the match, after Laurie Fishlock (67) and Eric Bedser (62) made valuable contributions. Such was Epsom CC's success in organising charity matches against most representative teams that their efforts were rewarded with more coverage in *Wisden* than any individual county side. The *Almanack* also managed to devote a quarter of its content to public school cricket, despite the widespread appeal of the game around the country as manifested in competitive leagues, amateur clubs, factory teams, office and other workplace elevens and the armed forces and civilian services.

* * *

By late 1943, nearly 300 children of London firemen had endured the pain of their fathers having perished while saving their fellow city dwellers from blitz raids. Each child was 'adopted' by a London fire station. The London Fire Service Benevolent Fund's Orphans Adoption Scheme donated £25 10s in National Savings Certificates to each child and bought annuities of 4/- per week up to the age of 14. These efforts were supported by a collection during a club match between Rediffusion and S.E.M. Beckenham for the Rediffusion Cup, part of the Holidays at Home Programme.

Although the blitz on London had caused much misery and pain, one more positive side effect was the improvement of the Ashton Playing Fields at Woodford Bridge, Essex. After the fields had been laid out in 1937, flooding at the low end became a recurrent winter problem. An ingenious idea to use some of the London debris caused by the Luftwaffe to raise these low-lying areas by 6 feet was implemented. The topsoil was re-spread and grass seeds planted. After three years the ground was finally ready to host a match between Patsy Hendren's XI and B.J. Brooker's Ilford XI on 8 August. Hubert and Gilbert Ashton, whose father had donated £10,000 towards the establishment of the playing fields and associated welfare and educational facilities, were in the Hendren XI, alongside Essex stalwart Jack O'Connor. Proceeds from the entrance fee of 6d were used to provide additional facilities for the children's playground at the Ashton fields.

Frank Woolley, serving as cricket coach to the temporarily Cornwall-evacuated King's School, Canterbury, had found the time to play in some Wings for Victory and Red Cross matches in the South West. Against G.L. Tonkin's Truro XI, he took two for 36 and scored a delightful 62. He raised a Masters and Boys team to play a St Austell and District XI in aid of the Red Cross, taking

Men play cricket in blitz-damaged London, October 1945.

six wickets for 5 runs. The war hung heavy in the great man's heart. His only son, Richard Frank, was killed in action on convoy duty in 1940 and his own Cliftonville home was destroyed shortly afterwards by a stray Luftwaffe bomb.

The second Birmingham Cricket Festival took place on 2–6 August. Prior to the previous year's gala, the Edgbaston ground had been in a derelict state, with the grass 18 inches high. An army of resolute volunteers turned it into a wicket worthy of top-class cricket. Once again Lieutenant Colonel 'Rusty' Scorer had assembled a fine collection of matches, with Warwickshire CCC lending the ground for free. Further interest was generated by A.W. Heath, a local magistrate, offering £1 for every six struck by a player in an innings, provided he hit a minimum of three. Further north, Leeds's magnificent Roundhay Park continued to attract crowds of 20,000 for its Sunday charity matches, making it the ideal venue for the city's cricket week, with appearances from county players currently engaged with northern league cricket and teams from Civil Defence and the Army.

Alec Bedser appeared in an England XI led by Les Ames, which took on a West Indies XI at Lord's on 29 May. A big match atmosphere prevailed, with a crowd of 18,010 paying spectators. It was in this match that three stalwarts of the post-war England team, Bedser, Trevor Bailey and Godfrey Evans, first played in the same side. Bedser excelled with figures of six for 27 in eight overs, including a hat-trick. He repeated the same feat for the RAF against the Metropolitan Police at Westcliff. Remarkably, his twin brother Eric had achieved two hat-tricks at Hove the previous summer. Alec, according to *The Cricketer*, possessed 'the necessary stamina ... his fast medium deliveries make haste off the ground. He knows too the value of length and he is one to keep an eye on.' Bailey was marked out as 'a thorough cricketer'. The match brought a chink of daylight through the clouds of war. 'Even in the midst of the greatest of wars cricket is still an incomparable game, and as the Home Secretary has put it: "Total war does not mean total gloom."' Oliver Stanley MP, Secretary of State for the Colonies, was in attendance, and £324 was raised for the Colonial Comforts Fund.

The Army had much the better of a drawn match at Lord's on 17 July against their habitual rivals, the RAF. Having been defeated heavily on Whit Monday, the troops moved up some big guns, including Gubby Allen, Errol Holmes, Stewie Dempster and Denis Compton. A crowd of over 20,000 saw Compton – having recently recovered from an operation on his varicose veins, and not having picked up a bat all summer – top score with an 83 full of quick footwork and beautiful strokes. *The Cricketer* purred, 'Compton always looks to have the best driving bat that was ever made.' With half centuries from Dempster and Maurice Leyland, The Army declared on 284 for six. Forty-one-year-old Allen then bowled with the venom of a man a decade younger to dismiss Ames and Gregory before the determined Bob Wyatt dug in to ensure a draw for the airmen.

* * *

Club Cricket Conference teams raised £1,598 for the Red Cross during the season. C.S. Davies, the Alexandra Park player, achieved a remarkable season's double of 3,026 runs and 214 wickets. His club had managed an admirable 115 matches in 1943. Len Newman's 130 not out was his 214th century in London club cricket, scored on his fifty-second birthday. Another significant achievement came from W.H. Chinnery, who on successive Essex Saturdays took ten for 36 and ten for 43 for Orsett CC against Jurgens CC and Hornchurch CC respectively. Nearby Buckhurst Hill CC could boast fifty-seven of their playing members in the services. One of them, Lieutenant Alan Lavers, an occasional Essex county all-rounder, was amongst the first gunners of the victorious Eighth Army to enter Benghazi. Four other members were serving overseas. Sadly, three of their cricketing comrades had made the ultimate sacrifice, including Major John Huskisson of the King's Royal Rifle Corps, who had been the 1st XI vice-captain. D.S. Jennings had survived a heart wound in France but was unable to resume playing. Despite the great drain on their playing resources Buckhurst Hill managed to continue playing on their delightful ground on the edge of Epping Forest; indeed, owing to an influx of new members, an extra XI was established. Sizeable crowds would sometimes flock to non-competitive southern club cricket. In early June, over 3,000 spectators saw Finchley take on the London Australians.

The necessity of filling club team sheets with players well into the veteran stage of their careers made for careers of notable longevity. Colin McIver, the former Essex wicketkeeper-batsman, was still captaining and donning the keeper's gloves for Ashtead, his Surrey club, aged 62. Arthur Paish, fast approaching his seventieth birthday, was still turning out occasionally for the Wagon Works Club, for whom he was employed as groundsman. In one match he made 60, at a run a minute. His former Gloucestershire county colleague, Percy Mills, 64, serving as coach to Radley College, managed the hat-trick in a minor match. C. Aubrey Smith, the noted film star who had captained England in his only Test match back in 1889, defied Father Time by pulling on the whites once more. Having given generous support to East Molesey CC's attempt to purchase their ground, he was persuaded to return to the game. He was permitted a runner but wrote, 'and didn't I get a wigging when I got home for playing against Doctor's orders'.

The summer afforded its fill of unusual feats. On 24 July, J. Walker opened the batting for Walton Heath CC against Burgh Heath CC at the Tattenham Way Ground. In the first twenty-one balls of the innings he raced to 50, those being the only runs on the scoreboard at that point. Lieutenant J. Yarranton RN took six wickets in six balls for a Navy XI in a services match, to reduce his opponents from 47 for four to 47 all out. A rare counterpoint to the general enterprise and dash of wartime cricket was witnessed in a match between Kingston Grammar School and MCC on 22 July. Proceedings began at 11.40 am and when lunch was taken at 1.00 pm, the Marylebone club's score stood at eight for 8. Refreshment seemed to perk up the remaining batsmen, as Peter Murray-Willis (41 not out) and A.W. Forsdike (39) raised the total to a semi-respectable 95 for nine declared. A remarkable 73 six-ball overs had been sent down by the grammar school boys, 34 of which were maidens. Kingston were dismissed for a mere 37, bringing an unlikely win for MCC.

An amusing incident occurred at Lord's in a match between Cross Arrows and United Hospitals. For this relatively minor encounter a wicket was cut close to the Tavern. R.H. Twining, the Middlesex wicketkeeper-batsman, persuaded the

R.H. Twining.

Cross Arrows captain to allow him to bowl his inaugural over on the famous ground. The batsmen ran one four as the ball failed to reach the long boundary, then the fifth ball of the over was struck in the same area and chased by two elderly and already exhausted fieldsmen, resulting in an all-run 6. However, one batsman was considerably fleeter of foot than his partner, thus they ended up at the same end, and a run-out of the striker was effected, with six runs to his credit.

Despite wartime exigencies, clubs on the south coast soldiered on. The Priory Club had been formed in Hastings in 1939, but 1940 saw all their rival local clubs suspend activities. Thus, the club arranged many service matches at the Hastings Central Ground, with Bill Edrich, Les Ames and Arthur Fagg appearing there in the early years of the war. The ground was one of the first to be affected by German bombing, but the damage was repaired without a match having to be cancelled. London Counties XI also appeared in 1940 and 1941, whilst 1943 saw three matches against members of the RAAF.

* * *

As in England and other Test-playing countries, so the game in far-flung countries soldiered on despite the constraints of war. The Argentine Sunday competition had to be suspended but the Saturday Championship provided some keen cricket, with Old Georgians edging out Buenos Aires. A charity match took place at Belgrano during the carnival festivities, with over $600 being raised for the Prisoner of War Fund. Many players benefitted from the coaching of the mercurial Hampshire all-rounder Len Creese, serving with the Army in the country. Creese was rarely far from the bizarre and tragic, having accidentally shot his county teammate Gerry Hill in the leg before the war. Hill described Creese as being 'as mad as a hatter', although that ebullience was drained when, having taken up a post-war position as groundsman at Hastings, he saw his precious grandson killed by a heavy roller.

What was initially thought to be the first recorded match in Ethiopia took place on 28 March 1943 between Major Welldon's XI and a battalion of the King's African Rifles. As the matting available was only 10 yards long, all the bowling came from one end, with the batsmen changing ends every eight balls. Hours of play were 9.00 am to 12 noon and 3.00 pm to 6.15 pm to avoid the high point of the heat. The intense glare and stony ground made fielding something of a problem. The KAR XI gained an emphatic win. In response to coverage of this match, John Nash, the Yorkshire CCC secretary serving with the Royal Signals, wrote to say that he had previously played in a match in Ethiopia, for Harar v Dire Dawa in January 1942, being dismissed first ball.

In Rhodesia, civilian clubs found it increasingly difficult to muster regular teams but managed to participate in the continuing leagues, which were augmented by RAF and Army XIs. The big match of the season featured RAF Rhodesia against the Rest of Rhodesia, with Flight Lieutenant A.P. 'Sandy' Singleton scoring a flawless 120 and taking seven wickets with his googlies for the flyers. Singleton, a Repton schoolmaster, who would captain Worcestershire in 1946, was the outstanding player in Rhodesian cricket, also demonstrating his unbounded enthusiasm for the game by his unselfish imparting of his knowledge to others, and the time he spent coaching in local schools.

The year 1943 was a successful one for cricket on the island of Mauritius, with the home club playing many service and Merchant Navy sides. J.F. Ireland, a Cambridge blue in 1908–11, scored 75 and 25 in his two innings. The bleak lava-strewn island of Iceland witnessed its first known cricket match on 12 August, when the RN and RNVR took on a team comprised of RAF, RAAF and RNZAF personnel. Gear was borrowed from a naval vessel. Surgeon Lieutenant D. Rice RNVR secured the loan of a sports stadium in Reykjavik, a hard football ground of baked lava mud. Coconut matting was nailed down over the pitch and the spectacle was witnessed by Icelanders and US troops, the latter bellowing phrases such as 'Get started' and 'Get that ball in'. At one point when a wicket fell a cry of 'Railway' could be heard. The puzzled players later learned this was a baseball expression meaning to sidetrack a man i.e. 'chuck him out of the team'. The airmen emerged victorious.

In Ireland it was proving difficult to maintain the standard of play seen during the previous three seasons. Poor weather was a factor, as was the loss of players on overseas service for some clubs. Phoenix's Jimmy Boucher, whose looping off breaks had previously claimed seven for 13 against the 1937 New Zealand tourists, and who many judges considered would have made a fine county player, had bamboozled his way to fifty-two wickets at an average of 6.3 by the middle of July. A further reason for the temporary stagnation of Irish cricket was the lack of cross-fertilisation with their counterparts on the British mainland. It was not until this season that the British Representative in Eire, Sir John Maffey, was able to raise a team to cross the Irish Sea to play Dublin University in the annual Trinity Week match.

Attempts were made by young RAF men training in the United States to convert the locals to the game. Americans stationed in the UK were also exposed to the beauties of cricket. History was made on Saturday, 18 September when two all-American teams played a match 'somewhere in England'. The sides were composed of USAAF officers representing two different stations. The fielding and throwing was of a higher quality than the batting, with totals of 92 and 35. Errol Holmes wrote: 'those of us Britishers who were fortunate enough to be there, will never forget the spectacle of our American friends playing keenly and enthusiastically and thoroughly enjoying an afternoon that had been devoted to England's National Game.'

* * *

The growing cricketing interest of American servicemen was symbolised by the presence at the England XI *v* Dominions XI at Lord's of the American Major General John C.H. Lee and his staff as guests of honour. Lee was a prominent advocate of the equal treatment and integration of African-Americans in the then segregated US Army, just as the Dominions players formed a cohesive unit regardless of race. That match was arguably the highlight of the 1943 season, as over 38,000 spectators crammed into Lord's over two fine August days. 'A better game of cricket could scarcely be imagined,' enthused *The Cricketer*, with fortune smiling first on one side, then the other. The first day had seemingly put the match beyond the reach of the Dominions, with England scoring 308 to their 115 all out. England batted on in the second day, with Walter Robins driving, hooking and cutting his way to a whirlwind 69. A declaration set the Dominions an imposing 360 runs for victory. Despite a fine innings from Stewie Dempster, England looked set for a comfortable victory at 218 for seven but Stan Sismey and Bertie Clarke put on 108 for the eighth wicket, leaving the final two wickets to make 34 for an unlikely win. With the clock pointing at a quarter to seven, 11 runs were needed with just one wicket remaining. New South Welshman A.W. 'Mick' Roper sent the last ball of a Jack Robertson over soaring up towards cover point. Trevor Bailey sprinted round to his left from extra cover, appeared to misjudge the flight of the ball, but managed to cling on to it. Both sides had covered themselves in glory for the manner in which they had gone about their business.

Shamefully the admiration shown by much of the cricketing public to the various West Indies cricketers who plied their trade and otherwise supported the nation's war effort masked a nasty undercurrent of racism. That paragon of racial integration and social harmony, Learie Constantine, fell foul of this during the very match that was being portrayed as a symbol of the Empire's common cause. In September 1943 it was reported that Constantine had been subject to an impromptu 'colour bar' at the Imperial Hotel in Russell Square. He had checked in, with his family and accompanied by Liverpool cricket impresario Charles Leatherbarrow, to take part in the big match at Lord's and been allocated rooms. Later the hotel's manager informed Constantine that he could only accommodate them for one night. One account suggested an American guest had exclaimed: 'The hotel is coming to something if you have to take niggers in.' Constantine replied that he had booked for four nights, to which the manager replied that he could ask the party to leave at any time. Constantine challenged the manager to eject him or declare him an undesirable person.

The manager offered the party alternative accommodation at a nearby hotel. To avoid further agitation, and at the suggestion of the Regional Officer of the Ministry of Labour, 'in the interests of peace and dignity' Constantine relented and grudgingly moved hotels. He subsequently sued Imperial London Hotels Ltd and the incident was raised in the House of Commons by Norman Bower,

MP for Harrow. The League of Coloured People took up the case with the Colonial Office, who put a ban on any venue exercising a colour bar. In October, Constantine spoke at a meeting to raise funds for Britain's first community centre for coloured people:

> With the advent of every war where a white man resorts to arms to settle his differences it does not require an extraordinary amount of imagination to see the opportunities opened up to the negro. Were I Paul Robeson I would sing the negro song of hope and faith 'Go tell them we are rising'.

The case eventually came to court in June 1944 and Constantine was awarded nominal damages of £5. He declined to sue further for defamation, considering that he had already drawn the British public's attention to the case and that their 'sense of fair play might hope to protect people of my colour in England in the future'. He expressed no bitterness and was rewarded for his stance by many letters of admiration and offers of personal accommodation for future London visits.

Aside from his appearances in the Bradford League and various charity match XIs, Constantine had been working for the Ministry of Labour supporting the welfare of West Indian technicians who had come to work in Liverpool's factories. His emollient character served to improve industrial relations between West African sailors and their employers in Merseyside and to persuade the League of Coloured Peoples to hold its annual conference in the city for the first time.

Constantine's companion during the unsavoury incident, Charles Leatherbarrow, had got through a tremendous amount of work organising and promoting charity cricket in the Liverpool district. As part of the Holidays at Home scheme he put together a North of England team to play the South of England at Gloucester over three days at the end of July. When a Lancashire XI beat a West Indies XI at Longsight by 30 runs on 18 July, the depth of quality available to raise teams in the county was demonstrated by the fact that on the same day a Charles Leatherbarrow XI *v* Blackpool Services fixture took place at Southport, with a liberal sprinkling of first-class players on display. A Rest of England XI which took on Lancashire at Stockport on 12 August included two West Indians, Ellis Achong and Manny Martindale. Three days later, when two sides with the same nomenclature met at Longsight, Martindale had become a member of the Lancashire XI whilst Achong remained with the Rest of England, being joined by fellow West Indian Edwin St Hill.

* * *

The eightieth edition of *Wisden Cricketers' Almanack* made a very welcome, if belated, appearance at the beginning of August. Increased production costs meant the price had to be raised to 6s 6d. There was an escalation of production numbers compared to the previous two summers, with 1,400 hardback and 5,600 softback editions published, a total increase of 2,000 compared to 1941. R.C. Robertson-Glasgow sounded a democratic note in proposing the abolition of the class distinction on the cricket field: 'The position of a cricketer's initials and the precise gate from which he should enter the field has long seemed vastly absurd. The pro's pay is direct, the amateur's indirect. To both cricket is the source (partly/entirely) of livelihood. To distinguish between them is surely humbug.'

Although much discussed during the war, a further generation of post-war professional cricketers would have second-class status thrust upon them by the game's governors before the meritocratic 1960s brought the abolition of the anomaly.

Plum Warner eulogised on the successes of the 1943 season in *The Cricketer Winter Annual*, although through typically south of England tinted spectacles, with 'Lord's naturally [being] the centre of the most important matches', although there 'was plenty of excellent cricket played in other parts of the country'. So, 'the game held its own extremely well'. Lord's had welcomed 232,390 paying spectators, with £3,450 13s 11d worth of net receipts being allocated to various charities.

* * *

Without the benefit of the domestic cricketing infrastructure, service personnel posted overseas continued to make extensive efforts to play the game. On 4 June, the Reverend G.L.O. Jessop scored 101 and took three for 36 for the 1st Royal Marines Group in their win over the 2nd Royal Marines Group. His innings included a six and sixteen fours. On the following day he hit 60 as the 1st Royal Marines lost to a strong Maadi Sporting Club XI, which included Kiwis Eric Tindill and Martin Donnelly. On 6 June, a Sunday, the clergyman marked the Lord's Day by hitting 112 as the Royal Marines defeated the Gezira Sporting Club, reaching his century in forty-nine minutes. By July 1943, the North African Campaign having come to a successful conclusion, Jessop had been transferred to Ceylon. The *Ceylon Observer* noted: 'Rev G.L.O. Jessop, who made several big scores in local club cricket, both in Colombo and Galle last year, is back in Colombo.' He was due to take part in a trial match which included cricketers from all three branches of service. As well as his cricketing and military duties, Jessop was also able to officiate at the wedding of Freda Litchfield, a WREN, to Major Wade of the Ceylon Army Service Corps. The ceremony took place at Christ Church, Galle Face, a place of worship also regularly frequented by Corporal L.W. Hall of the RAF.

Having attended a morning thanksgiving service in September 1943 to mark the third anniversary of victory in the Battle of Britain, Hall spent the afternoon playing cricket. On other occasions he watched and played at the Galle Face and Maitland Crescent grounds in Colombo. Keeping wicket on the matting pitches could be a treacherous enterprise, as several balls might stand up viciously, on one occasion catching Hall a nasty blow on the chest. However, his opportunities for play were few, as he was reluctant to forsake evensong at 6.00 pm for the pleasures of cricket. Despite this forbearance, the receipt of a copy of a 1943 *Wisden* from his friend, Doug Bird, provided much cerebral cricketing sustenance during Hall's time in Ceylon.

Prior to his noble death in July, another cricketer from a Christian milieu, Hedley Verity, had played for the Green Howards against the Gezira Club. Verity having taken five wickets, with his Yorkshire teammate Norman Yardley contributing 71, it was left to Laurie Hesmondhalgh to contrive two fortuitous boundaries in the final over to secure a one-wicket win. Tragically, Captain Hesmondhalgh's luck would run out a few weeks later as he was killed outright in the action that would also claim the life of his worthy teammate. It was reported from correspondents in Italy that Hedley Verity's hair 'had gone quite white' after a severe attack of dysentery but that the revered Yorkshireman was in good health once again. Sadly, this recovery would only prove temporary.

As the Allies celebrated the successful subjugation of Rommel's Afrika Korps with the fall of Tunisia on 13 May, thoughts of cricket long ago had helped to sustain the morale of one young enthusiast of the game. Corporal John Broom of No. 7 Light Field Ambulance RAMC, part of the 7th Armoured Division, the 'Desert Rats', had carried a copy of E.V. Lucas's classic *The Hambledon Men* in his kitbag from the Second Battle of El Alamein, through the Western Desert and Libya and on to Tunisia. Being able to cast his mind back to the country and the game he loved so much brought great comfort during the terribly trying experience of desert warfare. Broom, a follower of Essex CCC, would have been delighted to learn of the awarding of a DSO to the county's fast bowler, Lieutenant Colonel J.W.A. Stephenson, for his services in Tunisia. Stephenson was described by Home Gordon as 'the play-boy of first-class cricket, the joy-man whose energy is so great that when he has bowled and fielded until tea time he goes to the nets for exercise whilst his own side is batting'.

It was reported that Flying Officer Harry Parks, the Sussex all-round cricketer and county level footballer, was organising hockey, football and cricket matches around Tunis. Not every serviceman had such fulsome playing opportunities. Arthur Wellard, the lusty-hitting Somerset all-rounder, had used part of the £1,418 raised in his 1939 benefit match to buy a tobacco and confectionary business, a distinct gamble in wartime. Mrs Wellard was running the flourishing business while her husband was serving with the RAOC in Algiers. However, he was regretting that his unit was taking part in every sport except cricket.

In recognition of the contribution that the playing and watching of sport could make to military morale, the Egyptian Government built the Alamein

Club, 'presented by the people of Egypt to the Seaman, Soldiers and Airmen' of the Allied forces. Named after the decisive battle of the Desert Campaign, the club would eclipse the Gezira Club as the premier cricketing venue in the area. Lieutenant General Sir Bernard Freyberg, who had done much to encourage the playing of cricket by his New Zealand troops, attended the opening ceremony in May. The cricket ground had a fine pavilion, with a bell from El Alamein railway station installed at the front, which was rung to signal the start of play.

Gerald Pawle, formerly *The Cricketer*'s northern correspondent, worked for the British Admiralty's Directorate of Miscellaneous Weapons Development during the war. Colloquially known as the 'Wheezers and Dodgers', Pawle and his colleagues undertook anti-

Arthur Wellard.

aircraft research, providing devices such as vertical rocket mountings; anti-submarine research, producing radar deflectors and decoy; and amphibious assaults research, producing nets for landing craft. Pawle described efforts by the Royal Navy to provide cricket for its sailors stationed in Egypt. At the Alexandria Ground, surrounded by frequently sprayed lawns, flowerbeds and paths, the local club augmented their own extensive fixture list by allowing a succession of service teams to play on their 70-year-old ground. The fast outfield meant rapid scoring was possible. In one match between Royal Navy Over 30s and Royal Navy Under 30s, 450 runs were scored in three-and-a-half hours.

The RN ran a league competition of ten teams from May till September. RN Barracks, with a selection of Birmingham League and Durham League players, won nine out of ten matches to claim the title. Commander Richard White, a former Northumberland player, who had earned a DSO with two bars, played in occasional matches at Alexandria. White's father, Archibald, had captained Yorkshire before the First World War. Pawle lauded their efforts:

> I hope the organisers of the many games in Cairo and Alexandria realised how much it meant to men who had spent weary months of hard living and fighting in the wastes of the Western Desert – and to men of the Royal Navy who had probably not seen cricket in years, to be able to forget War for a few brief hours in playing or watching the game which, more than any other, brings memories of Home – and England at peace.

In a minor match in Alexandria between the Military Police and Clairwood, Dudley Nourse raced to 109 in thirty minutes. Describing it as 'probably the most hectic innings of my career', Nourse recalled, 'The mood to hit burst upon me and as I had already scored over 50 and had no particular wish to remain for any length of time, I set about the bowling.' One six-ball over saw all the deliveries hit out of the ground, followed by the next three balls Nourse faced in the following over.

Plans were made for New Zealand and South African teams to play three unofficial war Tests, the first of which took place on the second oval at the Gezira Sporting Club on 8 August. The Springboks took to the field full of the joy of renewed comradeship. Dudley Nourse recalled:

Dudley Nourse.

> It was difficult to know exactly who was in the war theatre until a game of that nature was arranged, when old friends would be unexpectedly met. Once the fellows, drawn from different units, were assembled, there were exclamations of delight as old pals saw each other again after long absences from contact.

Herbie Wade, captain of the successful 1935 tour of England, was summoned to lead the Springboks, with Nourse, Bob Harvey, Frank Nicholson and the redoubtable Major Bob Crisp making up a quintet of Test players. Despite facing this formidable array of talent, the New Zealanders squeezed home with an 8-run victory.

The second encounter took place the following Sunday. An official souvenir score card was produced with the Egyptian State Broadcasting Service giving regular wireless updates throughout the day. The Kiwis had been bolstered by the addition of Martin Donnelly. Despite his contribution of 47, the New Zealanders only amassed 152 runs and South Africa squared the series with an empathic nine-wicket win. Alan Burgess, a teammate of Donnelly's, recalled: 'He was good at everything. He was just one of those naturals. As far as the army went, he had to be an officer. He was just a good fellow.' The concluding unofficial Test was held at the Maadi Sporting Club ground. For this deciding fixture, New Zealand benefitted from the addition of Tom Pritchard whilst South Africa fielded a full side with previous or future first-class experience. Kiwi captain Bill Carson took the unusual step of inserting the opposition, but his judgment was justified as the South Africans were skittled for 114, with Herbie Wade top scoring with 40. Dudley Nourse commented: 'The wicket, matting over grass is not helpful to bowlers, but even so, Pritchard extracted some sort of assistance from it, which made me realise he would be an uncommonly good bowler on a pacy pitch.' In reply, New Zealand were tottering at 45 for three but Martin Donnelly and Roy Anzac Robinson, a 1916 baby, steered them to victory. One of the jubilant Kiwis, right-arm fast-medium bowler Neil Begg, later recalled the pleasure players derived from these encounters at the Egyptian country club grounds: 'the wickets at the Gezira and Maadi grounds were good and I remember with pleasure the dignified waiters bringing us cool drinks on silver trays at relatively frequent intervals. At the time I thought it was a fine way of waging total war.'

The final match of the NZ Base XI's season was against a strong Gezira Sporting Club XI, which included Essex duo Peter Smith and J.W.A. Stephenson, and Flight Lieutenant S.K. 'Shunter' Coen, the Springbok Test bowler. Martin Donnelly was once again in form, top scoring with 109 in ninety-three minutes. The master New Zealand batsman was also invited to play for the Gezira Club on several occasions that summer, finishing with the remarkable batting average of 355. He later recalled:

Roy Anzac Robinson.

> I could hardly get out. If I hit the ball in the air, some chap would fall over before he got underneath it, or if he got there, one of his colleagues arrived simultaneously! But I thoroughly enjoyed these very pleasant conditions; we'd come off the field pretty hot and sticky and there would be a little Arab or Sudanese boy waiting with a great hot towel … after the shower or bath. It was cricket in luxury.

Another emerging talent who had a successful Egyptian season was Jim Laker. The modest Yorkshireman struck 500 runs and took twenty-five wickets in seven matches in Cairo against the RNZAF, RAF and various Army XIs. Against the RAF, having discovered the ability to produce prodigious spin and bounce on the matting wickets of the Middle East, he turned in figures of five for 10, including the hat-trick.

Martin Donnelly.

The peculiarities of playing cricket in the searing Egyptian sun were highlighted by Dudley Nourse:

> It was during one of these games that I experienced a curious ruling. An appeal against the light was lodged while the sun was still shining brightly

from a cloudless sky. Pothecary was batting and a tall palm tree from behind the pavilion cast a shadow directly over the wicket. Pothecary appealed the light, there was a brief consultation between the umpires, and the players trooped off for the day much to the astonishment of those who had been able to come along to watch the game. It was odd.

Alf Gover.

Wartime cricket in the Middle East took on a form of its own as the matting wickets allowed the bowler a greater degree of spin and lift than traditional grass strips. For swing bowlers, their main weapon was nullified by the dry African airs. Across the summer of 1943, about 1,000 players took part in inter-unit games at the Maadi Camp. Each team was usually allocated two hours' batting time and eight-ball overs were standard. To avoid the glare from the blazing desert sun the action took place in the afternoon.

Lieutenant Colonel Michael White, the former Cambridge University and future Northamptonshire all-rounder, had not allowed the fighting in North Africa to dull his appetite for the game. On 26 April, within the sound of the guns of the final assault on Tunis, he played his first match overseas. This was the first of a weekly series, on a satisfactory matting wicket on hard earth, but the outfield 'had to be seen to be believed'. White put an appeal in *The Cricketer* for cricket balls, in whatever condition, to provide for his men.

Norman Preston, future editor of *Wisden*, received an airgraph from Lieutenant Alf Gover. Writing from a military hospital in Cape Town on 16 April, the Surrey fast bowler wrote: 'I have been "shoved" down here with a leg injury. It's a fine town, grand weather and scenery … I am hoping that this injury will not make any difference to my game. Otherwise I shall have to take up bowls.' His fellow Surrey opening bowler and brother-in-law, Captain Eddie Watts, also wrote to Preston of having been in at the denouement of the Tunisian Campaign. Watts noted of the country that if only there were a couple of sightscreens in the valley it could have been England.

* * *

Those far less fortunate servicemen destined to spend their war in prison camps resolutely carried on playing cricket whenever possible. In October, William Hickey devoted his *Daily Express* column to coverage of a triangular tournament between England, Australia and New Zealand at Stammlager 383. Hickey had received his information on a postcard sent by Sergeant Keith Hooper of Hull.

British soldiers playing cricket at Stalag VIIIB at Lamsdorf, Germany.

Two days were given to each match, with England vanquishing New Zealand, but both countries being soundly beaten by Australia.

D.E. Young, who had been a prisoner of war since 1940, wrote of the improvements in cricketing infrastructure at Oflag VI-B. The game had progressed from being played with tennis balls, home-made bats and a stool for a wicket. For the 1943 season real bats and stumps had been procured, and a matting wicket, real cricket balls and bats were available. It was also noted that it was 'pleasant to learn that *The Cricketer* is circulating throughout Young's camp'.

A report was received by *The Cricketer* about an 'England' v 'Australia' Test match at Stalag Luft VI, the northernmost prisoner-of-war camp within the area of the German Reich, situated in modern-day Lithuania. Headlined as 'Farthest North Test Match', a full two innings were played with the result having echoes of the Old Trafford Test of 1902, Australia nudging home by 3 runs. Incidentally, Fred Tate, whose misfortune in that match led to his moniker being applied to it, had died in February.

At Oflag 79, near Brunswick, Bill Bowes, Freddie Brown and their comrades, who had been transferred from Italian to German hands, kept up morale by organising sports. William Bompas, a Royal Artillery officer, recalled:

Cricket was played on four or five afternoons on the asphalt down the centre, with 6 and more or less out when the ball was hit onto one of the flat roofs. [Bowes and Brown] and a lot of club players took part, and the standard was really very good.

News from the Far East confirmed that Lieutenant Wilf Wooller, the Glamorgan all-rounder and Welsh rugby union international, who was serving with the 77th Heavy Anti-Aircraft Regiment, was safe. Wooller had taken a degree in anthropology at Cambridge before also playing centre forward for Cardiff City. Having been captured the previous February, after fifteen anxious months without any news it was reported that a message from Wooller had been broadcast from Tokyo and picked up in New Zealand. He had stated that he was well and had been able to play some outdoor games.

* * *

First-class cricket records were set during the 1943/44 season in India and New Zealand. An anonymous member of the Royal Navy, writing in *The Cricketer*, had arrived on the subcontinent in November 1943 during the first few days of the Bombay Pentangular Tournament. Making his way to the Brabourne Stadium to watch Muslims *v* The Rest, he found the ground to have few equals as a modern sporting arena. The members' pavilion had a small swimming pool attached. He noted that the crowd was far more demonstrative than the spectators at the average English county match. An electric bell was run each time an individual or team total was increased by a further 10 runs. The tournament's final, played over 3–6 December, made cricketing history as V.S. Hazare became the first player to score a triple-century yet end up on the receiving end of an innings defeat. Following on 448 runs behind for The Rest against Hindus, his 309 out of 387 also broke the tournament record, which had very recently been set in the Hindus' first innings, Vijay Merchant compiling 250. On the final day of the year, Merchant would break the all-India record, with 359 not out for Bombay *v* Maharashtra in the Ranji Trophy.

By the 1943/44 season, the four major New Zealand Cricket Associations had decided to arrange a full series of home-and-away matches. This arrangement proved successful and continued the following season. Wellington were subsiding to an innings defeat against Auckland at the Basin Reserve on 28 December when wicketkeeper Frank Mooney strode to the crease. In the face of a first innings of 438, the home side had made 167 and 111 for eight, with Mooney 5 not out. Shielding the final two batsman, Mooney put on 127 runs for the ninth wicket with Ray Buchan, a then record in first-class cricket in New Zealand, and another 113 with No. 11 Ted Knapp, taking his personal score to 180 in the process. This was the third instance in first-class cricket of both the ninth and tenth wicket stands in an innings yielding over 100.

Chapter 6

1944: Facing the Future with Confidence

'For the first time I realised how much more than a matter of runs scored and stumps upset the summer game is.'

Graham White, RASC

The year 1944 dawned with hopes of a second front being opened in western Europe and a faint prospect of the end of hostilities by the autumn. The world's cricketing calendar got underway with high-class matches in Australia. At the Sydney Cricket Ground a two-day match was staged between New South Wales and a Services XI, with Victor Trumper jnr excelling with five for 40 in the NSW first innings. Sid Barnes scored a runaway 104 not out in the state side's second innings. A further New South Wales *v* Services match at the end of January was notable for a second wicket partnership of 141 in fifty-four minutes by Barnes and Bill Alley. Lord Gowrie, the retiring Governor General of Australia, arrived at the ground an hour before his appointed time in order to watch the whirlwind hitting. A crowd of 19,096 raised £1,161 for the Soldiers' Comforts Fund.

Despite these encouraging performances, Jack Fingleton was fearful that the drubbings handed out by Australia to their English opponents in the immediate post-First World War Ashes series would be reversed after the current war. Fingleton feared for the development of the AIF soldier serving in the Far East, forced to 'accept … makeshift cricket when [he] can in tropical heat and on the poor jungle apologies for grounds'. Conditions were vile – humid, sticky heat interspersed with tropical downpour – but the sporting spirit of the men had kept the game alive. For Fingleton, the Australian game was also structurally unsound, with too few ex-players fulfilling administrative roles, and club matches lasting a mere two hours per innings. Fingleton's sentiments were endorsed by the octogenarian C.T.B. 'Terror' Turner, who declared: 'the true game is being sacrificed to provide the public with a "hit or miss" race for runs against time.' Sir Home Gordon responded by assuring Fingleton that Australian cricket was flourishing in England, with 500 players having put on their flannels in 1943 at Hove alone.

Gordon's assessment was confirmed by Flight Lieutenant B.R. Miles, an RAAF sports officer. Miles thought that Australia had little to fear from the resumption of Test cricket: 'It is interesting that the pessimism in Australia over the immediate future of cricket is not paralleled by optimism here.' The English public saw the potential of the RAAF players on show in the mother country. The Australians 'had acquitted themselves with marked success, given the lack of opportunity to practise and the time spent between matches on flying and operational duties'.

At the Wanderers Grounds in Johannesburg, Transvaal took on a South African Indian XI on 1 January. The fixture aroused great interest, as owing to the colour bar exercised in South Africa, opportunities for meetings between teams of European and non-white races had been few. Due to the country's racial divisions, only four of the Indian side had previous experience of a turf wicket. At Newlands, Western Province took on Combined Services in perfect cricketing weather. *The Cricketer* reported: 'the people who most enjoyed their holiday cricket were perhaps those who were lucky enough to sit on the grass under the oaks which fringe Cape Town's lovely ground at Newlands, almost in the shadow of Table Mountain, in perfect weather.'

Douglas Jardine, after successfully escaping the clutches of the Germans at Dunkirk, spent most of his war in India, firstly in Quetta, then in Simla. He joked that he was fortunate that the War Office had not posted him as Liaison Officer with the Australian Army. Jardine was able to play a few matches on the subcontinent, including captaining a Services XI against an Indian XI in a four-day first-class fixture on 11–14 February 1944. In a high-scoring game, with profits going to the Red Cross, Jardine was among the runs, but the highest scoring Services player was Joe Hardstaff with a second-innings 129. Gul Mohammad's 144 not out was the mainstay of an Indian first innings of 502, which enabled the hosts to emerge as victors by six wickets. A youthful T.C. 'Dickie' Dodds also appeared in this match. The future attacking Essex opening batsman had yet to receive his revelation from God to 'hit hard and enjoy it' as he was at the time a leg-spin bowler and lower order batsman. Being brought on to bowl first change in the face of a batting onslaught by Mushtaq Ali, Dodds was, in his own words, 'hit all over Bombay'. He asked Jardine if he might be permitted to move a fielder in order to stem the flow of boundaries and was refused:

> Next over someone was out, and I saw Jardine coming towards me. I was on the boundary and the crowd picked up his authoritarian figure heading in my direction. They chanted 'left, right, left, right' as he came. 'Dodds,' he barked, when within earshot, 'now listen to me. You and I are amateurs. It is only professionals who ask to have their field shifted when they are hit for four.' Then he turned round and marched back again. I was dumbstruck. Douglas Jardine was a man you did not forget.

In Bridgetown, Barbados, during the second of a pair of fixtures between the host island and Trinidad, 19-year-old Frank Worrell (308 not out) and John Goddard

(218 not out) established a new world record for the fourth wicket with an unbroken stand of 502. When Worrell passed the 210 that the Trinidadian Jeff Stollmeyer had made earlier in the match, a Barbadian in the crowd, unable to contain his joy, rushed onto the field and presented his hero with a large white chicken. As the leading light of post-war West Indian cricket emerged, so his pre-war predecessor, George Headley, continued to amass runs, as the Jamaican domestic season ended with him heading the batting averages with 639 runs at an average of 79.87.

British Guiana had dropped out of first-class cricket in 1940, unable to accept an invitation to take part in a triangular tournament alongside Trinidad and Barbados. This was mainly due to transport difficulties. By March 1944 they were able to resume competition,

Frank Worrell.

travelling to Port-of-Spain for two four-day matches. After putting up a decent showing in the first match, the lost years of first-class competition showed in the second, as they were routed by an innings and 217 runs. Elias Constantine, younger brother of Learie, struck a fine 139 to seal the Guyanese fate. Later in the year, British Guiana's Bourda Ground hosted its first first-class match since 1938. Clyde Walcott of the visiting Barbadians scored his debut first-class century.

The Madras Cricket Association assumed responsibility for the B. Subramaniam Memorial Cricket Nets Scheme. A four-winged net was put up on matting pitches of the Madras Cricket Club Ground at Chepauk. The nets were opened by Governor Sir Arthur Hope in October, the object being to meet a long-felt want of Madras cricketers. The nets scheme, the first of its kind in India, would provide systematic and regular practice for leading players and impart coaching and training to youngsters as well as providing free gear to deserving cases. A slip-catching machine had been donated. Mr Subramaniam, described as the 'W.G. Grace of South Indian Cricket', received initial donations of Rs 7,000/- in cash and equipment as India continued its rise to a pre-eminent position in world cricket later in the century.

Denis Compton continued to delight cricket-keen Indian crowds. On 10 September, assisting the Bombay Gymkhana in a whole-day fixture against G.I.P. Railway, the Middlesex man gave one of the most spectacular displays of hurricane hitting seen in the city for a long time. During his stay at the wicket for exactly two hours, Compton hit nine sixes and eighteen fours in his 174 not out with terrific drives, one hit smashing the scorers' table and damaging the score book into the bargain. A versatile sportsman, Compton had played in a services soccer international, England *v* Scotland, two days earlier, scoring 2 goals in a 5-4 victory.

* * *

With fierce fighting to be seen in north-western Europe from June onwards, the ongoing grind upwards through the Italian peninsula, the grim struggle to stem the Japanese advance at Kohima and continuing efforts to guard British shipping, it was inevitable that 1944 would exact a heavy toll of cricketing lives.

'Greater love hath no man than this, that a man lay down his life for his friends' is the most popular Bible verse used in twentieth-century war commemoration. Never was it more apposite than in the case of Foster 'Peter' McRae. McRae had made twenty-five appearances for Somerset from 1936 to 1939 as a right-handed batsman, with a highest score of 107 coming against Hampshire at Taunton. Joining the RNVR as a surgeon lieutenant, McRae was on board HMS *Mahratta* escorting an Arctic convoy off northern Norway in February 1944 when it was torpedoed by a German U-boat. Another erstwhile Somerset man, R.C. Robertson-Glasgow, described in *The Observer* McRae's final moments: 'Seventeen survivors scrambled on to a crowded Carley float, with their doctor, McRae. Suddenly the doctor said: "I appear to be in the way here" and as if he were interrupting some private matter, slipped into the water.' McRae perished in the freezing Barents Sea, never to be seen again.

London club cricket mourned the loss of Maurice Spearing, a sector captain of the London Fire Service, who was killed during an air raid on the capital on 20 February. Spearing had opened the batting and kept wicket for the Bank of England team and had been awarded his Club Conference cap in 1935. He had made several appearances for the British Empire XI in 1942 and 1943, having previously turned out occasionally for Cheshire. It had been due to the efforts of Spearing and his colleagues in the LFS that tens of thousands of lives had been saved and symbolic and venerable buildings such as St Paul's Cathedral delivered from destruction.

John Blake, a teacher of mathematics at Sherborne School, had played a few dozen matches for Cambridge University and Hampshire from 1937 to 1939. Having received a commission in the Royal Marines, he became part of 43 Royal Marine Commando. In February 1944, Blake and his comrades landed at Anzio, tasked with the job of capturing three peaks with bare, rocky, precipitous drops, to extend the bridgehead over the river Garigliano. Under mortar and shellfire, on the night of 3 February, D Troop fought through the night and seized Monte Ornito, with Captain Blake at the head of a bayonet charge which captured twenty prisoners. For this action he was awarded the Military

Cross, the citation for which referred to his 'outstanding gallantry and leadership ... without hesitation and heedless of the danger'. Four months later, Blake's commando unit had been transferred to the island of Vis on the Adriatic. During a diversionary attack on the island of Brač, designed to draw German fire from Tito's partisans in Bosnia, Blake was killed a few weeks before his MC was confirmed.

John Blake.

A death from a noble cricketing family occurred on 14 March when Captain Edward Mills Grace RAMC, grandson of his namesake, the famous Gloucestershire all-rounder, and great-nephew of W.G., died of typhoid fever while on service in Italy. Grace jnr had made four crossings during the evacuation from Dunkirk, bringing back the wounded from the hellish beaches, and had also seen service in North Africa. Although never achieving first-class status, Ted had scored 82 not out for Worcestershire Gentlemen against Gloucestershire Gipsies, his father's club. According to his father, also a Dr E.M. Grace, 'Whatever his limitations as a player, in sheer cricket spirit Ted Grace was a truly worthy member of the great family from which he sprang.'

Another name was added to the list of cricketing schoolmasters who had taught their final lesson. Squadron Leader E.H. Moss DFC was killed in action in March 1944. He was a Master at Radley College before the war and had played a few times

E. M. Grace.

for Oxford University. The cricketing world was still mourning the loss of Hedley Verity the previous summer. Jack Hobbs reported that his son, Captain Leonard Hobbs, had spent a whole day searching for Verity's grave, finding the Yorkshireman in a civilian cemetery. Young Hobbs arranged for Verity's name to be inscribed and took a picture to forward to Verity's widow.

Flying Officer David Merry RAFVR had played a couple of matches for Trinidad in 1941. Serving as a flying instructor, on 4 May his plane crashed

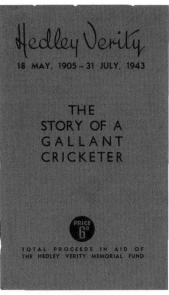

Hedley Verity was also remembered in a memorial match at Roundhay Park, Leeds, on 3 September 1944.

Flying Officer Dave Merry.

amongst the trees and burnt out 2 miles south of Penhold airport, Alberta. The pilot lost his life after ordering his pupils to parachute to safety and remaining behind to hold the aircraft steady so they could get out. Once again, a cricketer had lived to the biblical maxim of laying down his life for his friends.

Plum Warner had triumphantly declared on 17 June that 'the public seem keener than ever on their national game'. The BBC continued to broadcast many of the matches from Lord's to the Middle East, Italy and the Pacific Islands. The following day, Warner's mood of optimism was shattered as he became one of several Londoners who heard a cohort of deadly V-1 missiles nearing the end of their terrible journey: 'We have had the Flying Bombs, a hell of a row, and the bomb shrieking like an express train going through a station at 60mph. It is a bit nasty and disturbing and at Lord's we played (June 18) in spite of sirens.'

Three miles to the south, a mixed military and civilian congregation had gathered at the Guards' Chapel at St James's Park for Sabbath worship. The choir had struck up the Sung Eucharist when one of the flying bombs cut out

Play continues at Lord's as smoke from a doodlebug blast bellows in the distance behind the Nursery End.

and nosedived onto the chapel, destroying the roof, its supporting walls and concrete pillars. As the clouds of dust subsided, first-aid teams and heavy rescue crews arrived to find a scene of utter devastation. Doctors and nurses were obliged to scramble in between the concrete walls to administer morphine and first aid. Several rescuers and survivors later recalled that the silver altar cross had been untouched by the blast and candles continued to burn. The rescue services and Guardsmen from the barracks immediately began freeing survivors from the wreckage and carrying them out. One of the 121 fatal casualties, in what was to turn out to be the most serious V-1 attack on the capital, was George Kemp-Welch, who had played for Cambridge University, Warwickshire and MCC before the war. Kemp-Welch had married Stanley Baldwin's daughter in February 1934 and had received a commission in the Grenadier Guards in 1940.

A few yards from Kemp-Welch lay Lieutenant Harold Dods. Dods had been the outstanding batsman for Lincolnshire CCC during the ten seasons preceding the war, generally heading the averages. Dods, whose father was president of the club, was serving with the Scots Guards. He had only been married for four months and had been a member of Sir T.E.W. Brinckman's XI which toured the Argentine in 1937–38. Dods had made a first-class century at the Belgrano Athletic Club against the Argentine national team. His body was recovered from the wreckage of the chapel and buried in the churchyard near his family home at Dodington, Lincolnshire.

London schoolboy Don Hatcher recalled a V-1 attack rudely interrupting his enjoyment of cricket in high summer:

> What could be more relaxing, there had been no air raids for a couple weeks, it was a bright sunny summer's day, birds singing, butterflies fluttering by. I was lazing on top of the shed watching the two cricket matches going on in the London Hospital Sports ground. Dad was up in the tree next door helping our neighbour pick his cherries.

Then suddenly they became aware of an all-too-familiar rumbling dronelike noise. Hatcher turned to see coming, fairly low over the house, a doodlebug, 'silvery grey and spitting flame from its tail-mounted engine'. He reassured himself with the knowledge that if he could hear it, it posed no danger to him. Then there was silence:

> I looked up and could see its nose dipping towards the cricket pavilion, immediately looking back to the field I saw two empty cricket pitches with some thirty white blobs lying scattered round the edge of the field. There was nothing any of us could do but wait for the explosion and inevitable deadly blast!

Hatcher and his father remained in their perches waiting for the agent of doom to descend: 'Suddenly the Doodlebug coughed back into life, levelled out and chugged its way across the Crooked Billet and beyond towards Tottenham, leaving us white faced and shaken, to climb down from our perches and in true British style, go for a cup of tea.'

By the time their tea had been drunk, the cricket had resumed.

Bill Roach had opened the batting for the RAAF against an England XI at Lord's on 29 May. Ten days later he was dead, his Beaufighter NE200 having developed engine trouble off the Frisian Islands. At 1.57 pm on 8 June, Flight Sergeant Roach, the navigator wireless operator, had sent a message to the other plane on the mission: 'engine trouble Smithy'. The plane was last seen at 2.00 pm making a diving turn into the sea from a height of 50 feet, sinking immediately.

Following the death of Captain R. Alexander, killed in Italy, the North of Ireland club sustained two further losses. Lieutenant Ronald Morgan of No. 15 Platoon, 1st Battalion Royal Ulster Rifles, 6th Airborne Division, was killed in Normandy, last seen by his comrades on 7 June. Morgan was among soldiers who entered the town in Sainte-Honorine. His platoon withdrew from the area in accordance with orders. Other platoon members saw Morgan begin the retreat. When they re-entered Sainte-Honorine on 11 July, they found Morgan's body. On the same battlefield, his brother, Lieutenant Harry Morgan, No. 1 Medium Machine Gun Platoon, one of the club's leading bowlers who had played a number of times for the Gentlemen of Ireland, lost a leg. Harry had played four first-class matches for Ireland, taking eighteen wickets at 10.38.

Major Bill Carson of the 5th Field Regiment of the New Zealand Artillery had established a world-record third-wicket partnership of 445 with P.E. Whitelaw in only his second first-class innings, scoring 290. Having been wounded in Crete in 1941, winning the MC in 1943 and being mentioned in despatches, Carson's shoulder, hip and ankle were severely damaged in battle. He was evacuated, but died on 8 October from jaundice en route from Bari to Alexandria. Lieutenant M.J.W. Cassy was killed in action in Italy in October while serving with the Grenadier Guards. He had played for Oxford against Cambridge in the 1941 match between those two universities and subsequently several times for Northamptonshire in their wartime matches.

Glamorgan County Cricket Club could point proudly to the contribution that a Welsh cricketing contingent had made to the success of Operation Overlord. John Madden-Gaskell had made one first-class appearance for the county back in 1922 before his business career took him to Taunton. In 1942, aged 46, he was appointed as a staff captain with the Royal Engineers. By the time of Overlord, Madden-Gaskell had risen to the rank of major and as Deputy Assistant Quartermaster General he oversaw the provisioning of food and equipment for the operation, receiving the MBE for his contribution to this task. Meanwhile, 21-year-old Jim Pleass of the Royal Corps of Signals worked as a wireless signaller in the invasion force that landed at Arromanches. His landing craft narrowly avoided a German mine. Jim and his comrades had to look on in horror as an adjoining vessel in the flotilla was smashed to pieces, killing all of its occupants. Once the beachhead had been established, Jim lined the beach signallers with the heavily armed cruisers, helping to direct their fire at precise targets. Within a week, the invasion secured, Jim returned to the UK. After the war he was able to make his county debut and go on to represent Glamorgan on 171 occasions. Hugh Vaughan-Thomas, younger brother of the broadcaster Wynford, played one match for the county in 1933. He became an expert on the landing of armoured assault craft known as Buffalos, and was involved in both the Normandy landings and the subsequent crossing of the Rhine. For this work he was awarded a military OBE in 1946.

After nearly two months of anxious waiting, RAAF cricketers were informed that their captain, Flying

Keith Carmody.

Officer Keith Carmody, was a prisoner of war in Germany. Norman Preston wrote: 'Whatever experiences he has gone through, he must have cherished the memories of his wartime cricket snatched between breaks of operational duties.' A Beaufighter pilot in Coastal Command, Carmody was last seen by fellow Australians at 3.45 am on 13 June after his plane had been hit off the Dutch coast. Reports suggested he had it under control as it descended and there was every chance of him reaching land. Having recovered from injuries sustained during his crash-landing, Carmody was a leading force in a series of cricket matches played at Stalag Luft III. The first 'Kreige Test Match' between England and Australia was played on 12 August, resulting in an England victory with a second encounter

Prisoner of war Test match at Stalag Luft III, Belaria. (*Courtesy Tony Barker*)

on 25 August having the same outcome. This was much to Carmody's chagrin, as he had spent precious energy in watering and scraping the pitch to make it of an acceptable standard, as well as coaching some of his teammates. The sporting season was brought to a premature halt on 8 September as the camp sports field was closed for good, as the German authorities grew alarmed at the advance of the Red Army from the east.

Bob Crisp was wounded in Normandy and was evacuated to England. A shell had struck his right arm and Crisp reckoned he would not be fit again for bowling until the following season. Another South African Test player, Lieutenant Colonel Pieter van der Bijl, considered in his day one of the tallest men at Oxford University, was a veteran of the 'Timeless Test'. A slow-footed and dour batsman, he showed considerably more alacrity on the battlefield, running his jeep under fire to bring back to safety half a dozen wounded men. For this action he was awarded the MC in February 1943. Van der Bijl had his spine and ankles fractured in Italy in August 1944, but doctors considered permanent disability unlikely. Although he recovered enough to enjoy a long and distinguished teaching career, he would never take to the cricket field again.

Kent were fortunate not to lose a triumvirate of captains, with both Geoffrey Legge and Gerry Chalk having already paid the ultimate price of war. In March 1943, Bryan Valentine, who had been awarded the MC in 1942, had been posted to the King's Own Scottish Borderers and took part in the Normandy landings in June 1944. The following month he was badly wounded in the leg shortly after the Battle for Caen and returned to the UK, where he was nursed by his wife, Elizabeth. Valentine later returned to Europe and after the conclusion of hostilities captained a British Liberation Army XI against the Netherlands in a two-day match at Haarlem in August 1945.

Geoff Rabone, who had performed well for various New Zealand XIs in 1943, was not available for the 1944 season. Serving with Bomber Command on the night of 7 August, his Lancaster bomber was shot down over Beuzeville in Normandy. With the aid of a French farmer he was sheltered in an attic of a farmhouse by the French Resistance for five weeks, until the British arrived to liberate the area and arrange his return. On his return to England, he visited the Fernleaf Club, a favoured watering hole of New Zealand servicemen. He met Bob Metcalf and the beer flowed freely that night.

In contrast, Flight Sergeant Harry Walters of 149 (RAF) Squadron of the RNZAF, who had played one first-class match for Auckland and was a frequent member of the New Zealand Services team, was shot down during a bombing raid and his body was lost in the English Channel on 25 August. Wisden noted: 'Walters was a most attractive batsman, and his passing meant a big loss to New Zealand cricket, for he promised to be a Test player of the highest order.'

One Kiwi fortunate to escape unscathed was Alan Burgess. During the Battle of Monte Cassino, the Canterbury man witnessed the US Air Force drop 1,400 tonnes of bombs on the historic hilltop abbey. 'We watched that bombing from the hills behind it. The whole town was just flattened, it was all rubble.' Burgess was relieved to get out of the battle unscathed. 'You were frightened to put your finger up or it would get shot off. Yeah, I had a couple [of close scrapes. ... A couple of pings at me. Sniper stuff that missed; that hit the wall behind me, you know, that sort of thing.' One of the future experiences of Burgess's long life was a return to Monte Cassino to commemorate the seventieth reunion of those who had taken part in the Italian campaign.

Captain Herbert Oliver 'Peter' Huntington-Whiteley had played in the Eton *v* Harrow match and been a member of the Gentlemen of Worcestershire tour to Berlin in 1937. The grandson of former Prime Minister Stanley Baldwin, Huntington-Whiteley undertook more daring and dangerous visits to the Continent while serving with the Royal Marines 30th Assault Unit, known as Ian Fleming's Commandos. He was killed during special operations at Le Havre on 12 September. Another cricketer with Worcestershire connections, Captain Cedric Humphries, perished in 1944, killed in action at Pannenschopp, aged 30. His two brothers, Gerald and Norman, had also played for the county.

The most prominent cricketing casualty of the Normandy campaign was Glamorgan captain and secretary Maurice Turnbull, the fifth, and mercifully the final, England Test cricketer to lose his life on active service. Had the war not intervened, it is probable that Turnbull would have risen to a prominent position in cricket administration. Literally a man for all seasons, Turnbull had combined his duties at Glamorgan with playing squash, hockey and fencing to a high level. Furthermore, he remains the only player to represent England at cricket and Wales at rugby union. Turnbull's less physically energetic pursuits included bridge, poetry reading and classical music. A devout Roman Catholic who rarely missed Sunday mass, he also found the time to run an insurance business and write two books with his namesake, Maurice Allom.

Leading resistance to a German counter-attack on the recently captured village of Montchamp, Major Turnbull was killed instantly by tank fire. His body was spotted lying in a ditch by one of his men, Sergeant Fred Llewellyn, who found a photograph of Turnbull's wife and three children in his wallet. Llewellyn made sure the wallet and other personal effects were faithfully sent to the family.

Major Maurice Turnbull, Welsh Guards, (*Glamorgan Cricket Archives*)

News of Turnbull's death filtered through to Cardiff Arms Park, where Glamorgan were playing. As the news spread around the ground – then little more than a tree-lined meadow with a stand at either end – the spectators who had gone there to seek a pleasurable relief from wartime cares spontaneously rose and stood in a minute's silence for their fallen leader. From a game that bred leaders of men, Turnbull was the sixth county captain to be killed in the war, following Peter Eckersley, Bob Nelson, Gerry Chalk, Geoffrey Legge and Harold Dods. Turnbull had ensured that he had attended Mass and taken Holy Communion in the days leading up to the fatal attack. He had written to his wife shortly before his death:

> If anything should happen to me you must promise me to accept 'gladly' (Father Hubert's idea) which means sorrowfully but not resentfully, facing the future with confidence, knowing that I shall be with you as much as I am at present, which is saying a lot. My love to you all, and more to you dearest heart. I love you to the whole of truth.

* * *

The role military chaplains played in sustaining and enhancing the spiritual lives of their men was central to the conduct of the war. Field Marshal Montgomery, himself the son of a bishop, had stated, 'I would as soon think of going into battle without my artillery as without my Chaplains.' There was a widespread and long-held belief that cricketing and Christian values were entwined. Playing the game encouraged ethical behaviour, honesty and integrity. Partly for this reason, many northern towns had Sunday school and church leagues representing various denominations. The opportunity to play organised cricket in such leagues was often based on regular church attendance. Bill Bowes, the Yorkshire and England fast bowler, spoke at a sportsman's service held at a Methodist Chapel in 1935, stating that the teaching of sport ran 'parallel with certain Christian ideals' and that cricket was 'a game every Christian should be interested in because it demanded self-discipline, self-control and team spirit'.

Amongst those cricketers who continued to perform this crucial role in maintaining the fighting men's morale was the Reverend Francis Browne, the former Cambridge University and Sussex bowler. Browne, known as 'Tishy' due to his bowling action reminding people of a famous racehorse, was senior chaplain to the 56th London Division in Italy. The Reverend E.T. 'Tom' Killick sailed for West Africa to take up the post of Senior Padre (Church of England) of Royal Air Force West Africa Command. Meanwhile, the Reverend Jack Parsons, vicar of Liskeard, was invalided out of the Army in September, having served as a chaplain to the forces since January 1940.

Parsons, who had won the Military Cross during the previous war, had had little hesitation in once again volunteering his services, this time with the Royal Army Chaplains' Department. He told his Church Council: 'Believe me when I tell you that I have had as clear a call as any man ever had to go. My duty … is to be among the troops during this crisis in our country's history.' Parsons was attached to 4th Battalion, Dorset Regiment, and quickly won the respect of his men. One officer described him as a 'rock-like figure of great faith and inspiration' whilst another recalled a 'wonderfully sympathetic friend and wise counsellor' whose non-compulsory church services were packed and who also ran battalion sports.

Transferred to the post of senior chaplain within 77th Division, Parsons was despatched to North Africa in the spring of 1943. His ship was torpedoed in the Mediterranean and he lost all his kit, including his cricket bag. While he was preaching at an Easter Day service for British personnel manning a PoW camp at St Cloud, Parsons noted German prisoners watching through the barbed wire. A true man of God, he then arranged to take an evening service for them. Holy Communion was taken and the Lord's Prayer recited, 'I in English, they standing rigidly to attention, in German. After the service, every German officer and other rank filed past me and shook hands.' This service became a regular occurrence, as Parsons saw the decline of Nazi influences amongst the prisoners. 'The religious instinct of those German people had been suppressed by Nazism and now sought freedom of expression.'

The Reverend J.W.J. Steele had made seventeen first-class appearances for Hampshire during the 1938 and 1939 seasons, taking fifty-seven wickets with

Left to right: the Reverend R.B.S. Gillman, vicar; Lieutenant General Miles Dempsey, C-in-C Second Army; the Reverend J.W.J. Steele, chaplain, Second Army. (*Museum of Army Chaplaincy*)

his medium pace bowling. By 1944, Steele had risen to the rank of Assistant Chaplain-General of the Second Army, one of the most senior ranks a chaplain could attain. On 4 June, Steele conducted a service at Christchurch, Portsdown, at which the commanders of the Second Army were present. Steele's words placed the prospects for the success of the forthcoming Operation Overlord in the hands of God:

> Lord, we desire to place ourselves and what we are about to undertake in Thy hands. Guide, direct and prosper us, we beseech Thee; and if Thou seest that this undertaking will be for Thy glory, grant us good success. Make us and those who act with us to feel that, unless Thy blessing is with us, we cannot succeed, and that, except the Lord build the house, their labour is but lost that build it.
>
> The war could only be won with God on our side, indeed if He were not, then any victory would be hollow.
>
> To Second Army there had been given a glorious part in a great task. To relieve the oppressed, to restore freedom in Europe, and to bring peace to the world. Equipped with all the power that modern science can give; and entrusted by our country with the man and the weapons for the accomplishment of this task, let us rise to a full sense of our responsibilities.
>
> As we stand upon the threshold of the greatest adventure in our history, let us now offer to Almighty God all our powers, of body, mind and spirit, so that our great endeavour may be thoroughly finished.

Four years later, the prayers having been answered, Steele returned with the Second Army's commander-in-chief, General Sir Miles Dempsey, to unveil two memorial stained-glass windows as a permanent reminder of this historic occasion.

* * *

Although the 1944 fixture list for the English season was broadly similar to those of the previous four wartime summers, the Normandy landings and subsequent campaign in north-western Europe meant that fewer top-class cricketers were available for domestic sporting action. Home Gordon wrote: 'A cricket season always starts with joyous anticipations. This one of course depends on the Second Front and therefore expectation is fraught with anxiety for those taking part in that Great Adventure.' London Counties XI would need to call on more club players rather than established county stars to fill a team sheet. However, the West Country would see more high-class cricket than previously, with G.O.J. Elliott developing an impressive fixture list for his West of England XI.

Elliott had had unsuccessful trials for Gloucestershire as a young man and had become a regular in the Gloucester City XI. He went to France in 1940 with the Gloucester Regiment, was seriously wounded during the evacuation, and brought back by hospital ship with a broken neck. His doctors believed his cricketing days were over. As he lay in bed encased in plaster of Paris he wrestled with the problem of how to restore first-class cricket to a decent level. He realised that many prominent players were in the forces or undertaking war work in the West Country, so endeavoured to combine them into a West of England XI. Elliott was discharged from the Army and returned to his post at the City Treasurer's Office in Gloucester. He enlisted the support of F.O. Wills of the famous Bristol tobacco company, Bev Lyon and R.J.O. 'Jack' Meyer. A collection of pre-war stars was collected to entertain the West Country cricketing public. K.G. Bird glowed that Elliott had provided a 'tremendous infusion of energy into the life-blood of the game at a time when … it fell to a low ebb'. He revived interest in the game in the West Country and gave pleasure to many thousands of people. Charities benefited to the tune of £3,080 in 1944.

Among those who would miss the English summer were the Bedser twins. Eric and Alec had been despatched to North Africa. The former wrote to Norman Preston, 'Life would not be worth living from our point of view if we were separated. This may sound peculiar but anyone who has a twin can appreciate what I mean.' As the Surrey pair departed the domestic cricket scene, so they were replaced with the arrivals in England of Wally Hammond, Bob Crisp and Alf Gover, with Alf having fully recovered from a knee operation.

Plum Warner, in response to press reports that the MCC Advisory Select Committee, under the chairmanship of Sir Stanley Jackson, might recommend a post-war cup competition, dismissed the desirability of such a contest: 'we dislike the idea of a Cup. Cricket needs no such stimulus. Honour is enough.' Eschewing other suggested alterations, such as making permanent the eight-ball over, trialled during the 1939 season, Warner concluded, 'What cricket needs is at least twenty-five years of quiet, sensible government.' Ex-Worcestershire professional Fred Root was scathing: 'Present-day league, local and work cricket is booming, but if dynamite is not introduced into first-class cricket it will not find its niche in the post-war world.'

Cricket in England would revert to the six-ball over from 1944 onwards. This fixed for decades what had previously been a moveable feast. The original laws of cricket, written in 1744, had stipulated a four-ball over. In 1899, the number was increased to five, then six the following year. Australia had used the eight-ball over since 1918 and South Africa since 1937. Further recommendations in the committee's report, published in February, included:

1. A resumption of county cricket at the earliest possible date.
2. MCC to press the government for relief of Entertainment Duty on gate receipts, which could potentially cripple county finances.
3. No reduction of the number of first-class counties, and no two-league championship format.
4. No county cricket to be played on a Sunday.
5. An emergency plan for the first post-war season should time not be available to arrange a normal programme.
6. Temporary relaxation of qualification rules for county players.
7. No change in the format of first-class matches.
8. Minor alterations to declaration laws.
9. A new ball to be available to the fielding side after fifty-five overs.
10. Removal of appeals against the light.
11. Some discussion of a regional county competition to run alongside the traditional championship. (This came to nothing.)

Whilst Warner and his fellow traditionalists strove to maintain the sanctity of the English first-class game, grassroots clubs continued the grim battle for survival. H.G. Dorman of the Club Cricket Conference and Sir Lawrence Chubb of the National Playing Fields Association were successful in lobbying to prevent 50 acres of sports grounds in the Wembley area being taken over for building and post-war planning. The Minister of Health ordered a public enquiry, which was held at Wembley on 27 June, the result of which was that he declined to sanction the proposal of Wembley Borough Council, saving the grounds from building development.

Publishing and printing difficulties held back the launch of the 1944 *Wisden* until the end of July, with Hubert Preston assuming the editorship. Preston, known by the nickname HP, was deaf for much of his life, using an ear trumpet before battery-operated hearing aids became available. His first *Wisden* ran to 7,000 printed copies.

The goodwill displayed between Australian and English cricketers, a far cry from the contentious and divisive 1932/33 Ashes tour and its aftermath, was given voice by Australian Prime Minister John Curtin. On 10 May, Curtin was made an Honorary Freeman of the City of London. In his acceptance speech, after referring to the national characteristics of physical stamina, endurance in adversity and unconquerable spirit, he turned to cricket:

> You have some evidence of that at Lord's now and again. Lord's is to Australia what it is to this country. We would refuse to contemplate a world in which there would be a jurisdiction over Lord's which would prohibit the playing of Test Matches. … We are defending the city of London and those 22 yards of turf which we hope will be used time and time again, so that the Motherland and Australia can decide whether the six-ball over is better than the eight-ball over.

* * *

The British Empire XI returned to the fray once again, with Harry Halliday in form against the club for whom he had starred in 1943. Playing for an Ordnance XI at Feltham, the young Pudsey native bowled throughout the Empire innings, sending down twenty-five overs for his six for 70. Despite then carrying his bat for 76, he ended up on the losing side. The match was notable for the inaugural appearance behind the stumps of Empire stalwart Harry Crabtree, who managed to effect three stumpings off the bowling of Bertie Clarke.

On 2 July, four players more accustomed to playing under the colours of the XI were on the opposing side when the travelling team met an Essex XI at Chelmsford. Harry Crabtree, Sonny Avery, Ray Smith and Stan

Bertie Clarke.

Nichols had the best of a drawn game in which Tom Pearce top scored with 116 for the home side. Ray Smith returned figures of five for 41 against the team he regularly captained. A Coventry and District XI overcame the British Empire XI in a two-innings fixture by six wickets, the main contributions coming from Arthur Fagg (92 and 30) and Tom Goddard (five for 42 and seven for

56). Three days later, Fagg put in an appearance for the Empire XI against Combined Universities at Stockport, top scoring with 137 in a total of 453. Emrys Davies, considered by John Arlott to be one of the best eleven county players never to be picked for England, also made a century. Derbyshire drew with Nottinghamshire at Derby on 12 August.

The British Empire XI season extended to 1 October, on which occasion Harry Crabtree scored a century, enabling him to become the first batsman to record 1,000 season runs for the club, his tally of 1,086 coming at an average of 32.90. On the bowling front, Bertie Clarke once again led the way with 102 at 9.10. Joe Hulme topped

Jack Lee.

the London Counties XI averages with 1,034 runs at 73.85 in his twenty innings whilst Jack Young was the leading wicket-taker with eighty-eight at 7.88. Private Jack Lee, the former Middlesex and Somerset all-rounder and a regular for the London Counties XI, was killed on 20 June in Normandy while serving with the 208 Company of the Pioneer Corps. When the club was wound up in 1946, the remaining funds were given to his widow, Agnes. She was in sore need of the solidarity of her husband's professional colleagues as shortly after his death the tobacconist and newsagent's business she ran was completely destroyed by a flying bomb.

* * *

Most English county clubs persisted in ticking over on a wartime footing, ensuring a continuity of presence that could elide back into a full-time presence once hostilities had ceased. An Essex County Services XI was formed to temporarily take the place of the Essex County Cricket Club for the remainder of the war. Fixtures were arranged against Cambridge and Oxford Universities, Sussex, the RAAF and West Indian and New Zealand XIs. The chief aims were stated as keeping county players in practice for their post-war careers and to develop promising young players. At the end of October news was received of Lieutenant Colonel Brian Castor; the county's secretary had broadcast a message from a Malayan prisoner-of-war camp stating he was safe and well. Returning to the club at the end of the war, thence to the secretaryship of Surrey CCC, Castor would live to be 85.

Leicestershire's former Grace Road headquarters had been occupied by a state secondary school, but the local education committee decided that it was in the public interest that, after the war, the club should return to the ground they vacated in 1901. The Aylestone Road Ground, which the club had played on for the previous four decades, had been left to drift into a state unfit for cricket. Fifty-five-year-old Aubrey Sharp, who had made his Leicestershire debut back in 1908, continued to captain the county during the season. In a Whit Monday fixture against Northamptonshire he came up against 51-year-old R.H.D. 'Bertie' Bolton, the Chief Constable of the county. Elsewhere in the East Midlands, Derbyshire CCC's pavilion had been so badly vandalised by children that their projected fixture against Nottinghamshire on 12 August would have to be played at the LMS Railway ground in the town. More optimistically for Derbyshire followers, Gilbert Hodgkinson was resurrected from the obituary pages of *Wisden*. Hodgkinson had been badly wounded in the head and taken prisoner while serving in France in 1940 and news of his death was carried in the 1943 *Almanack*. By the spring of 1944 he had been repatriated and was hoping to turn out for his county again. In the dying embers of the era of an obligatory amateur captain, he would lead his county in the 1946 season.

Sixty-two-year-old Jack Hobbs prepares to take to the field for Surrey Colts, whom he captained, against King's College School Wimbledon. (*Historic Sporting Pictures*)

An indication of the improving status of the professional cricketer was the election of Jack Hobbs to the Surrey Committee. With typical modesty, Hobbs remarked, 'I regard it as a high compliment to the professional cricketer.' His elevation was contemporaneous with the passing of the 1944 Education Act, synonymous with the Conservative Education Secretary R.A. Butler, which sought to enhance the aspirations of children from humble beginnings, such as that from which Hobbs had emerged. One of Hobbs's

Reg Simpson.

committee colleagues, colts captain Andrew Kempton, was to experience the promise of youth and the anguish of loss in 1944. One of his charges, 19-year-old Aircraftman 2nd Class Brian Wildbore, died on 4 September. More encouragingly, the season marked the debut of the 14-year-old Tony Lock, who 'showed promise'. Another pre-eminent professional, George Hirst, retired as coach of Yorkshire CCC, to be succeeded by Emmott Robinson.

Reg Simpson had returned to the UK and was in good form, scoring 41 for Nottinghamshire *v* a Services XI at Trent Bridge on 24 June. His services were in great demand. Over a period of nine innings in nine days Simpson scored 529 runs at Trent Bridge, Lord's and Edgbaston. On 16 July, Northamptonshire came close to being the first team to beat the RAAF in 1944. Peter Murray-Willis inserted the Australians and they collapsed to 64 for six. Some good hitting from Bob Cristofani raised the total to 122. Strong all-round bowling and fielding, with Cristofani once more to the fore with four for 17, bundled out the hosts for a mere 53. Northamptonshire managed to fulfil thirteen fixtures – seven at home and six away. Three home matches were played at the Spinney Hill Ground, one on the ground of the True Form Shoe Company, two on the Corporation Ground in Kettering's North Park and one at Wellingborough School. An away match against Sussex at Horsham was the first inter-county match south of the Thames during the war.

Every prospect pleased in the charming surroundings of Priory Park, Chichester, when the match between Sussex and C.S. Dempster's XI drew a large crowd. Local enthusiasts emphasised that had it not been for the ban prohibiting entrance from Hampshire, only a few miles distant, the attendance would have doubled. Those present generously threw twenty pounds into the charity collection sheet which Dempster and Mercer carried round to receive contributions for Sussex, while the charities of the RAF and RNZAF also substantially benefited. The loudspeaker was tactfully used to convey interesting information. The increasing personnel needs of Operation Overlord meant that Dempster had to invite fifty players before securing eleven names to make up his team, losing Ken James, Ted Badcock and Stan Nichols at short notice due to service demands.

The Middlesex and Essex *v* Kent and Surrey match finished in an exciting draw, with Doug Wright holding out with the bat for half an hour to ensure Kent and Surrey finished on 194 for nine. Earlier, 17-year-old Luke White had top scored in the Middlesex and Essex innings with 77. The Kent and Surrey captain on this occasion, off-spinning all-rounder Jack Davies, had augmented a First in the Classics degree he had taken at Cambridge in 1934 with a further degree in Psychology in 1939. His intermittent appearances in wartime cricket were limited due to his work with the War Office. Davies eventually rose to the rank of colonel, serving as Chief Psychologist in the Directorate for the Selection of Personnel, and receiving an OBE in 1946. Davies's work was vital in the war effort, devising tests that ensured Army recruits were best placed in roles that would match their skills and psychological profile. His preoccupation with psychology had been demonstrated in the Kent *v* Derbyshire fixture at Gravesend in 1939. Les Ames had signalled a six after stumbling over the boundary while taking a catch. Davies reckoned this act of sportsmanship was that of 'a mature individual who had passed beyond the realm of any preoccupations with self, or with unlimited success, power or brilliance'.

Middlesex CCC reported a credit balance of £524 7s 8d for 1944 as members continued their support. Kent CCC's run of wartime financial surpluses continued, although the profit was reduced to £15 2s.8d. A total of 115 matches were played at the St Lawrence Ground, along with the now customary athletics meetings and baseball match for the benefit of American troops, and £46 12s 7d was raised for a prisoners of war collection during the Buffs match on August bank holiday. The club received many letters looking forward to a resumption of normal patterns of the cricket season, especially the Canterbury Week. According to the annual report: 'the youngest lad on our ground staff ... states that during several years' service in the Near and Middle East he has seen some wonderful sights, but none so good as the St Lawrence ground when it is all set out ready for the Week.'

Over 40,000 people watched the seven days' play at the third Birmingham Cricket Festival. In the middle of a rather sunless summer, the weather relented and £2,514 was raised for war charities. In true festival spirit, boys were permitted the use of the outfield during the intervals, and 'some great Test matches were carried through amid shrieks of approval', according to R.I. 'Rusty' Scorer, who provided regular updates by loudspeaker. As the festival was aimed at the general public looking for a wartime diversion, between overs and during breaks in play, Scorer would describe the nature of the dismissals, the peculiarities of the ball, and the tactical moves by each side. A great innovation was the printing on the reverse of the scorecard a plan of the field, and Scorer explained to the crowd the various field alterations, and why they were necessary for the different types of bowler and batsmen. '[I]n fact he educated the ordinary spectator to the mysteries of the game, while the expert probably felt satisfied at hearing his own opinions endorsed,' commented *The Cricketer*. Scorer's innovations proved popular. Human dramas were also broadcast:

> The announcer's voice tells the crowd that he has a small child of three called Judy, who has lost her daddy. She is wearing a pink frock and a hair ribbon. She is quite all right, he has given her an apple to soothe her, but would her parents come round and collect her.

Not since the South African Test match of 1924 had Edgbaston housed such a large crowd as the near 12,000 gathered for the Festival XI *v* RAF match.

At the conclusion of the festival, the Reverend A. Birkmire, Senior Chaplain to the Birmingham Garrison, conducted a sportsman's service in front of the pavilion, highlighting the deep Christian vein in wartime British society. Such was the interest in this episode that several readers contacted *The Cricketer* to learn further details. Music was supplied by an RAF Maintenance Unit band and the service opened with 'O God, Our Help in Ages Past' followed by a prayer and a lesson. After an address by the Reverend Birkmire, the closing hymn was 'Eternal Father, Strong to Save' and the service ended with a benediction. On a previous occasion when a service of this nature was held at Birmingham, a large crowd waited several hours to attend it after the cricket had been rained off early in the afternoon.

Worcestershire managed to host a plethora of matches at the County Ground, including a fixture between an All-England RAF XI and a Worcestershire XI on 5 August. The match was memorable for a brilliant 117 by Wally Hammond, the RAF skipper. He hit one six high into the trees at New Road and was said to be at his pre-war best. A festival of sorts was also possible at Canterbury where, on the August bank holiday, a Canterbury Services XI took on Lieutenant W.H.V. Levett's XI. Frank Woolley received a message from the 96-year-old F.A. Mackinnon, who had played a Test on Lord Harris's 1878/79 tour of Australia: 'My congratulations to you, Frank Woolley, and to all for keeping the flag of dear old Canterbury Cricket Week flying. Am with you in spirit today, and hope to meet you all in the flesh next year.' The distinguished Kent veteran scored 15 from one over in his 35. Another match between St Lawrence-Beverley and the Army at Canterbury, under leaden skies, commanded an attendance of 2,000.

* * *

Club Cricket Conference teams struggled on into a fifth wartime summer. A.W.T. Langford wrote of the preparedness of southern clubs in cricketing and war effort terms, 'What effect the invasion of Europe will have on cricket it is impossible to say, but the clubs have wisely planned a full season for, after all, a match can always be cancelled if national needs necessitate such action.' Clubs that did not belong to any recognised league or associate found themselves outside the Priority Buying Certificate Scheme for the distribution of sports gear. The Board of Trade, in consultation with MCC, arranged for such clubs to participate in the scheme. Applications for equipment would be filtered through a 'parent club', usually the nearest county club, which would forward the consolidated application for equipment to the Board of Trade as early as possible, and no later than 31 January 1945.

The perennial issue of Sabbath play arose once more. Mr Stanley Christopherson, President of MCC, told the Conference that he was in favour of Sunday cricket providing that no gate money was taken and play did not begin before one o'clock. 'With this opinion the great majority of church people of all denominations agree.' While many CCC clubs were raising money for the

Red Cross, the particular achievement of Cheam CC was remarkable. Despite having only a third of their pre-war membership strength, their match against Surrey Colts raised £628 7s 4d for the charity. The Buccaneers managed to play over twenty matches against clubs and public school sides. The write-up of the club's fortunes in 1944 in *The Cricketer* was marked by a mention of the only player to score a century against them during the season being referred to as 'Halliday', the by then well-known Yorkshire professional, whilst every other player or opponent was referred to by his initials.

Australian Prime Minister John Curtin's visit to England enabled him to attend the first big match at Lord's in 1944, Army *v* Civil Defence Services on 13 May. A crowd of 14,000 saw veteran Maurice Leyland top score for the Army with 64, but some lusty lower-order hitting from Edward Scott (91 not out) saw Civil Defence home by two wickets. Curtin's citizens continued to create a favourable impression. The RAF *v* RAAF match at Lord's led seasoned observers to comment that Bert Oldfield and Bill O'Reilly had natural successors in the forms of Stan Sismey and Bob Cristofani. Sismey's neat, undemonstrative glovework and agility accounted for Bob Wyatt while the latter's seven for 39 demonstrated lively variations and masterly analysis of batsmen's weaknesses.

The RAAF team continued to thrill spectators. The knowledge that they and their mates could face imminent death led to an electrifying approach to the game. On 15 July the Antipodean flyers came up against a team of men tasked with managing the worst excesses of their Teutonic pilot counterparts, the British Civil Defence XI. Keith Miller had reached 96 when an air-raid siren signalled the arrival of a flying bomb. After it had landed south of the ground, the Victorian all-rounder struck a four to hoist his century before another device fell to earth as he saluted the crowd. In a wonderful match, Laurie Fishlock made 122 for the CDS as Clive Calvert nearly bowled the RAAF to victory with four for 30, following on from his 55 earlier in the day. Eventually CDS clung on for a draw with nine wickets down. This, and other demonstrations of high-level cricketing skill from Miller, Carmody and their comrades, prompted Pelham Warner to consider the possibility of a 'Test' series between the British and Australian armed services, the genesis of the 1945 Victory Test series.

The innovation of the umbrella field was also drawn up by the RAAF's captain, Keith Carmody. He had noted the frequency with which opposing batsmen had snicked the ball, only for it to remain in the air for a few feet before falling to the ground. After discussions with Stan Sismey and Mick Roper over drinks in the Strand Palace Hotel, he employed a new-look close fielding cordon either side of the wicket, the field deriving its nickname from its resemblance to the shape of an umbrella. Carmody recorded a cartoon representation of the field placement in a log book he kept while he was being held as a prisoner of war.

As tens of thousands of troops massed along the south coast in preparation for Operation Overlord, a crowd of nearly 28,000 enjoyed a thrilling finish on

There we were...

Carmody Umbrella field. (*Courtesy Tony Barker*)

a perfect summer's day at Lord's as Australia took on The Rest. Len Hutton set off The Rest at a good tempo before Walter Hammond, making his first wartime appearance at the ground, was cheered all the way to the wicket. His 46 included a straight drive off Cristofani into the pavilion. Trevor Bailey took two wickets in his first over to put the Australians on the back foot in the pursuit of the 281 needed for victory. A stand of 132 between Jim Workman (105) and Keith Carmody (86) swung the match Australia's way, the former scoring the second wartime century by an Australian at Lord's. Their last batsman made his way to the wicket with three minutes left on the clock and 5 runs to win. After Alan McDonald carved a 3 over extra cover's head off Bailey's bowling, Ted Baker nudged a couple through the leg side to bring about a famous victory.

A couple of days later, another large Lord's crowd enjoyed England *v* Australia. Ross Stanford of the RAAF, who had been awarded a DFC and was now serving as a member of the famous 617 Squadron, scored 51 in an Australian total of 243. Len Hutton led the way to an English victory with a polished 84. The two matches raised £1,683 once Entertainment Tax of £759 and expenses had been deducted. A good wicket and a fine day were tempered with a cold north wind when The Army met the RAAF at Lord's on 17 June. A foretaste of the exuberance Godfrey Evans would bring to the post-war game was in evidence. *The Cricketer* noted he was 'a smart wicket-keeper, and good on the leg-side, but he must learn to adopt a quieter method. He appears to "jump about" too much.' Reg Ellis, the South Australian left-arm spinner, bowled tightly for his five for 34 in twenty-two overs to see his side to a 77-run victory.

Some 4,000 spectators saw the RAAF rack up 304 for four on the first day of a two-day match against the West Indies at Edgbaston in early July.

Twenty-one-year-old Clive Calvert made a chancy 141 for the Australians and, although handicapped by a pulled leg muscle, Learie Constantine hit a six and seven fours in his 54 not out in the drawn match. At the close of play on the second day, the Sabbath, a sportsman's service was held by Major the Reverend A. Birkmire, with Constantine reading the lesson. Sadly, the broad-featured Calvert would not enjoy similar luck on 16 December that year, when the Lancaster in which he was serving as a wireless operator crashed into the Baltic Sea during a mine-laying operation, claiming the lives of all eight crew members. Calvert's body was never recovered.

Clive Calvert.

In June, Learie Constantine captained a West Indian XI against an England XI at Lord's. Ernest Bevin, a friend of Constantine, was amongst the spectators, as was the Colonial Secretary, Oliver Stanley. Despite going down to a heavy 166-run defeat due to a century from Walter Hammond, Constantine scored a whirlwind 42, including a six into the members' stand. His ovation reassured him of the popularity amongst the decent majority following the racial discrimination he had encountered the previous year at the Imperial Hotel. In September 1944, Constantine captained an 'All-Blacks' team composed of players from the West Indies, Sierra Leone, the Gold Coast and Nigeria against an Anglo-Scottish side in Edinburgh. Following the match, Constantine gave a talk on the 'West Indies and the War'.

On 20 July, a team of Canadian servicemen took on a Lord's XI. Les Todd gorged himself on some inexperienced bowling to make 151 as the hosts ran out winners by 213 runs. On 7 and 8 August, an England XI took on firstly the Australians and then a Dominions team at Lord's. The first fixture attracted 16,000 spectators. Hammond's masterly 105 featured perfect timing. The England skipper's successful summer allowed younger spectators to admire the master in action after a long absence from top-class English cricket. One observer emphasised the link wartime cricket could provide between past glories and the future followers of the game:

> but for these games many a young cricketer would have no opportunity to see a first-class player in action and would be doomed to grow up without that priceless heritage. ... Imagine arriving at the age of fifteen, having seen nothing of the majesty of W.R. Hammond, not a glimpse of the cricket of R.W.V. Robins!

Miller made some glorious strokes all round the wicket in his 85 and the crowd was also treated to scintillating fielding from both teams and outstanding glovework from Sismey and Evans. In the Dominions fixture, eight Australians featured alongside Stewie Dempster, Bertie Clarke and Ted Badcock in a keenly fought draw which featured a century from Laurie Fishlock. Nearly 6,000 spectators attended. Matches were usually contested either on a fixed amount of time per innings, or with the team batting first enforcing a declaration when they felt appropriate. A rare experiment in limited-overs cricket occurred at York on Saturday, 12 August in the final of a Northern Command Inter-formation competition between Northumbrian District and East Riding and Lincs District. Players, including Maurice Leyland, played an innings of thirty eight-ball overs each. A week later, the Royal Navy put out only its third totally representative XI into the field. They had the better of a drawn match, with the White Ensign flying proudly from the top gallants of the Lord's pavilion.

An aggregation of the major matches at Lord's saw Les Ames top the batting averages with 67.09, whilst Jack Robertson had compiled the most runs with 859 in his twenty-seven innings. Other significant players having a dozen or more innings at headquarters included Denis Compton, Laurie Fishlock, Maurice Leyland, Cyril Washbrook, Bill Edrich, Bob Wyatt, Harry Halliday, Les Todd, Bertie Clarke and Trevor Bailey. Ted Badcock headed the bowling averages and others claiming twenty-five or more wickets included Doug Wright, Les Todd, Alf Gover, Bertie Clarke, Trevor Bailey and Stan Nichols. Keith Miller headed the RAAF batting averages in Lord's matches, with Reg Ellis, Bob Cristofani and Mick Roper being the leading wicket-takers.

* * *

The game remained resilient in its further-flung outposts. RAF and RN teams joined the Philadelphia Cricket Association to compete against the domestic teams. In Chicago, the Illinois Cricket Association was reduced to five clubs due to the loss of players to the forces or war work. Many veterans had to be coaxed out of retirement by energetic secretaries. Chicago CC won the championship for the fifth time whilst Winnetka CC won the K.A. Auty Cup. Meanwhile, the gospel of the game was spread to Mauritius, as the island's Football and Hockey Club played a strong Navy XI. J.H. Bowkett for the club side carried his bat of 18 in a total of 67. Once the Navy had knocked off the runs, reaching 80 for no wicket, Bowkett came on fifth change to take all ten wickets for 14 runs.

Across the Middle Eastern oilfields, cricket was being played. In Iran, matches took place despite summer temperatures of 110°F to 120°F in the shade. The usual protocol was to play two hours on each of two evenings for each match, from 4.45 to 6.45 pm. Service sides played against staff from the Anglo-Iranian Oil Company.

Alec Waugh wrote of plentiful good club cricket taking place in Baghdad. The local side, the Casuals, had recently celebrated their twenty-first anniversary. They benefitted from their own ground – an oval surrounded by oleanders and featuring a matting wicket. Similar to neighbouring Iran, two-day matches took place from 4.15 to 6.30 pm, the light becoming poor in the final half hour. The Casuals were captained by S.N. Hare, an employee of Royal Dutch Shell in Baghdad, who had played a few times for Essex in the early 1920s (and still holds the county record for the ninth wicket partnership, 251 with Johnny Douglas against Derbyshire at Leyton in 1921). During the war the presence of Paiforce (Persia and Iraq Command) added to the variety and zest of the fixture list. The GHQ of Paiforce also ran a series of league matches for units. Sir Godfrey Rhodes, who had earned the soubriquet 'The Saviour of Stalingrad' for his inauguration of the 'Aid to Russia' service in 1941, topped the 1944 batting averages.

In Uganda, a triangular tournament took place between Europeans, Goans and Indians, with the hope that Africans would soon be strong enough to compete. Bushbucks Cricket Club had been formed as a memorial to the late Reginald Wickham, son of the old Somerset cricketer the Reverend A.P. Wickham. Young Reginald had been killed in a car accident in September 1938, having been a great driver of the organisation of the game in Uganda. The first memorial match was played on 31 December 1944, when the Bushbucks met an ITC XI, with a toast of cider being drunk to Wickham during the luncheon interval.

The Northern Cricket Union of Ireland oversaw five league competitions comprising forty-one clubs. With impending events on the war fronts, and the consequent shortage of players, the annual match between teams representing the British Army in Northern Ireland and the Province of Ulster, played during the past four seasons, had been allowed to lapse. Some leading clubs had gone out of existence. However, an organised league and cup competition were maintained. Gross receipts for the first four wartime seasons of £241 12s 6d were handed to the Red Cross Fund of the Governor of Northern Ireland, the Duke of Abercorn. Annual matches between a Services XI and Ulster had taken place throughout the war. Continued strong interest in the game was demonstrated at the final of the Northern Ireland Cricket Union Challenge Cup in August. The competition, with a history stretching back to 1887, saw its 1944 climax contested in front of 7,230 spectators as Waringstown, Co. Down CC beat Cregagh CC, a Belfast club.

Sir John Maffey, the British Representative in Eire, raised an XI to play a two-innings match against Dublin University. The match coincided with the Fall of Rome and the opening of the Second Front. College Park, Dublin, despite being in the centre of the metropolis, was, according to *The Cricketer* correspondent J.C. Picken, 'picturesquely situated, and the surrounding trees and the buildings of the University add to its seclusion'. A band played during the afternoon for a large and fashionable crowd composed entirely of civilians. No aircraft or balloons littered the neutral Irish skies as the match swung backwards and forwards before Maffey's XI won by nine wickets.

The Leinster Senior League continued with eight teams, Leinster winning the league and Pembroke the cup. Twenty-year-old Bill Haughton was forging a reputation for attacking strokeplay, with a 'grand eye and very strong wrists and forearm', according to 'Bystander'. He had made 68 in thirty-five minutes, 87 in fifty-one minutes and 57 in forty minutes for Dublin University. Haughton's strength was put to further post-war use as he represented the Irish national team on twenty-nine occasions at field hockey.

* * *

The balance of power between the strong northern English leagues began to tilt slightly towards the western side of the Pennines. The Central Lancashire League decided to reinstate professionals for the 1944 season. Nine of the fourteen clubs decided to avail themselves of this opportunity whilst the Lancashire League maintained its strict wartime non-professional policy. The Central Lancashire League got off to a lively start, with Heywood being dismissed for 8 runs, with Robert Rae claiming seven for 2. Learie Constantine was in good form for Crompton whilst Charlie Hallows, Edwin St Hill and Norman Oldfield showed that the league was regaining its former strength.

Radcliffe maintained their unbeaten form in the Central Lancashire League, with one eight-wicket win over Heywood witnessing 49 not out by Charlie Hallows and five for 37 from Manny Martindale. The reintroduction of professionals into the league proved a great success. Crowds were higher, as was the standard of play. Radcliffe sneaked the championship from long-time leaders Werneth. The experience of Charlie Hallows and Manny Martindale had much to do with Radcliffe's success, Hallows averaging 50.84 for his 661 runs whilst Martindale claimed seventy-one wickets for 8.67.

Rishton won the Lancashire League, their first success since 1912. The club had Arthur Ramsbottom to thank for his 803 runs and fifty-two wickets at 6.67. Blackpool succeeded Blackpool Services as champions of the Ribblesdale League. The Liverpool district, which had sustained heavy bombing, was harder hit than most. Liverpool, for example, instead of fielding four Saturday teams, had to be content with an occasional Sunday match. Birkenhead Park, New Brighton and Northern were still without their grounds.

The Bradford League pointedly opposed MCC's decision to revert to six-ball overs for the 1944 season. 'Many valuable minutes have been saved in the limited time at our disposal to provide attractive relaxation for the present day supporter,' wrote F. Milton Watmough. Len Hutton was in good early season form for Pudsey St Lawrence, with a century against Brighouse, whilst his future post-war English opening partner, Cyril Washbrook, was racking up the runs for Eccleshill.

Although predominantly playing in the Central Lancashire League in 1944, Learie Constantine appeared at Windhill in May to captain the side. He hit a whirlwind 36 in seventeen minutes, with four sixes and two fours, after taking two brilliant catches and claiming three for 37 to take his side to a five-wicket victory over Baildon Green. His Caribbean colleague, Ellis Achong (six for 82), gave able assistance.

Saltaire had promised to have the finest team in the league, having agreed terms preseason with Bill Voce, Tom Goddard, Bill Copson, Harold 'Doc' Gibbons, Arthur Fagg and T.D. Hounsfield, but travelling restrictions severely handicapped the ability of four of their stars to appear regularly, only Copson and Hounsfield being frequent players. They succumbed to Spen Victoria for only 63 runs, George Pope (five for 33) and Arthur Booth (five for 28) bowling right through the innings. Les Ames was slightly less successful in the Bradford League than in the big matches at Lord's, finishing ninth in the averages with 39.33. The heaviest scorer was Vic Wilson of Undercliffe, followed by Len Hutton of Pudsey. Saltaire's Bill Copson was the highest wicket-taker with 76.

Spen Victoria, who had entered the league in 1931, emerged as winners of Division A, with Pope and Booth the keys to their success. In doing so they became the first club to win the B and A divisions in consecutive seasons. Only sixteen balls were sent down in the final of the Priestley Cup as 7,000 disappointed spectators were forced to wait until 16 September for the contest to be settled. Spen Victoria completed a fine double by overcoming Yeadon by 72 runs. George Pope top scored with 76 before claiming six for 36 in front of 8,000 spectators. The availability of match fees of up to £25 plus the prospect of lucrative collection money led some county secretaries to express concern about losing stars to the Bradford and other northern leagues. Overall this failed to materialise, with most players of first-class standard rejoining their counties from 1946 onwards.

Slaithwaite contested the Huddersfield and District League's Sykes Cup Final against Broad Oak at the Fartown Ground on 5 August. A crowd of 7,652 contributed to gate receipts of £250 as Slaithwaite emerged victorious by eight wickets. The sum of £50 raised for the Red Cross was the highest for any match in the Huddersfield area. Golcar won the league title. Longton won the North Staffordshire League and Sunderland Police carried off the Durham Senior League Championship. By the end of July, the Birmingham League was distilling into a three-way contest for honours between West Bromwich Dartmouth, Mitchells & Butlers, and Dudley. West Bromwich Dartmouth's eventual success owed much to Eric Hollies, who took eighty-one wickets at 8.12. George Paine, the Warwickshire player, was in good form for Kidderminster, making scores of 101 not out and 50, alongside bowling figures of four for 68 and six for 54 to beat Aston Unity and Walsall.

* * *

On 1 July, the Notts Women's Cricket Association was able to recommence operations after a five-year lacuna. A match in aid of the Red Cross was arranged to take place at the University College Ground against a Leicestershire and Rutland XI. The resumption of play was credited to Miss Eileen White, who had been captain of the Boots Athletic team for a dozen years. White had also opened the batting for Nottinghamshire and the Midlands. Across the Atlantic, the women's game was making progress in Trinidad. Sister Caro Brown, of the island's Colonial Hospital in San Fernando, wrote to *The Cricketer*:

> I have started a nurses' cricket club. Cricket is a favourite game out here. … You would be very critical of our pitch. It is rough savannah – what we would call common land, only we have nothing so rough. The heavy rainfall, the heavy soil, and the rough scrubby grass make it very hard going. The actual pitch is prepared with special soil or something and has a length of matting on it. Anyhow, we play good cricket.

Wilfred S. White, writing in *The Cricketer*, complained of the Board of Trade's policy of assembling huge stores of sports equipment to be sent to countries on the Continent to help them get their sports up and running after the war: 'Whilst helping other countries surely our own clubs, who have struggled to keep the game alive and grounds in order at home, might be allowed to purchase their minimum requirements from the manufacturers.' There was little doubt that the game was bringing huge benefits to a country at war. The *Daily Sketch* of 25 August reported that army psychiatrists had stumbled upon the idea that watching a cricket match could be a cure for war fatigue.

> A number of boys in hospital blue from a Midlands military establishment centre were so much improved after attending a match at a famous county ground that more cricket matches are now being specially organised for them.
>
> 'Cricket is the best nerve sedative of all games' a psychiatrist told me, 'all the factors contribute to this – the spaciousness of the pitch, the comparative leisurely pace of the game, the soothing contrast of white flannels with the green carpet, and the pleasant thud of the leather ball on the willow as it is snicked through the slips or slammed to the boundary.'

There was cause for optimism that the 1945 season would take place amidst a great sense of domestic normality. On 16 September, Double Summer Time and blackout regulations were relaxed after five years. It was also announced that the Home Guard would be stood down. H.D.G. 'Shrimp' Leveson Gower, that doyenne of festival cricket, expressed the hope that the Scarborough Cricket Festival could be revived for September 1945. He was taken to task in *The People*: 'All present indications are that big-time cricket will be considerably attenuated in 1945, let alone festivals lasting several days.' Fortunately for the thousands who would enjoy the bracing Yorkshire late summer air at the North Marine Road Ground, Leveson Gower's sanguinity was well founded.

* * *

By May 1944, many cricketers who had enjoyed some measure of organised cricketing opportunities while stationed in Egypt were now fighting their way up the Italian peninsula. Opportunities for matches were still seized upon. A NZ Army Pay Unit played against the Eighth Army Rest Camp at Campobasso. Later in the summer, the Eighth Army having advanced northwards, on a piece of ground levelled by bulldozers and with a matting wicket, several county cricketers featured in an Army *v* RAF match. Harry Parks and the Bedser twins played for the RAF, renewing acquaintance with Tom Dollery, recently recovered from a bout of malaria. The wicket was described as 'a bit sporty' but Parks managed to make 50.

Tom Pritchard was establishing a fine reputation in services cricket in Egypt. Playing for a NZ Base XI against a Maadi Sporting Club XI, which included RAF players, the fast bowler took nine for 6, including a hat-trick and six wickets in one eight-ball over. The *New Zealand Free Lance* purred:

> Never before in the Middle East has there been such a display of fast bowling. It almost bewildered the 'Tommy' batsmen. Pritchard took five of his wickets with six balls, for no runs. His final delivery sent all three stumps flying through the air for yards. Pritchard's bowling in this innings would have shaken batsmen much better than the airmen.

On 11 September the *NZEF Times* reported on the success of John Simpson, who had been a successful fast bowler in Auckland senior cricket before the war. Showing his true all-round prowess, Simpson hit 66 out of a total of 104 for the NZ Advance Base XI before stumping four and catching two of the opposing British unit batsmen.

The principal attraction in Middle East services cricket in 1944 was a series of three matches between Cairo and Alexandria which featured such talents as Pritchard, his Kiwi comrade Eric Tindall, South African Dudley Nourse and future England great Jim Laker. The Yorkshireman had already carried his bat for 106 not out and taken six for 10 as the South African Air Force XI were bundled out for 29. During the same season, in a match between Cairo City and Helwan at the Gezira Club, Laker claimed five for 7, including the prized wicket of Nourse. Across the whole year, Laker claimed 221 wickets at an average of 5.7 while amassing 960 runs. This outstanding return prompted Captain Peter Smith, the main organiser of cricket in Alexandria, to accurately prophesy: 'Laker, with his immaculate length off-breaks, used to play for Saltaire as a batsman. He should now walk into most county sides as a bowler.' In late 1944, Laker was selected to play in a match at the Alamein Club between English and Australian servicemen. Contested in the spirit of a Test match, a vociferous crowd of 10,000 cheered on their national teams. None present could have imagined that twelve years later, Laker would set an all-time first-class record of nineteen wickets in a match.

A late-season match took place between a South African XI, containing five Test players, and an invitational team from the Alamein Club. The local club side called on Tom Pritchard and Bob Crisp, the former taking four for 41 in the South African XI total of 117. The final high profile match of the 1944 season in Egypt was a two-day fixture between a British Forces XI and a British Empire XI at the same ground. There were seven New Zealanders included in the Empire team, which scored 279 in their first innings. In reply the British Forces side totalled 286 for nine. Empire went on to score 170 for five, before declaring. The match ended in a draw. The 1944 season had been one of the best on record in Egypt, largely due to the opening of the Alamein Club. Sam Pothecary set the record score for the club with 148.

Peter Smith.

It was reported that Ron Aspinall, the Almondbury all-rounder, had scored 2,000 runs and taken 200 wickets in Egyptian cricket in 1944. Aspinall would have to wait until he was 27 to make his first-class debut, his star shining brightly before injury ended his career prematurely. He eventually became a familiar sight on English county grounds, umpiring in over 700 first-class and one-day matches. Peter Smith, the Essex all-rounder, captained Alexandria in inter-area matches against Cairo, claiming more than 300 wickets and hitting over 2,500 runs, but perhaps his greatest assistance to the game was the coaching of young cricketers in the services.

Aside from the delights of the Egyptian sporting clubs and the feats of the feted and famous, cricket continued to provide spiritual solace for many servicemen. Graham White, writing of a service match in Italy between two RASC units played on a bumpy pitch in the blinding light, surrounded by a sun-baked, turfless outfield, reminisced:

for the first time I realised how much more than a matter of runs scored and stumps upset the summer game is – and how much of one's enjoyment of it is due not upon who wins or how well so-and-so bowled, but upon a host of little things which, strictly speaking, are not a part of cricket at all. Until then I had only appreciated these things in a vague, subconscious way.

White's senses were transported back to an archetypal English summer's setting:

Now I began to see them more clearly – the refreshing sight of close-trimmed turf and the resilient feel of it under the feet. The tall elms, standing like sentinels around the green, their shadows stealing slowly across the grass as the sun goes down at the day's end. The busy hum of the mower, and the rich scent of new-cut grass …

The musical clink of cup against saucer in the cool depths of the pavilion. A pleasant sound at all times, but who would not exchange all Beethoven's symphonies for it when the score stands at 270 for 4 and the thermometer is 80 degrees in the shade!

Opportunities to play cricket were carved out in the most inauspicious of conditions. Lieutenant P.S. White of the Royal Artillery wrote of how, armed with a strip of coconut matting 22 yards by 5, and a bag of cricket gear, 'one can have a game going in a matter of a few minutes on any old flat piece of desert'. This was particularly handy when on the move. On several occasions an innings was completed during one evening with the match being finished the following evening 200 miles away. White whimsically mused, 'Who knows, the day may come when the touring side will take their own wicket with them and not only toss for innings but also toss for wicket – ours or theirs – what fun!'

This keenness was shared by many troops on overseas service. L. Griffin, a former cricket coach at Charterhouse School, recounted some of the lengths to which men serving in the Middle East would go to arrange a cricket match. Two of Griffin's unit, builders by trade, had managed to obtain enough concrete to lay a serviceable wicket. At another location the unit's coconut mat had been placed on a vehicle track, whilst their chaplain, Padre Oliver, produced a gramophone, the cooks provided tea and 'everything had the appearance of a village green'.

G.R. Hollingworth wrote of his regiment's cricketing relaxations in the toe of Italy: 'Free from parades, and with little to occupy our time, it was inevitable that someone should eventually suggest forming a cricket team.' A full kit, minus wicketkeeping gloves, was available to Hollingworth, but no ground nor matting was provided. Once a suitable area had been found and cleared three days were spent scouring every salvage dump in the area, and eventually, on the verge of despair, they succeeded in finding some matting. Fixtures were arranged with several local units. The first XI was largely experimental as only two members had experienced any cricket at all for four years. Matches took place between five and eight in the evening. In one match an admixture of malaria and a surfeit of peaches laid low three of the bowlers. After enduring the sporting pitch conditions for several weeks, the team's final match took place on a grass outfield in the grounds of a hospital.

Lieutenant Edward Crutchley wrote to his father about a match played on 19 August 1944 against a New Zealand XI:

George Mann got a side together from the Brigade (Guards) and we played against a New Zealand team who, to our disgust, had been playing and having nets fairly frequently! ... We lost. George elected to bat and we were all out for 108 (Crutchley 45). The New Zealanders made 109 for 7. It was a good match played on the Siena football ground. We all enjoyed it more than I can say.

George Mann, a future England captain, had won the MC in 1942, and was later awarded the DSO due to 'consistent courage and outstanding leadership' in the Allied advance from Rome to Florence.

A ground was also established in Naples, inside the city's racecourse, whilst in Rome a wicket was cut at the football stadium. The Royal Palace at Caserta also contained a cricket pitch. While playing at this venue Eric and Alec Bedser made a pilgrimage to the grave of Hedley Verity. The great man had been laid to rest in a cemetery above the town down a peaceful country lane. The Bedsers and Frank Smailes, a pre-war colleague of Verity's in the great Yorkshire team, arranged to have a marble headstone erected, of which a photograph was taken and sent to Verity's widow in Leeds.

The Bedser twins were serving in the War Crimes Intelligence Branch, with one of their investigations involving the murder of three RAF servicemen who had been attacked while on leave in Naples. In March, Mount Vesuvius erupted, blowing 200 feet off the top of the mountain. Eric and Alec assisted in the evacuation of the local population, recalling, 'The lava came shooting down. You couldn't get within 100 yards of it.' Their Surrey teammate Arthur McIntyre had been wounded in the Anzio landings, and was recuperating in a convalescent home near Bari. Transferred to the role of Army physical training instructor, McIntyre helped establish a service ground there; its perfect situation by the Adriatic was complemented by a monumental effort to flatten and smooth the playing surface with a bulldozer and heavy roller. The wicket was of matting over a concrete surface, and sightscreen and scoreboxes were made and erected. Seating accommodation was built for several hundred spectators. Marquees were set up for serving refreshments and loudspeakers provided a running commentary on the action. Scorecards were printed and convivial lunches were enjoyed by the spectators.

The Carpiquet Aerodrome on the Normandy Bridgehead provided a remarkable setting for a cricket match. A completely gutted hangar served as a pavilion and a shell-pitted runway partially covered with thin strips of coconut matting as a pitch, with tent pegs affixing it to cracks in the concrete. Most remarkable of all was the fact that it was in full, if distant, view of the forward German positions, about 5,000 yards away. The outfield was in the process of being de-mined by a team of trained Alsatian dogs. Ralph Cobbold, who had played for Cambridge University in 1927, captained one team, and Derick Heathcoat-Amory the other. Heathcoat-Amory would be captured during Operation Market Garden and later serve as Chancellor of the Exchequer in the MacMillan government.

In October 1944, Jack Chegwyn, a New South Wales cricketer who would make a post-war reputation organising scratch XIs to tour the remote bush districts, took a team to tour northern areas under RAAF control. One unfinished match in Queensland was against an Army team with many pre and

British soldiers playing cricket in France, 1944.

post-war Test stars in attendance (see image on opposite page). They included Colin McCool, Bill Alley and Bill O'Reilly (third, fourth and fifth from left, back row), Ron Saggers (far right, back row) and Stan McCabe, Vic Jackson, Don Tallon and Jack Chegwyn (third to sixth from left, front row).

In November, a side consisting of members of the RAF and the South African Air Force from various Air Schools across the Union embarked on a tour of the Cape Peninsula. The Western Province Cricket Union arranged for the team to enjoy net facilities at Newlands. Pupil Pilot Menzies enjoyed the accolade of bowling 'Tuppy' Owen-Smith, one of Wisden's 1930 Cricketers of the Year, for a first-baller. On 11 November, the team played a Royal Navy XI captained by Vice-Admiral Sir Robert Burnett, C-in-C South Atlantic. Two days later they played an Eric Rowan's Eastern Province Fortress side at Newlands, affording an excellent day's cricket which covered two innings. 'A most successful and happy venture', according to two leading lights, Flight Lieutenant K.G. Williamson and Pilot Officer Richard Altham, son of Major Harry, the eminent cricket historian. 'What could be a more profitable and pleasant way of spending a wartime leave in this distant and most attractive land?'

Jack Chegwyn's Cricket XI, 1944. (*Australian War Memorial*)

Military progress in Europe now meant that the prospect of Allied victory, and the concomitant resumption of pre-war rhythms of life, could now be realistically entertained. It would be difficult indeed to name a district inhabited by British servicemen that had not witnessed some attempt, however primitive, at a cricket match. Thus Pelham Warner believed that the peacetime game would be more popular than ever. In particular, the development of air travel would make it possible for Australian cricket followers to witness Tests in England, and vice versa. He argued that standards might take a few years to return to pre-war levels. 'In judging young cricketers some of the critics are rather harsh. They forget that the young player of today has only an occasional match and that regular net practice is almost out of the question.'

* * *

At Stalag Luft III in Lower Silesia, the venue of the popular 1963 film *The Great Escape*, inmates had laid a concrete pitch with a 6-yard gap in the middle due to a shortage of concrete. Sackcloth was laid in the absence of matting, creating a sporting wicket. The small playing area and soft sand outfield was, according to one of the players, P.A.W. Thomas, 'almost a travesty of the real game but it re-awakened the spirit of cricket amongst us'. Nearly 300 out of the 800 prisoners played five matches each. Two were county class and about thirty good club standard; the rest very indifferent. 'For a month cricket filled the thoughts of many of us – we read and re-read the few books there are here, talked endlessly of it and lived again happy memories of long ago days.' A league was organised based on a block or hut basis, each named after an English county side. Flight Lieutenant Keen was one of the star players. In one match he claimed the wicket of Marcel Zillessen, the inspiration of the James Garner character The Scrounger in the *Great Escape* film.

One escapee of whom no news had been heard since 1943 was Flight Lieutenant John Jewell, nephew of renowned Worcestershire player Maurice Jewell. He had escaped from a prison camp in Italy in 1943 and on 1 June 1944 his uncle was told by the Air Ministry that his relative was safe. The younger Jewell had played two first-class fixtures for the county, as well as appearing in various service matches at Lord's.

Spirited inner resistance to the vicissitudes of captivity endured in the Far East prison camps. Glamorgan's Wilf Wooller, who had been captured on Java, arrived in Changi camp in September 1943. He was eager to get down to some keen sport:

> Despite the fact that I was down to almost eight stone and had occasional bouts of fever, I also took part in some of the camp sports. We made a pair of cricket pads, two bats, a set of stumps and found a cricket ball in order to stage an odd game of cricket. The highlight came on Christmas Day [1944] when we staged an England versus Australia Test match in front of bemused Japanese guards.

For Wooller, the matches allowed his mind to escape to happier times and cheerier places: 'All you heard was the bowler's footsteps, his shoes scuffling the dirt, the swish of the bat, a little click, dead silence. That was a Brahms lullaby compared to the chaos and bedlam that went on the rest of the day.'

This was to be the final big cricket match organised in the Japanese camps. As the tide of war started to turn in the Allies' favour, an order came banning the playing of sports and holding of concerts as they promoted excessive morale amongst the captives.

The renowned and heroic Australian doctor E.E. 'Weary' Dunlop also took part in that match. He recorded:

> Incongruously, I was asked to captain Australia in a 'Test' match, Australia *v* England. It was played with a tennis ball and odd local rules. Single wicket, 18 yard pitch, no running, no stumping, 8 per side. All scoring by strokes to particular objects, over the hut 'six and out' etc.
>
> We got the father of a hiding, licked by 4 wickets, an innings and about 60 runs. The England team included 'Fizzer' Pearson and Norman Smith (Yorkshire 2nd Eleven and Colts). Fizzer Pearson, the star turn, absolutely

annihilated us with his fast bowling. There was an awed silence as I went to the wicket and some talk of 'an international' (Rugby)! I ingloriously just broke my duck both innings and almost entirely shed the remaining skin on my blistered feet from the horse race. Now I can hardly walk.

E.W. Swanton recalled the same encounter:

With the Australian innings comes sensation, Captain Fizzer Pearson, of Sedbergh and Lincolnshire, the English fast bowler, is wearing BOOTS! No other cricketer has anything on his feet at all, the hot earth, the occasional flint being accepted as part of the game. The moral [*sic*] effect of these boots is tremendous. Captain Pearson bowls with shattering speed and ferocity, and as each fresh lamb arrives for the slaughter the stumps seem more vast, the bat even punier. One last defiant cheer from The Hill when their captain, Lieut-Colonel E.E. Dunlop, comes in, another and bigger one from the English when his stumps go flying.

The Bombay Pentangular Tournament resumed, attracting huge crowds, with an opening day attendance of 30,000 enjoying Hindus *v* Parsis at the Bradbourne Stadium on 21 November. The Europeans, despite fielding Reg Simpson, Dick Howorth, Denis Compton and Joe Hardstaff, succumbed to Parsis thanks to a 215 from 20-year-old Rusi Modi. Modi, already a renowned run accumulator, would score an aggregate of 1,008 in only five matches in the Ranji Trophy in the 1944/45 season, a record that would stand for over forty years. In 1946, Modi took part in the first post-war Test matches in England, despite not being fully acclimatised to the vagaries of the British weather. John Arlott described him as 'tall, painfully thin, grey of face and huddled into an overcoat, tending to tremble'.

Chapter 7

1945: Cheerful Careless Cricket

'No Hitler can kill the love of cricket which is inherent in the English people ...
Cricket will flourish as never before in all its long and splendid history. It is ...
a great part of the life of the English people.'

Pelham Warner

Whilst the failure of Operation Market Garden in the autumn of 1944 had dashed hopes of a swift end to the war, hope still remained that victory in the early spring of 1945 would allow for a full programme of matches for the English season. However, Norman Preston recognised that 1946 was a more realistic target date. The uncertain state of the European situation caused a hold-up in organising a full 1945 fixture list. To fill the void, the British Empire XI went ahead and planned forty-five matches. Wartime sides such as the RAAF, London Counties, West of England and Coventry and District were not willing to carry on at the expense of a County Championship, but happy to organise themselves once more for a final farewell.

Despite the continued omission of the championship, 1945 promised a much richer diet of cricket than had been the case for the previous five wartime seasons. The ban on playing in coastal areas having been lifted, Hampshire had arranged their first fixtures since 1939. As the pulse of county cricket was beginning to beat with a more typical rhythm, so the Club Cricket Conference reported an anticipated upsurge in preseason planning. The imminent expectation of victory in Europe allowed for a more expansive programme, which included the welcome return of first-class cricket to England after five barren years. In all, eleven first-class fixtures would take place, although none formed part of an official competition. The Australian Services XI would play nearly fifty matches and 414,000 people would pass through the Lord's turnstiles.

The Club Cricket Conference AGM took place on 24 February at The Polytechnic in London's Regent Street. Here it was announced that £6,564 had been raised for the Red Cross Fund during the previous season. Thought was given on how to bridge the gap between club and county cricket, with a similar body to the Sussex Cricket Association being mooted in other counties, notably Derbyshire. The gap between school and club cricket was also being addressed by Ealing Dean CC, who had written to all local schools promoting the club and its activities. The club had run seven teams in 1944 and had increased its fixture list to 160 matches for 1945. The game's future would depend on the appeal it made to youth. Pelham Warner reckoned that efforts had focussed largely on public and secondary schoolboys, and more should be done for the elementary schoolboy cricketer. Grass or good quality matting wickets needed to be provided, alongside organised coaching. Complimentary tickets to county matches should also be given to schoolboys, he argued. Cranleigh CC ran a scheme whereby a youth could pay 2s 6d for a membership, which entitled him to coaching two evenings per week plus the use of the nets on other evenings. As future visions were offered, East Molesey CC got on with the more prosaic task of arranging a ten-day cricket festival. Club Cricket Conference members arranged more Home Weeks than previously. The St Lawrence Beverley combination was to play one more season before reverting once more to separate playing entities.

Wimbledon CC had resumed play after a five-year hibernation, welcoming back I.S. Hampton and D.E. Young, who had been captured at Dunkirk. The BBC CC too was running a few matches, having closed down at the outbreak of war. Dulwich CC also planned to restart. After three and a half years in the Far East, Jack Marriott, the Barclays Bank fast bowler, was home again and was appointed captain of RAF Atherstone. Marriott had previously played Middlesex 2nd XI alongside Compton, Robertson and Edrich, as well as for Longton in the North Staffordshire and District League. The *Staffordshire Advertiser* of 1 June 1940 described him as:

> a young giant who bowls a fast ball from a great height and often makes it bore in from the off. He has played for Barclay's Bank and has a Club Conference cap. … At first sight I should place Marriott as one of the best fast bowlers we have had in the district. In four matches he had taken 20 wickets for 92 runs.

Post-war, Marriott would serve as secretary of Barclays Bank Sport Club until his retirement in 1975.

Jack Young of Middlesex completed the rare feat of taking all eleven wickets for 57 in a twelve-a-side match for A.E.G. Baring's XII *v* Kolster Brands. Baring's XII also included Bev Lyon, Lionel Tennyson and Jack MacBryan. Len Newman completed his 227th century when he made 103 not out for Alexandra Park *v* Kenton and surpassed 1,500 runs for the season. Whilst the great majority of the sides were still

John Marriott. (*Barclay's Bank Archive*)

below pre-war strength, A.W.T. Langford was confident that the 1946 season would be approximately normal. He marvelled 'at the way in which the clubs overcame apparently insurmountable difficulties and in some instances actually contrived to turn out teams of considerable strength'. It was anticipated that the number of active clubs in the Club Cricket Conference would rise from 600 in 1945 to 1,000 in 1946.

Although the war's end seemed in sight, still several pages of *The Cricketer Spring Annual* were filled with the obituaries of young men cut off before their prime. Sergeant Navigator K.C. Campin, who had made his debut for Bedfordshire in 1939 aged just 16, was killed in a flying accident in Scotland. Meanwhile it was reported that his county teammate, Squadron Leader Alec Cook DFC, had been killed in action over France in August 1944. Stanley Dearlove, secretary of Goodmayes CC in Ilford and for many years the club's outstanding bowler, was killed by enemy action in November 1944.

* * *

For British and Commonwealth service personnel stationed overseas, and therefore unable to play a part in the domestic cricketing victory celebrations, the game was played whenever the opportunities arose. On 10 June, a match was played at Caserta, Italy, staged by Lieutenant R.E. Henty of Surrey 2nd XI and Honor Oak CC. A matting wicket and rough outfield was the stage as none of the players, which included the Bedser twins and Arthur Wellard, wore flannels. Alec Bedser took five for 42 and he and Eric visited the grave of Hedley Verity, whose loss they felt 'was such a grievous blow to English cricket'.

An East Italy *v* West Italy match took place on 30 June and 1 July on Bari's beautiful Army Cricket Ground. The presence of many well-known cricketers including New Zealander Bill Merritt, Basil Allen, Arthur McIntyre and George Emmett meant much attraction was afforded to the fixture, with it being broadcast to service personnel throughout Italy. The marquees, refreshment tents, flags and bunting as well as the band of the 615 Regiment RA all helped to give a seaside cricket festival atmosphere. On 28–29 July, a CMF Army XI played an RAF XI, with Emmett (62) and McIntyre (82) featuring for the soldiers.

Signalman Peter Hollingworth wrote of how cricket was organised in the Argenta Gap, starting with just one tennis ball. 'A bat was carved from a plank and with a petrol can for wickets we managed very well – until the ball literally fell apart.' A bat was then fashioned from a shell-torn tree. One match was played with the new bat, 'a close match in a small farmyard where a line of haystacks constituted the off-boundary and mid-on fielded at the pig-sty door'. Eventually a ground was hewn in a field of clover. The first match, between Royal Signals and The C.O.'s XI, saw the latter all out for 12 on a 'wicket possessed of the devil'. The ball would stop dead in the clover so the only way to score was with lofted shots.

Another field was found, with the farmer being gifted twenty cigarettes and 2 ounces of tobacco to scythe down the playing area. Troop funds paid £18 for a full length of matting and men made and painted a splendid scoreboard, whilst sightscreens were made from old identification strips. The unit eventually acquired four bats, three of poor quality and one Gunn & Moore – a veteran of the Nile Delta, Western Desert and Sicily bound up with insulating tape. Out of forty men in the troop, two teams were raised which played around the area. They were unbeaten in 1945.

A familiar sight to passers-by on the sea front at Naples was a number of practice nets erected adjacent to an army transport unit, whose commanding officer was Major I.C. Maconachie, the Northumberland captain. In a match played at the Italian Naval Academy at Leghorn, two sides represented the officers and ship's company. Gerald Pawle, former Northern Correspondent of *The Cricketer*, and later a notable author of cricket and other books, hit three sixes and thirteen fours in his 76. Major J.W. Martin of Kent performed the hat-trick for an Army XI *v* RAF at Bari Ordnance Depot Ground, San Spirito, on 8 September. A CMF XI beat a MEF XI at 51 Rest Camp, Rome, on 17–18 August by an innings and 13 runs. A good sprinkling of Test and county players took part, including Bert Sutcliffe, Norman Yardley, Peter Smith, Ron Aspinall, Jim Laker, George Emmett, Tom Pritchard, Arthur Wellard, Bill Merritt and Arthur McIntyre. Elsewhere in the Mediterranean, as part of VJ Day celebrations, a team of Australian servicemen played the Rest of the Rock on Gibraltar.

Air Vice-Marshal B.E. Baker, serving in East Africa, relayed information of a remarkable feat that took place on 17 February at RAF Seychelles when an RAF XI playing HQ Garrison BNCO dismissed their opponents for 5 runs. L.A.C. Juneman, a wireless operator from Battersea, took nine for 0, hitting the middle stump six times. Baker proudly stated, 'My RAF team which I have started in East Africa has just defeated Nairobi, Entebbe, and Uganda Kobs.'

From the opposite coast of Africa, Flying Officer F.M. Saunders reported on services cricket in Sierra Leone. The Brookfields Ground in Freetown resembled an English one, with a concrete stand and grass outfield, although the wicket was matting. Other grounds were laid out on service sites, varying in quality. 'Fielding is an adventure which can easily end in minor disaster for the over enthusiastic,' commented Saunders. All three services played each other twice, and also played against the Sierra Leone Civilian XI and the Sierra Leone Cricket League XI. The league XI was comprised of native Africans whose bowling was fast and accurate, although their runs came from cross-batted hits or deflections. 'They have all the physical attributes to make good cricketers, but in their attitude to the game and the spirit in which they played it they have a great deal to learn,' thought Saunders. The Reverend Tom Killick was prominent in the matches as well as Stanley Profitt, who had played a handful of matches for Essex in 1937, and Harold Day, the former Hampshire batsman who had played Rugby Union for England.

N.E.H. Knight of the Royal Artillery, serving with the 14th Army, felt less forgotten upon receiving cricketing news:

> what a joy it is to receive *The Cricketer* out here. Is it still jungle and paddy-field I see lying there head? Nay, surely it will be through the enchanted woods and pastoral ground of Kent the path stretches; onwards towards that day when the Rising Sun shall mean nought else but the return of glory to our summer game.

Captain Sonny Avery, the Essex opening batsman, had also been dispatched to the Burma Front. He echoed the importance of reading material, particularly sporting related, for the men: 'The lads haven't been treated at all well, although things have improved slightly just recently; they deserve the best we can give them.' Avery appealed for a cricket match to be arranged in England in aid of 36th Division. 'Most of the troops, now that the war in Europe is over, seem to feel they have been forgotten.'

An airstrip, from which planes had taken off to fight the Japanese fleet in the Battle of the Coral Sea in May 1942, was the improvised ground for one of the eleven matches played by an Australian team that toured northern Air Force stations. Airmen based at Iron Range, 200 miles from the tip of Cape York, cut up tent flies and sewed

A.V. 'Sonny' Avery.

them together to make matting for the wicket. Organised by Jack Chegwyn, the tourists were captained by Stan McCabe, who headed the averages with delightful batting. Second to Bill O'Reilly in the bowling averages was 52-year-old Clarrie Grimmett, who on one occasion bowled for two hours without a rest. This was one of the final appearances of the prematurely wizened spin wizard. Later in the year he announced his retirement from the game.

Playing opportunities for troops of the British Liberation Army in Germany were less forthcoming. Leslie Compton used his week's leave in May to play for Arsenal against Maidenhead United, and the British Empire XI *v* Slough. A corporal in the Middlesex Regiment, attached to the 15th Scottish Division,

Compton had seen action in the battles for the Falaise Gap and Nijmegen, and taken part in the Seine, Rhine and Elbe crossings. He complained he had yet to find a cricket ground in Germany.

Initially a prohibition on fraternisation between British troops and German civilians had been enforced by the War Office. A handbook issued to all members of the British Liberation Army (BLA) warned in particular of German women exploiting their feminine charms in return for food and clothing. This ban proved unworkable, with Field Marshal Montgomery finding it unnecessary and cumbersome, and it was lifted in July 1945. One member of the BLA wrote to *The Cricketer* with more encouraging news from Germany:

> With reference to teaching German children cricket, my batman has set up some stumps, carved a bat from a plank and each evening an admiring crowd of boys hang around our office waiting for him to come out and teach them. He is very patient with them, and they all enjoy it tremendously.

T.C.D. Hassall of Wareham suggested that cricket be taught to German children. 'Would it not be immensely worthwhile to help the healthy rehabilitation of German children, if taken young enough, to teach them to play cricket at a very early age?' Learning the spirit of cricket from a young age would, apparently 'have a great influence of the understanding of international affairs'.

The cricket season for some members of the British Liberation Army started early. Lieutenant J.F. Mendl reported that a match was played near the Reichswald, just across the Dutch-German border, on 25 March. One BLA soldier had written, 'If the material is available I shall have a cricket ground built here by German soldiers, as it seems likely that we shall be spending some time as occupation troops.' *The Cricketer*'s Notes and Comments section recorded that exposure of the German people to the game could only be advantageous: 'It is surely not too much to hope that our national game will play an important part in the re-education of the Germans.'

* * *

Cricket was already established in Turkey by 1939 and the war brought a flood of new British blood to the embassy in Ankara, complete with stumps, bats, balls and sundries imported from Cairo. Matting was laid on a football field made of dust, ash and clumps of tough vegetation, situated 3,000 feet above sea level. With summer temperatures well into the nineties, sudden dust and thunderstorms would tear across the ground, choking, blinding or soaking players and spectators. The Turks preferred the spectacle of American diplomats and airmen playing baseball on the neighbouring field, just a solitary native spectator crouching on the boundary to watch the English game. Players were transported by bus for the 2-mile journey from the Embassy Club to the ground as there was no petrol for private cars.

Fast bowlers could manage no more than three over spells and grubbers were frequent. Boundaries were short, with the small totals of less than a hundred containing many sixes. A.W. Newsom, a Wiltshire Queries CC player, emphasised how, despite the conditions, the matches could transport the mind back home:

> It doesn't matter in the least who wins. Once in a dust-storm the scorebook blew away altogether but we played on. All that matters is that for a time we are each of us back on some field at home. I am sure that each of us stretches his imagination with violence enough to be transported from the middle of the Anatolian desert to Chalfont, Corsham, Ottery St Mary, Blackpool, Wallsend, Nottingham or wherever he would like to be. In war the isolation of belligerents in the neutral country is astonishingly complete, but for an hour or two we can forget it over a game of cricket.

Conversely, Captain J.N.H. Foster, who had played wartime cricket in lands as diverse as Gibraltar, Palestine, Egypt, India and Rangoon, found himself at Lord's watching Hammond bat. 'Did I enjoy it any more than some of the games in which I had played in Syria, the Desert or Palestine? I don't know. There is always a tremendous satisfaction in playing on a ground that you have made yourself.'

Much cricket was played in Khartoum in the Sudan between 1943 and 1945. The one good standard ground at Gordon College was put at the disposal of the military whilst other grounds had poor outfields and bumpy wickets. A league was operated with nine teams, with hours of play restricted from 3.00 to 6.00 pm due to the heat and gathering gloom. The league was won by the RAF in 1943, Royal Signals in 1944, and RAF in 1945. Each team had two or three good club-standard cricketers. Khartoum Cricket Club members were chiefly Sudan government officials and other British civilians.

V.H. Cockerham reported on the damage done by the war to cricket in New York. 'Things were pretty bright until the US entered the war.' There were two leagues with twelve clubs in all but this declined from 1942 onwards due to loss of players to the forces. Five clubs 'quit play' and only three could continue on a regular basis – Brooklyn, Staten Island and General Electric. It was impossible to purchase new equipment and the US Navy took over Brooklyn's ground.

Cricket had continued in Holland despite the German occupation. There had previously been keen interest in the game before the war. In 1939, a Netherlands team had played a two-day match at Lord's against an MCC side captained by Percy Chapman. In 1940, after the hiatus occasioned by the invasion, plans were drawn up to play a regional competition of four teams. This system was adopted by the Dutch Cricket Association. This was successful and formed the basis for subsequent war years. At times it was feared that the Germans would interfere with the summer game but fortunately that never happened. They were disinterested in cricket, apart from one notable occasion. On The Hague CC ground they watched fielding practising using the Kachaball Fielding Machine. The Germans thought it great fun and afterwards had a try. The first German who endeavoured to catch the ball got a nasty hit on his knee and was not seen again. A second split his finger when trying to hold a catch and a third was so badly hit by the ball on his head that he was completely knocked out.

For the first season following liberation English cricketers managed to fix up a few matches, with many units playing Dutch sides. The enemy occupiers had stripped the country bare so the liberators saw to it that the grounds were mown and other repairs undertaken to make cricket possible. When news had come through on hidden radios of the death of Hedley Verity, Dutch cricketers removed their caps in his honour and out of respect for the sacrifices that English cricketers were making on their behalf. Previous cricketing ties had sustained a continuing bond of comradeship during those dark years.

Major F.E. Templer, briefly commanding officer of the 15th King's Parachute Battalion, wrote of the splendid welcome the Dutch afforded British cricketing troops. Every man who wished to was given the opportunity to play during the summer of 1945. Many played against native Dutch cricketers, with honours being fairly even in these encounters at brigade or regimental level, but the hosts were more successful against unit XIs. An all-Holland XI beat a Services XI by over 100 runs, then a BLA XI by an innings despite the presence of Bryan Valentine and Arthur Brodhurst, the Cambridge University and Gloucestershire player. The British players were hampered by lack of practice, having recently arrived from Germany, and the bacchanalian hospitality of their hosts in the evening between the two days of play.

At the Woodvale Club in Belfast, a Town v Country match was held on the second day of the VJ celebrations in aid of the Hedley Verity Memorial Fund. Ideal cricket weather blessed the occasion, with spectators enjoying a magnificent view of the surrounding hills. With the ground, umpires and hospitality provided for free, a cheque for £117 2s was forwarded to Yorkshire CCC for the family of 'A man of outstanding personality and charm of manner [who] made very many friends here'.

* * *

The game remained resilient on the Indian subcontinent, with the additional spice of British servicemen in some matches. Denis Compton was in action in a four-day match for the C.K. Nayadu XI v Cricket Club of India XI at the Brabourne Stadium, Bombay. Due to four centuries in the CCI XI innings, the Middlesex man's 106 was not enough to stave off an innings defeat.

Commander G.F. Osborne RNVR witnessed what he termed a 'Test Match' between Ceylon and India on 1–3 April, thirty-seven years before the first official

Test between the two nations. He was 'genuinely surprised by the show put up by Ceylon' in the drawn match whilst asserting that the Indians would need to up their game when they came to England. Ceylon had been bundled out for 107 in the first innings before dismissing India for 179. They had proceeded to 225 for seven before the match ended in a draw. Osborne's verdict on Sri Lankan cricket was one with which cricket lovers have come to concur in the four decades since the nation's inaugural Test match in 1982: 'That Ceylon can produce the talent is quite clear. Quick of eye and most supple of wrist their out cricket was a joy to watch. And was played as they ... enjoyed every moment of it.'

Many Englishmen serving with South East Asia Command had the opportunity of playing good cricket in Ceylon and it was the general opinion that S.S. 'Sargo' Jayawickreme, captain of the Sinhalese Sports Club, was the outstanding cricketer. Osborne's judgement was corroborated by K.S. Ranga Rao, the Honorary Secretary of the Board of Control for Cricket in India. Rao expressed the view that Ceylon should be granted Test match status and given a place at the Imperial Cricket Conference. Ceylon Cricket Club established a new record of matches in a season, playing eighty-one, fifty-four of which were against service teams, with Paul Gibb making a succession of rapid scores. Gibb was to return to England after the war and make the physical move south from Yorkshire to Essex and the hierarchical move from amateur to professional status. To acknowledge this change in circumstances, MCC forced him to resign his membership. Eventually Gibb took work as a bus driver in Guildford before dying of a heart attack in 1977.

Previously expressed worries about the future strength of Australian cricket were somewhat assuaged by the emergence of two players in a series of two-day matches played across the 1944/45 holiday period. Ray Robinson drew attention to Bill Johnston, with his 'lively left-arm pace off the wicket', and Private Ray Lindwall, who 'kept up his pace well' for a Services XI against NSW despite being hampered by an inoculation shot in the arm. Another playing prospect was to utilise his talents in a higher service. The Reverend Fraser Withington, whose slow bowling took two good wickets in the Melbourne Christmas match, had been ordained in 1944 after two years with the Australian Imperial Forces. Known, inevitably, as the 'sporting parson', Robinson wrote, 'he approaches the crease with a zigzag run, and imparts enough episcopal worm to the ball to turn it from leg after it has dipped from the off in the air.'

For five years the MCG had been occupied by the RAAF and an official announcement was made that the ground would be retained by the airmen until the conclusion of the Pacific war. The Victorian Cricket Association had played its annual Christmas and New Year fixtures at Richmond, Fitzroy, St Kilda and Princess Oval (Carlton). Herbert Sutcliffe, twenty years after he first set foot on Australian soil with Arthur Gilligan's Ashes squad, visited Melbourne early in 1945 and was entertained by the Richmond Cricket Club and Victorian Cricket

Association (VCA) officials. He attended the match between Richmond and Melbourne and was made an honorary member of the former club.

It proved impossible to resume the Triangular Inter-colonial Tournament in the West Indies for 1945, but the Barbadians were able to visit Trinidad. A pair of matches, stretching across February and March, marked the first appearance together of the legendary 3Ws, who would elevate the West Indies onto a higher plane in world cricket. Frank Worrell was a cool, confident batsman beginning to touch greatness. Twenty-year-old Everton Weekes, a former groundsboy at Kensington Oval, had joined the Barbados Regiment in 1943 and was quickly noticed in Army cricket and invited for trials with Barbados in January. He made an impressive 53 in the second match. Completing the future famous triumvirate, Clyde Walcott struck 102 in the first match.

* * *

The Bradford League had chosen, by the narrowest margin of the chairman's casting vote, to continue with the two-division scheme for 1945, instead of reverting back to the one league that had existed between 1903 and 1937. It was agreed by twelve votes to ten to revert to one division for the 1946 season. The eight-ball over was to be persevered with, a measure reckoned to save a valuable twenty minutes of time in the half day available to league cricket. MCC remained open to further consultation on the desirability of the continuation of the eight-ball over in minor cricket. The league continued to suffer a mini exodus of players across the Pennines, with George Pope and Jim Smith leaving the West Riding for the Lancashire leagues.

The broad, sunlit uplands previously promised by Winston Churchill seemed a distance away in the West Riding as the league programme began in snow, hail and rain. Stan Nichols took seven Bingley wickets for 40 runs for Farsley. However, due to rain delays and transport difficulties, the Essex man had to leave the match before being able to bat, his colleagues only amassing 54 all out in the face of Robert Rae (eight for 15). Kiwi Stewie Dempster made some amends for his poor 1944 form with 57 not out for Idle. Learie Constantine was back as captain of Windhill, for whom Les Ames played an early season merry innings of 55 as the team beat Bowling Old Lane. Later in the season he made a faultless 118, including three sixes and eight fours, against Undercliffe. Another former England wicketkeeper, Arthur Wood, hit 80 in the same match, as Undercliffe achieved an eight-wicket victory. In contrast, Eddie Paynter, who had made 4,401 runs in the previous five wartime seasons, had only mustered 65 runs in eight innings. By June, Jim Laker was back in action for Saltaire, scoring 57 against Pudsey. He was on the losing side thanks to 52 not out from Len Hutton.

The Bradford League continued to provide a fertile hunting ground for other Test-class players. In their first five matches Tom Goddard had captured twenty-five wickets at 5.36 whilst Stan Nichols had twenty-six at 7.03. George Dawkes, the promising Leicestershire wicketkeeper who had made his first-class debut as an 18-year-old in 1939, was singled out for his pluck and keenness. Having dislocated a finger in a midweek match, he turned out for Windhill on the Saturday, and the following day at Coventry, where he was unfortunate enough to fracture his jaw. He still played in a match two days later despite playing with a strapped-up finger and his mouth padded with cotton wool, effecting five stumpings and playing a forceful innings.

By mid-August, seven clubs were in contention for the A Division title. A meeting between Saltaire and Windhill at Roberts Park attracted 4,000 spectators. Seventeen-year-old Victor Munden, who had been introduced to the league by George Dawkes, took five for 45 for the visitors. Undercliffe clinched the title on the final day of the season, pipping Pudsey St Lawrence by one point. The Priestley Cup was won by Yeadon. Johnny Lawrence, with seven for 44, enabled Bingley to defeat Great Horton to claim the B Division title.

The talented 17-year-old leg-spinner Eddie Leadbeater had been approached by several Bradford League clubs, therefore Huddersfield and District League club Almondbury had offered him a contract for the 1946 season, making him the youngest professional in the country. Leadbeater took twenty-one wickets for 75 runs in three matches over Whit weekend. Edwin St Hill had returned to Slaithwaite as a professional after several seasons in other leagues either side of the Pennines. The Trinidadian topped the bowling averages with sixty-five wickets at 7.32 apiece. On 1 August a great crowd assembled to watch his benefit match, against a side raised by Learie Constantine. The great man made 109, including seven sixes.

The adulation that St Hill received, having been one of the 338,000 men rescued from the beaches of Dunkirk in 1940, contrasted with the reaction in some quarters to his appointment as the club's professional for the 1934 season. The *Colne Valley Guardian* had published an editorial saying, 'What does it matter what colour a man's skin happens to be, providing he can play good cricket and, by his personality and example, raise the standard of the whole team?'

The Sykes Cup Final saw an attendance of 4,750 at Huddersfield's Fartown Ground, as Kirkheaton took on Huddersfield. Fred Berry, who had previously played for Surrey, took seven for 26, earning himself a collection of £10, as Kirkheaton were

Edwin St Hill.

dismissed for 102. However, H. Webster replied with seven for 22, and a collection of £11, as Huddersfield were dismissed for a mere 54. Willie Watson, attempting to break into the Yorkshire team, was plying his trade in the league, scoring a fighting 74 for Paddock against Dalton in mid-August. Thongsbridge welcomed back Harold Beaumont from three years' imprisonment by the Italians and Germans. He was soon back in form in a local derby against Holmfirth.

Stone and Nantwich were in a position to rejoin the North Staffordshire League due to an easing of transport restrictions. Despite discussion at the AGM, the ban on collections for amateur players was retained. Professionals were allowed just two collections per season, a restraint that would be lifted after the war. Some, such as league president Sir Ernest Johnson, felt that a grievous error had been made in barring professionals for four years after the last war – a lesson that should be heeded now. On 9 June, Silverdale were bowled out for 6, with Harry Hancock, the former Staffordshire player, taking seven for 0 in five eight-ball overs. On 14 July, the biggest gate of the war was achieved in the North Staffordshire and District League, with 3,000 witnessing Bignall End's visit to Knypersley. Spectators enjoyed bright sunshine, a picturesque environment, a needle match and an exciting win for the home team, who went on to claim the league title. Eric Hollies continued to dominate Birmingham League batsmen, with nine for 25 in 20.4 overs for West Bromwich Dartmouth v Smethwick. The following match he took seven for 5 against Dudley. Hollies ended the season with ninety wickets at 6.82, topping the averages. This enabled West Bromwich Dartmouth to claim their fifth consecutive league victory.

In the Central Lancashire League, on 21 July, J.P. Whitehead took seven for 20 against Stockport, including a hat-trick. Remarkably, K. Dean took one in the same match for Oldham, whilst E.D. Dewson of Middleton recorded one on the same day. Dewson had recently returned from a German prisoner-of-war camp. Controversy veiled the conclusion of the league season as table-topping Milnrow were deprived of the championship due to fielding unregistered players. This handed the title to Heywood, who were led by Bill Farrimond, the Lancashire and England wicket-keeper. Farrimond also headed the league batting averages with 412 runs at 58.85.

The imminent availability of professional cricketers who would be demobilised from the forces concentrated the minds of administrators of competitive northern clubs. John Kay, Honorary Secretary of the Central Lancashire League, was a member of Middleton CC. The club suggested a standard payment for league professionals, in the clubs' own interests, as 'Few clubs can afford to pay the salaries now regarded as usual, without the aid of social efforts throughout the whole year.' For the salaries commanded, a professional should be expected, in addition to his playing efforts, to talent spot and coach younger members. At the end of the war Kay intended, if necessary, to invoke the aid of the Ministry of Labour to ensure that all players engaged in first-class cricket at the outbreak of war and still under the age of 35 be directed back to their pre-war positions, leaving the veterans free to go into the leagues and pass on there the benefit of their experience.

In the *Daily Sketch* on 6 January, L.V. Manning dealt with the same questions under the alarmist headline 'This may be the last chance for County Cricket'. Manning claimed: 'Cricket can only avoid losing its best talent after the war by co-operating with the leagues instead of still regarding them as poor relations.' Conversely, the leagues were regarded as the rich relations by many southern counties, able to outbid them in the engaging of professionals. An agreement had been reached between Lancashire CCC and the leagues operating in the county whereby the latter agreed not to engage any member of the Lancashire staff unless the county consented. There was little evidence of widespread tempting of men from county clubs. County pros had been better paid pre-war than league professionals.

The average payment in the principal leagues was £16 per week, or £320 per season. Some overseas players received considerably more than this, reducing the amounts paid to home professionals. In the principal counties a regular member of the side would receive around £8 per match for thirty matches. With the addition of a winter retainer, he would receive £420 across the year. The addition of talent money in the leagues and a benefit match could add to this. In general, a successful benefit match would trump talent money. Also a player who excelled for his county might well be picked for England, Players *v* Gentleman and festival matches. So, with no prospect of regular county cricket in 1945, some older professionals accepted contracts from league clubs, but there was a smooth transitional exodus of professionals from league to county through 1945 and 1946.

The Lancashire League continued with the eight-ball over. Jim Parks had signed up for Accrington and produced a stand-out nine for 25 against Ramsbottom. The league also waived their rule that all amateur players must serve a one-year residency qualification by allowing Billy Sutcliffe to join Ramsbottom. On the field, Albert Nutter, the Nelson professional, took ten for 13 against Lowerhouse and still ended up on the losing side. This was the first ten-wicket feat in the Lancashire League since Learie Constantine's ten for 10, also for Nelson, in 1934. It was swiftly followed by Ellis Achong's ten for 71 for Todmorden against Burnley on 4 August. Church had opened up a lead at the top of the league, the all-amateur team receiving an extra point for wins against teams that employed a professional. This lead would be maintained until the end of the season.

* * *

At the other end of the cricketing spectrum of the gritty northern leagues, public school cricket had suffered a 50 per cent decline in standards of play during the war, according to Lieutenant Colonel G.H.M. Cartwright. This was ascribed to a shortage of gear, wartime restrictions on travel, the evacuation of many schools to remote areas, the focus on cadet training and reduced quality of coaching. For Cartwright, if the regaining of pre-war standards were not attained, 'English cricket, which has its roots in the Schools, will suffer'. As Victory in Europe was confirmed, with scenes of jubilation across Britain, Pelham Warner argued for the swift resumption of the Gentleman v Players match, 'a game of long tradition and great prestige in which it is still the ambition of every cricketer, be he amateur or professional, to take part'. Warner appeared keen that the egalitarian waves that would sweep Attlee's Labour Party into power in July would not lap at the shores of cricket's class divide. He dressed up his desire for the return of the fixture as the 'need [for] keen hard cricket in preparation for the strenuous games in Australia'. When the series did resume in July 1946, the Players promptly demolished their opponents by an innings and 140 runs. It would not be until the coronation year of 1953 that the amateurs could muster a victory. Home Gordon held a discussion with Bob Wyatt regarding the abolition of any distinction between amateurs and professionals. All players would get their expenses in county cricket and those who desired it, the additional fee hitherto only allotted to those belonging to the remunerated body. The idea was to proceed no further for a decade and a half.

For the first time since 1940, the historical picture gallery of the game was rehung in the Long Room at Lord's, Warner averring, 'after nearly six years they appear more attractive than ever, and being a warmth and colour to the walls which have been sadly lacking during the war.' This familiarity was reinforced by the commemoration of the fiftieth year of service of J. Gladwell, a member of the groundstaff, who had begun service there on 11 June 1896. Warner agreed with suggestions that a memorial cricket museum to those who had lost their lives in both world wars be established at the ground but pointed out the necessity of undertaking remedial groundwork first. It was envisaged that leading cricketers would donate items of interest, and 'Lord's the headquarters of cricket, to a greater degree than hitherto, should be made a sanctuary of the game.' Also back at Lord's, watching the British Empire XI play the RAAF, was Freddie Brown, recently released from German captivity and due to marry in June. He appeared thin and worn, having lost considerable weight. His fellow former inmate Bill Bowes had returned home, but having lost 3 stone during his incarceration, he declined MCC's invitation to play for England against Australia at Lord's at Whitsun.

Major Robert Melsome, who had been an Army stalwart in peacetime inter-service matches, was another who made the pilgrimage to Lord's after a long captivity. He attended the Sir Pelham Warner's XI v Second Army match. The Second Army flag was flown for the first time on a cricket ground and a tablet, bearing the Second Army insignia and its corps and divisional signs worked in

RAAF take to the field at Lord's *v* a British Empire XI, 12 May 1945. (*State Library of Victoria*)

coloured enamel, was presented to MCC. Its inscription read: 'Presented to the Second Army to the MCC on the occasion of the match at Lord's.'

* * *

Although somewhat overshadowed by the glamour of representative Australian, New Zealand and West Indian XIs, the British Empire XI still had a valedictory wartime season to complete. They had a fine seven-wicket win over an Army XI at Westcliff-on-Sea. Centuries by Harry Crabtree and R.N. 'Nobby' Hunt enabled them to hit off 229 in just under two and a half hours. Hunt had made eleven appearances for Middlesex in the 1920s and had once taken all ten wickets for Barclay's Bank against National Provincial. The Empire XI also triumphed on the same ground on 7 July, passing the RAF score with ten wickets still in hand. Harry Crabtree, that fine servant of wartime cricket, again took full advantage of his home ground with 90. He received a letter of congratulations from Stanley Rous, Deputy Chairman and Honorary Secretary of the Red Cross Sports Committee:

> Dear Crabtree
> I heard with great pleasure of your wonderful innings against the Army at Westcliff on Saturday – 116 not out is indeed a great achievement. I am sure you must be very proud of having contributed so largely to the victory of the British Empire XI, and I congratulate you most warmly.

Despite previous suggestions that the XI could continue into the post-war era as a festival and touring outfit, the decision was taken to bring proceedings to a fitting end once the 1945 season had been completed. A farewell dinner was

Bertie Clarke executes a dashing pull shot against the RAAF at Lord's on 12 May 1945. (*Australian War Memorial*)

held at which silver tankards were presented to the unsung heroes, umpire E. Fletcher and scorer E. Hoskin. The achievements of the British Empire XI deserve more than a footnote in cricketing history. Over six seasons they had entertained an anxious and war-weary British public to the tune of 238 matches, raising over £15,000 for charity. Their two leading lights, Harry Crabtree, with 4,328 runs, and Bertie Clarke, with 665 wickets, played occasional county matches after the war. However, the wartime seasons were their 'finest hour'.

Clarke became a GP in Northamptonshire and played for the county in 1946–47 and later for Essex in 1959–60. More intriguingly, he incurred a three-year prison sentence for illegally terminating a pregnancy. Following his release Clarke carried on playing league cricket well into his sixties, his last major appearance being for an Old World XI *v* Old England at The Oval in 1983. Crabtree played a handful of matches for Essex before becoming a major influence in cricket coaching, working on an MCC programme to encourage cricket coaching in state schools. A member of the Essex CCC committee, he was awarded an MBE for his services to the game and his *Wisden* obituary concluded: 'His friendliness and enthusiasm reassured and inspired many a young cricketer.' The Empire XI's regular captain, Ray Smith, enjoyed more successful seasons with Essex before taking on a coaching role at Felsted School and eventually moving to Henley-in-Arden to run a restaurant with his family.

* * *

Stan Squires, the Surrey batsman, claimed to be the only first-class cricketer to have taken part in a match in the Hebrides. An RAF sports officer, Squires was responsible for the laying of a concrete wicket, complete with matting, at one station and, when weather permitted, a good time was enjoyed. A sand dune half the size of a house at cover point presented quite a problem but also raised many a laugh. The fielder would lurk out of sight and then emerge as the batsman set off for a second run, causing a run-out. Squires was experimenting with wearing contact lenses when batting. Described as 'invisible glasses', they had been used by many airmen in the war. Post-war he continued to wear them while representing Surrey.

Wing Commander W.H.N. Shakespeare had managed to arrange eighteen summer fixtures for the RAF but the Army had to be content with a modest six matches, three of which were to be against the RAF, RAAF and RN. The war situation removed many of the players who had made up the strong Army teams in the early years of the war and it was difficult to raise sides of even moderate strength. Two of those absent were S.C. 'Billy' Griffith and Hugh Bartlett, friends since school, who had both landed in Holland with the Airborne troops the previous summer. Griffith was awarded the DFC for his efforts in the Glider Pilot Regiment during the Battle of Arnhem. A Desert Air Force team organised by Wing Commander Shakespeare, Honorary Secretary of the RAF Cricket Association, played six matches in a tour of England. The tour was sponsored by Air Marshal Sir John Slessor. A Commandos tour, in aid of the Commandos Benevolent Fund, also took place. This included two matches against the New Zealand Services XI. Amongst those appearing for the Commandos were Trevor Bailey and Ken Graveney.

* * *

The notion of a post-war tour of England by a New Zealand Services rugby team had been mooted by General Bernard Freyberg, the head of 2 NZEF. Stewie Dempster had advocated a similar enterprise by Kiwi cricketers. The *Egyptian Gazette* of 13 March 1945 discussed the potential strength of the New Zealand cricket contingent in England for the forthcoming season: In addition to Martin Donnelly, Tom Pritchard, Bill Merritt, Ken James, Ted Badcock and Stewie Dempster, two more New Zealand Test cricketers were expected in England. They were H.G. 'Giff' Vivian, vice-captain of the 1937 NZ tourists, and Linsday Weir, known as 'Dad' due to his premature balding and aged look. Both had seen service in North Africa and Italy with General Freyberg's NZ Division. Donnelly had been summoned from Italy to take up a post with the Prisoner of War Repatriation Unit, based in Kent.

Freyberg placed Donnelly in charge of drawing up a list of suitable candidates, but stated that men from later reinforcements would not be available for selection in preference to those who had contributed more to the war effort, thus excluding Bert Sutcliffe. The New Zealanders wanted to play with a spirit of thanksgiving for the success of the collective war effort, rather than serious competition. To that end, eleven recently released PoWs played for the side at various points: Ru Morgan and Frank Fortune (Wellington); Bill Vincent, Jack Jacobs, Bob Webb, Bill Sibley and David Thomas (Canterbury); Fred Byerley (Auckland); Herb Barker (Taranaki); Murray Sharp (Poverty Bay); and Jim Everest (Waikato). Alan Burgess recollected, 'it took a lot for the POWs to come out and play … you couldn't expect them to make big scores, their minds weren't on it.' Murray Sharp was a tall right-hand batsman and right-arm leg-spin bowler from Gisborne who played first-class cricket for Canterbury either side of the war. Private Sharp joined the 22nd Infantry Battalion of 2 NZEF and was captured in the battle at Ruweisat Ridge in July 1942 while serving with the 22nd Infantry Battalion and held as a PoW at Camp PG 57 at Gruppignano, Italy. He was later moved to Stalag 344 Lamsdorf, where he was active in many of the cricket matches played at camp. Bill Vincent of 20th Battalion and Armoured Regiment had been held in the same Italian camp, where he skippered the New Zealand team. Vincent appeared for the New Zealand Services in 1945 as a middle-order batsman and was considered the best fieldsman in the side.

With the backing of the New Zealand Government an organising committee was formed. The XI on the field would rotate dependent on availability. Nine of them had played for the NZEF Base team while stationed at Maadi Camp in Egypt. Alan Burgess recalled, 'it was a split-up sort of a business, we often did not know who would be playing until you got to the ground.' The four senior professionals in the NZ Services side – Ken James, Stewie Dempster, Roger Blunt and Ted Badcock – had been resident in England in 1939. The quartet had played in New Zealand's inaugural Test match in 1930. Now into their forties, they stood in stark contrast to the youthful servicemen who made up the rest of the team. Team members received no extra pay for most of the matches, turning out instead for the love of the game and to celebrate their deliverance from the evils of fascism.

Badcock was fortunate to have made it to the end of the war. Serving in the Auxiliary Fire Service in Salford in May 1940, he had been called out to deal with a blaze that had broken out at a textile merchant's warehouse on the banks of the river Irwell. Having been lowered down by rope to the edge of the river to moor a fire float, tons of masonry and bales of blazing material fell into the water just behind him. The *Manchester Evening News* reported:

> Section-commander Fred [Ted] Badcock of Salford AFS was saved from injury by warning shouts from the crowd watching from the New Bridge-street bridge. He had swum from the river fire-boat to the side of a blazing building to take hold of a rope which had been thrown down to keep the boat in position … When he was making his second attempt to catch the

rope the crowd saw a wall about to collapse above him. They shouted and Badcock swam to safety as the wall collapsed. Going back again he caught the rope and swam back with it to the boat.

Badcock would subsequently continue his firefighting service.

In all, thirty-nine players would represent the NZ Services XI in thirty-five matches from May to September. Their travels took them from picturesque village greens to established Test venues. *Wisden* noted the Kiwis played 'free and entertaining cricket and became warm favourites everywhere'. Gate receipts were donated to various charities and the rebuilding of the pavilion at East Molesey CC. The NZ Services XI appeared at the home of cricket on 7 June against a strong Lord's XI, which included Bill Edrich, Laurie Fishlock, Errol Holmes and Gubby Allen. As well as the established stars of the team, the match afforded the opportunity for four Kiwis to play on the historic turf who, until a few months previously, had been prisoners of war. Another player of modest standard, George Sage, a senior B grade cricketer, realised his boyhood dream to play at Lord's. Veteran Ted Badcock shouldered the load of the bowling, sending down forty overs for his six for 69. Despite an opening stand of 124 between Stewie Dempster and Roger Blunt, the match was drawn.

The growing mood of egalitarianism that would see the Labour Party achieve a landslide general election victory later in the month was yet to permeate the Lord's authorities. When Sir Pelham Warner's XI met the New Zealand Services XI on 12 July, Ted Badcock, as a professional, was required to step onto the

Ted Badcock and Stewie Dempster, June 1944. (*Courtesy Rob Franks*)

ground from a gate to the side of the Members' Stand. In solidarity, a handful of Kiwi amateurs, including Neil Begg, accompanied him through that entrance.

A match on Ripley's historic green, on the south-western fringe of the New Forest, witnessed the first occasion on which the man whose Hampshire burr would come to give colour to so many summers, John Arlott, spoke on the BBC. He described the bowling of Ted Badcock as being as 'steady as the Rock of Gibraltar'. Iain Gallaway, who would himself grace the cricketing airwaves for many decades, later recalled that the locals knew 'every hill and hollow' of their green. Delightfully, strawberries and ice cream were served in a marquee and the local vicar arrived in time to say grace.

Arlott captured the atmosphere beautifully:

> So that was Ripley, with the flags around the marquee, a real New Zealand flag amongst them, some cheerful careless cricket after tea with the game won and lost – strawberries and ice cream, salad and beer and deck chairs, shooters, googlies and the frantic arguments of small boys 'You told me Fishlock was going to play.' 'So he is.' 'No he ain't.' And the New Zealanders laughing and not worrying about losing.

Lindsay Hassett, whose first-class bowling aggregate would amount to a mere 18 wickets, found the New Zealand Service XI batting to his liking when appearing for the AIF at Eastbourne, claiming five for 31 as the Australians crushed their Antipodean neighbours. Due to the competing attraction of the Australian Services team, and the focus on domestic post-war reconstruction, the NZ Services team did not gain the publicity or accolades they deserved.

Mr Peter Fraser, the Scottish Highland-born prime minister of New Zealand, was due visit Britain for the Conference of Empire Premiers, and was keen to visit East Molesey cricket ground. The club had recently received a grant of £100 from the New Zealand Government. This unusual gift was the result of the club having purchased the freehold of its ground as a memorial to Captain F.E. Smith, late of Dunedin and Wellington, an East Molesey player who was killed at El Alamein. The plan had received the blessing of *The Cricketer*:

> East Molesey and General Freyberg have pointed out one of the ways in which the mistakes of the last war in failing to invest in the social fabric. … Why build more war memorials? Why spend money on setting up stones when it can be spent much better in keeping the stones off the grass? What better and more fitting memorial … could every town and village possess than an English field preserved for ever from the apostles of ribbon-development.

A match between the club and a New Zealand XI was witnessed by a host of notables including the High Commissioner for New Zealand, Sir Stanley Jackson and H.D.G. Leveson Gower. The proceeds of the match were in aid of the new pavilion.

The players were introduced to the eminent First World War General Lord Birdwood as part of the day's official proceedings. It was a special occasion and according to a report in the *Auckland Star*, 'the Prime Minister of New Zealand, Mr Fraser and Lieutenant-General Sir Bernard Freyberg sent messages wishing the club every success.' Over 3,000 spectators turned out to support the match. Many Kiwis from the various service units in London were in attendance. During the lunch break the Minister of Labour, Mr George Isaacs, made a speech which was concluded with the quote 'one outward thing that holds us in the Empire together is the Crown'.

The high point of the tour came at Scarborough's bracing North Marine Road Ground, as the traditional festival was revived for 1945, New Zealand Services XI taking on H.D.G. Leveson Gower's XI. The crowd during the middle Sunday swelled to 10,000. The 48-year-old warhorse Ted Badcock bowled 57.5 overs to take six for 166. Len Hutton made 188 in front of the Yorkshire crowd. A sporting declaration by Ken James gave Leveson Gower's XI a sniff of victory, which they seized. Bill Edrich recalled the match: 'the New Zealanders played carnival cricket – that was a summer of such cricket. They made a sporting declaration and were beaten after a tremendous fight.' Also as part of the festival a Yorkshire XI drew with the RAF, Herbert Sutcliffe scoring 8 batting at No. 5. This was the Yorkshire master's final first-class appearance.

The *New Zealand Free Lance* of 29 August 1945 highlighted the favourable impression the team made: 'The good play and sportsmanship which have characterised the matches the New Zealanders have played so far have made them welcome everywhere.' So welcome in fact that Alan Burgess was asked to stay and play county cricket, but his mother had suffered a stroke and he wished to return to New Zealand.

* * *

As the final English season of a fixture programme dominated by service XIs and wartime combinations was played out on grounds around Britain, the first-class counties were able to turn their minds to the immediate and future structure of the English game. In March, an MCC subcommittee chaired by Colonel R.S. Rait Kerr published an interim report on Lancashire's proposal for a knockout competition. 'Many of the keenest supporters of county cricket are not concerned with the position of their county in the Championship Table,' wrote Pelham Warner, 'or with the outcome of a Knock-Out Competition. For them each match is to be regarded on its merits.' He bemoaned the highly competitive age, with many people preferring matches when something was at stake, rather than the inherent interest of the match. Left to Warner and his ilk, cricket would remain in a sempiternal Golden Age. The subcommittee recommended a trial period of two seasons for a cup competition. Warner expressed concern about cramming too many matches into a season which also featured a tour by one of the Dominions. On the other hand, a knockout match might lead to 'high tension' cricket, which would be a good grounding for Test matches.

The subcommittee recommended the unimaginative title of 'The Cricket Cup'. They rejected the opportunity to play the matches over one day or two days, or to have time limits on innings. Walter Robins was quoted as being supportive of a proposal for a knockout cup: 'I believe we have a chance to put on the map the kind of cricket a large section of the public have wanted for some time.' The *Daily Herald* saw the proposal as a blow to the 'ultra-conservative elders of the game'.

R.C. Robertson-Glasgow, writing in 1945's *Wisden*, was typically eloquent in his condemnation of the idea:

> While the fate of the world was being determined, English cricket was the scene of an interesting little battle, which ended in the rout of the 'hustlers' and the triumph of conservatism over the heresy that progress and speed are synonymous. The defeat of the *soi-disant* progressives, with their programme of one-day and time-limited matches for first-class cricket, was a certainty so long as the issue of debate rested with the majority opinion of practising cricketers.

The traditionalists were to win the day. On 12 June the decision was made to defer any decision on a cup competition until a normal County Championship season had been completed. Eighteen years would elapse before such a competition was inaugurated.

Inter-county matches during the summer of 1945 tended to be regional in nature, the basic petrol rationing for civilians having been restored on 1 June after a three-year hiatus. Fixtures such as Lancashire *v* Derbyshire, Leicestershire *v* Derbyshire and Sussex *v* Hampshire were feasible, but not those between northern and southern counties. The Sussex Cricket Association (SCA) had been formed to encourage young players and provide more enterprising cricket. Punctual starts and crisp observation of intervals were also insisted upon. The county had been hit hard by the war, with three quarters of its recognised clubs being temporarily closed down due to evacuation, the ploughing up of grounds, absence of players in the services and, according to W. Walker writing in *The Cricketer*, the 'unwelcome attention of the Hun'. Under the auspices of the SCA, matches became keener and provided a graduated ladder through which a player might pass to district level, East *v* West Sussex and Association *v* County XI. There was also provision of youth matches to prevent players unable to break into a 1st XI from drifting away from the game. The SCA had managed to put together a cricket week at Lewes, during which they played St Bart's Hospital, Alexandra Park, the Australians, the Buccaneers, and Gravesend. Whilst it was hoped that these moves would eventually lead to Sussex winning the County

Championship, of far greater importance was the 'restoration of the game itself to its former grandeur, and the planting in the minds of young players of the ethics and traditions of "cricket" which will prove no small aid to England in regaining her dignity, greatness and peace'. In May, forty-two boys were invited from local clubs and schools for a weekend of tuition at Littlehampton, receiving coaching from the Langridge brothers, which included batting technique taught via group exercises. In a further boost for Sussex cricket it was decided that the Hastings Central Ground would not be lost and the club could look forward to a new era under the captaincy of Billy Griffith.

County grounds had suffered from physical neglect and, in the cases of Old Trafford and The Oval, bomb damage. Plans were afoot for the redevelopment of the Manchester ground, with the aim of holding 40,000 people, which would have made it the biggest in the country. However, a fundraising appeal failed to raise the necessary monies, and sixty German PoWs were paid a small three farthings per hour to prepare the ground for the Victory Test in August. They painted the stands and scoreboards whilst a German signwriter created all the public notices such as 'Transfer to Stands' and the words and figures for the scoreboards. A crowd of 76,463 would attend the match over three days.

A.F. Davey had estimated the cost of restoring The Oval to be in the region of £50,000. Stakes had been driven into the turf and cages of barbed wire had been set up in preparation for housing German prisoners of war. Although these guests never materialised, the ground was in a sorry state when a new groundsman, Bert Lock, was appointed at the end of the war. Concrete posts were dismantled and holes filled in. Mounds of debris were cleared and 45,000 turves of grass brought in from Hoo marshes in Kent. Throughout the winter of 1945/46, Lock toiled so the ground would be ready for its first first-class season in seven years. Warwickshire appealed for £50,000 for improvements to Edgbaston, although the long-term plan for the ground's reconstruction had been estimated at £201,150. Very wisely the committee had decided to lay out a car park on newly acquired land, which would accommodate approximately 700 cars. Northamptonshire aimed to raise £10,000 to put the county in a sound position.

In Wales a fund was started to endow hospital beds in South Wales and Monmouthshire in memory of Major Maurice Turnbull. On 18 August, a memorial match took place in honour of Glamorgan's lost captain and secretary at the Arms Park between Glamorgan against a West of England XI led by Wally Hammond. This allowed the club to bid a public farewell to a man who had been its very lifeblood for a decade or more. A further monument to Turnbull's work came in 1948, when the Welshmen lifted the County Championship for the first time, under the leadership of Wilf Wooller, who had endured his own grim war. Having entered captivity as a strapping 6ft 2in, 14-stone multi-sportsman, he

Wilf Wooller (left) with Eaglestone and Hever. (*Courtesy Glamorgan Cricket Archives*)

returned home 60lb lighter and suffering from severe stomach cramps. Despite his privations, Wooller lived to the ripe age of 84.

Worcestershire took on an RAF XI at New Road on 4 August. The flyers, led by Bill Edrich, lost to the hosts by two wickets. The lack of sightscreens somewhat hampered the batsmen but allowed a very large crowd to squeeze into every seat as burning sunshine bathed the picturesque ground. The silver band of the RAF played during the intervals and Arthur Gilligan gave a wireless commentary on the match. The county's committee invited young cricketers to trial matches on the County Ground during the holiday season. The New Road venue was put to good use during the victory summer, with fifty-five matches taking place, from the county fixture through to works and colts matches.

During the war Hampshire's playing activity had been confined to one match but the county had already arranged seven before the 1945 season arrived. The vagaries of wartime team selection were in evidence when a previously wired telegram arrived at Hove to inform the committee that Army Chaplain the Reverend J.W.J. Steele was unavailable. Steele was already on the field leading his county against Sussex. The rise of the respectable professional was furthered as George Gunn was appointed to the Nottinghamshire committee to replace the late Sir Julien Cahn. Leicestershire had arranged use of Grace Road for nine home county games, in agreement with the headmaster of the secondary school which then occupied the site. Northamptonshire played nineteen matches in 1945, bringing their wartime total to a highly creditable forty-five.

'Every member of the side is agreed that the Trent Bridge ground is the finest in England,' proclaimed Lindsay Hassett at a reception given to the Australian Services XI by the Lord Mayor of Nottingham during the match with Nottinghamshire. Trent Bridge showed few scars from the bombing of 1941 when 223 incendiaries were dropped on the playing area. Fires had burnt out some of the buildings behind the pavilion, with the cost of repairs estimated at £5,000. The match also marked the first appearance for the county since 1939 of Bill Voce. The historic Trent Bridge pavilion was de-requisitioned by the military authorities. It had been used by ATS staff serving in the Army Postal Service. The commentator's box had served as a medical room and, according to Dorothy Pelmear, one of the ATS postal workers based in the area, 'worst sacrilege of all, we drilled on the hallowed turf! What would Denis Compton et al have thought of that?'

Yorkshire, the pre-eminent county side of the 1930s, were looking to rebuild an ageing and war-ravaged team. A Yorkshire Colts match at Huddersfield on 9 August featured promising players. One was 'Wardle, a 22-year-old miner from Denaby Main, [who] is being spoken of as a possible successor to Verity'. The obvious gaping and aching hole left by the great man's death was initially filled by 43-year-old Arthur Booth. Booth, who had plied his trade in the minor counties after being unable to dislodge the great man from the side, was written off as being too old to succeed to the coveted left-arm spinning berth. He did his cause no harm in the Roses match at Old Trafford on 2–3 July, taking ten for 66 in the match. Bill Bowes was also back in action having last worn the white rose on that solemn occasion at Hove in 1939.

The return fixture, a three-day match at Bradford Park Avenue on 13–15 August, was set aside as a memorial tribute to Hedley Verity, and a subscription list for his widow Kathleen was opened. Sir Stanley Jackson appealed for generous support, saying Verity would have had a benefit match in 1941 had war not intervened, describing 'this opportunity of showing respect and gratitude to the memory of one who always played the game and did his duty to the end'. The total receipts were £3,000. On the opening day Bowes bowled finely but had to retire soon after the luncheon interval with a pulled muscle, taking no further part in the match. He had, however, claimed his 1,500th first-class wicket, a feat that must have seemed a forlorn hope during his captive years. The country's premier county side was also granted a match against the Australian Services at Sheffield on 23–24 July. Miller and Hutton scored centuries in a drawn match.

A match took place at Mexborough on 18 June in which Hutton, Bowes, Barber, Wood of Yorkshire, as well as Paynter, Martindale, the two Popes, Copson and Mitchell took part. Hutton scored 124 in under two hours. Emmott Robinson and Wilfred Rhodes umpired, as the latter was able to view his future successor in the pantheon of Yorkshire slow left-arm bowlers, Johnny Wardle, at close quarters. Further promising prospects for Yorkshire included Alec Coxon and John Whitehead, who had emerged as effective opening bowlers during the war. Coxon, of Saltaire, was 28 years old by 1945, blessed with tireless energy and the ability to swing the new ball either way and, when the shine wore off, to bowl off and leg cutters. Whitehead, a 19-year-old engineering cadet from Preston, impressed for Yorkshire against Australian Services. He had previously appeared for Lancashire, but Yorkshire discovered he was born at Upper Mill, a few yards inside the border. One observer noted: 'After a shuffling, hesitant run of about nine steps, he sends down quite a fast ball. At the moment of delivery, the action is perfect, with the right shoulder finishing well down the wicket.' This blend of those keen to make their initial mark on the county, such as Booth, Coxon and Whitehead, and the old guard intent on one last hurrah – Bowes, Sellers and Leyland – would be sufficient to see Yorkshire lift the 1946 championship, suffering just one defeat.

Kent CCC recorded a significant loss, contrary to the position during the wartime summers. The annual report stated: 'It has been possible to maintain the ground in good condition, but the buildings need paint and repair. These will be effected as soon as possible after they have been de-requisitioned.' Ninety-one matches were played on the St Lawrence Ground, with a crowd of 7,000 present to see Kent v The Rest on 8 August, with £216 11s 5d being collected for a local hospital. Amongst their number was 97-year-old F.A. MacKinnon. Kent won by 104 runs. Despite the grievous loss of Gerry Chalk, the report noted, 'Luckily most of our 1939 players are still available.'

John Dewes of Cambridge University began the season in fine form, with consecutive scores of 154 not out, 89 not out, 126 not out, 128 not out and 104. Although he was run out for 35 in his next innings, the university side still beat a New Zealand Services XI by five wickets. Dewes was also prominent in a splendid Royal Navy victory over the Army at Lord's on 18 August, appearing alongside Tony Mallett and Trevor Bailey.

* * *

The RAAF players who had forged a favourable wartime reputation had been booked for twenty-two 'big' matches, including occasions when some of the side were due to play for a full Australian Services XI or a Dominions XI. The team was much changed from that which had thrilled the British public during the previous two seasons. Keith Carmody, George Wall and Bruce Collings were in German captivity at the start of the season, whilst Ken Ridings, Clive Calvert, Charlie Walker and Bill Roach had been killed in action.

Mick Roper proved to be in good form for the Australian airmen during the season. He was also involved in an unusual dismissal. Playing for South of England v RAAF at Lord's on 30 June, Gubby Allen was given out 'handled the ball'. R.C. Robertson-Glasgow reported in *The Observer*:

A singular incident closed Allen's innings. He played one from Roper in such a way that the ball seemed to him likely to roll back on to his stumps. With his bat he narrowly prevented this from happening; then with his hand he returned the ball towards Roper, who, after a moment or two of reflection, appealed to the umpire. In fact, Roper was appealing for 'bowled' but the bowler's umpire rightly deeming that an appeal covers all contingencies, gave Allen out under Law 29.

On 1 August an RAAF XI raised by Wing Commander the Reverend Dave Beyer visited Dulwich to play the Public School Wanderers in an all-day match. A collection was taken for the St Stephen's Church (South Dulwich) bomb damage repair fund. To augment the RAAF players who had thus far entertained the English

Australian Services fast bowler Mick Roper signs autographs during a match against the RAF, 1945. (*Australian War Memorial*)

cricketing public, four Australian state players who had been serving in the AIF had become available: Lindsay Hassett, Dick Whitington, Cec Pepper and Bert Cheetham, the last of these having survived the 168-day Siege of Tobruk.

The AIF team was in action early in the season with a match against Bexhill at Eastbourne. Having practised for three weeks in glorious weather, the Aussies were forced to take to the field in wintry conditions on 28 April, their sweaters still being on order from the outfitters. Nevertheless, they proved far too strong for the Sussex men, who subsided to 39 for nine in 17.4 overs. The Australians were generous in expressing appreciation of the facilities for playing which had been afforded them, for the mutual benefit of the restoration of cricketing prowess of both nations. All-rounder Richard Holmes had recently been released from a four-year spell as a prisoner in Germany. His camp, Stalag 344 at Lamsdorf, was 'one of the bad ones', but he refused to elucidate, telling Norman Preston, 'I want to forget all about it.' Holmes did relate news of 'Tests' played on dirt wickets in the camp, some matches being watched by crowds of 5,000 inmates. Cec Pepper really let himself go in a match at High Wycombe, scoring 100 in forty-seven minutes. In one wartime match in Australia, it was claimed, Pepper had reached three figures in ten minutes, hitting ten sixes. North of England had a fine victory over Australian Services at Blackpool's Stanley Park on 16–17 August, winning by an innings and 89 runs thanks to 171 from Norman Oldfield and eight for 92 in the match from Eric Hollies.

Cec Pepper and Keith Miller stride out with intent. (*Australian War Memorial*)

The Australian Services XI also pitched up at that traditional end-of-tour venue, the Yorkshire spa town of Scarborough. H.D.G. Leveson Gower's XI were soundly beaten by an innings and 108 runs on 5–7 September. Cec Pepper smote 168 in a total of 500, becoming the last player to clear the tall Victorian terraced houses of the adjacent Trafalgar Square. The combined batting prowess of Hutton, Fishlock, Edrich, Wyatt and Robins was insufficient to put up much of a fight as South Australian Reg Ellis took ten for 67 in the match. The Australians played a farewell match at Hove where, in the words of Padre Dave Beyer, 'war-time Australians virtually graduated in English cricket'. Proceeds went to the Sussex Maternity Hospital.

To those Australians who played the game in such an enterprising and crowd-pleasing spirit fell the honour of convening five times that summer to play in a series of 'Victory Tests' against a representative England XI.

Bill Edrich articulated the mood of optimism which gave context to the series:

> Those of us that were left alive and young enough to still take part in the first class game turned to and began to oil our bats again in 1945, and eagerly discussed the possibilities of putting the game on its feet once more. It was obvious that no proper County programme could be fixed up for that season; players were in uniform, grounds were requisitioned, officials were filling other posts. But, with almost miraculous swiftness and adaptability, Sir Pelham Warner and other authorities improvised a series of 'Victory Tests'.

The first unofficial Test match at Lord's, commencing on 19 May, was the first first-class three-day match in England since 1939. Total attendance was well over 70,000, with £1,935 being raised for Red Cross and RAAF funds, despite the removal of £957 in Entertainment Tax by the government. Pelham Warner was particularly aggrieved by the tax, which amounted to 3½d on a shilling and 10½d on a two-shilling admission. The most poignant moment of the match came when Australian airman Graham Williams walked out to bat at No. 9 with Keith Miller going well at the other end. Miller later recalled the moving scene:

He was given a great ovation that compares with anything ever given Bradman, Lillee or Richards. But it was not the sort of clapping and cheering that greets a hundred. This is different. Everyone stood up. They all knew about Graham's captivity. He was a big fella, but he was gaunt from his experience, and he just walked round for a while as if in a trance. ... Whenever I think of it, tears still come to my eyes.

Two weeks before this match, Williams had been freed from a German PoW camp after four years of captivity. He had been seized early in the war when his plane crashed in the Middle East and had survived on starvation rations. He was 31kg below his pre-war bodyweight when he walked out to the middle at Lord's. Despite being so weak that he had to be given glucose between overs, Williams went on to score 53 runs at a-run-a-ball and take two wickets in his forty overs.

Warrant Officer R.G. Williams RAAF. (*Australian War Memorial*)

The match had a thrilling climax to complement the occasion, with Cec Pepper smiting Australia to victory as the clock pointed to seven o'clock. The standard of play was excellent, given the fact that players had been at war for over half a decade. Pelham Warner, writing in *The Cricketer*, waxed lyrical at the scintillating play and its wider significance as England emerged into its New Jerusalem:

> That Hassett ... Pepper, Miller and Sismey will be seen in future Australian teams we have little doubt. ... The match proved conclusively that no Hitler can kill the love of cricket which is inherent in the English people. ... Cricket will flourish as never before in all its long and splendid history. It is ... a great part of the life of the English people.

The ebullient mood was shared by the physically ailing Australian Prime Minister John Curtin, who articulated the quasi-spiritual bonds that the game of cricket sustained between the countries of Commonwealth and Empire:

> I cannot forbear tendering my warmest good wishes to English cricket in the coming season, and particularly to all those gracious people who will assemble at Lord's where tradition so richly nourishes and perpetuates our great game. ... My sincere good wishes for the reopening of a series which I hope will never again be interrupted.

When Curtin died in early July, the flag was lowered to half-mast at Eastbourne, where the Australian Services XI were playing H.D.G. Leveson Gower's XI.

Lindsay Hassett and Stan Sismey.

The wider press was slow to pick up on the emerging excitement the matches generated, with C.B. Fry complaining how little prominence was given to the match in 'our great London press', despite the large crowd. This was surprising, given the potential for an increasing thirst for post-war leisure. In March 1943, Winston Churchill had reckoned that at the end of the war some 7 or 8 million people would have between £200 to £300 due to them through the Wings for Victory War Savings campaign, insurance payable to families whose home had been destroyed by air raids and war gratuities due to members of the armed forces. In response, *The Observer* had predicted: 'Leisure will be large, and leisure, like peace and freedom, is a vacuum which has to be filled if it is not to be an affliction. The discovery of improved living, of wide and eager enjoyment, is the prime need of civilised society, the end beyond the end.'

A month passed before the second match took place, on 23–26 June. Over 48,000 spectators thronged Sheffield's Bramall Lane Ground as England levelled the series thanks to a Hammond century and two five-wicket performances by northerners George Pope and Dick Pollard. Hammond's innings on the wet Sheffield pitch was judged the best of the summer by Norman Preston. Set 330 to win on the final day on a challenging batting surface under Yorkshire cloud cover, Australian hopes seemed forlorn, but a doughty 93 from Jim Workman took the total to 221 for four before he fell to Pollard, with the rest of the wickets being mopped up despite some dogged resistance. Pollard, drawn from Crompton in the Lancashire League, demonstrated that a diet of wartime league cricket had been a good grounding

George Pope.

for higher competition. He was a striver with the right temperament, who would lead the series wicket-taking table with twenty-five in his four appearances. Army duties would restrict his chances in 1946 but he was able to make his Test debut against India and negotiate special leave, alongside Bill Voce, to make the boat for the 1946/47 Ashes tour.

The third match saw a comfortable win for Australia, as England sought to blood its youth who had never played serious competitive cricket. John Dewes, Luke White and Donald Carr were all aged under 19 and lacked experience against the high-quality fast bowling the Australians possessed. Lord's spectators numbering 78,000 surpassed the gate for the previous series match on the same ground. The Australians continued to draw warm plaudits, with *The Cricketer* noting, 'The Australians are pleasant and sportsmanlike opponents under their captain and fine batsman Hassett, and they are doing their own and our cricket good.' As momentum gathered through the series an extra 2s 6d was charged for entry to the two Lord's grandstands for the third and fourth matches. At just a shilling for basic entrance to the ground for a full day's play, Lord's compared favourably to Stamford Bridge, where ninety minutes of Chelsea FC fare would cost 2s 6d. Even better value was to be had by several Australian service personnel, with 1,000 complimentary seats set aside for them per day.

The fourth match in the series took place at Lord's on 6–8 August. Over 30,000 paying spectators on day one meant that the gates closed by 11.40 am. Attacking brilliance from Miller and dour defence from Sismey raised the Australians to 273 for five. An even larger crowd on day two saw a Cyril Washbrook century before the match drifted to a third-day draw.

The series denouement took place at the newly repaired and repolished Old Trafford on 20–22 August. Gates were again closed behind 28,000 people. In a low-scoring match that saw England win by six wickets, Lancashire's Eddie Phillipson, later to serve as a popular county and Test umpire, was the star performer, taking six for 58 in the second innings to set up the England win.

The excitement generated by the Victory Tests and other big matches at Lord's during this celebratory season was not to everyone's taste. Michael Hughes-Morgan and A.R. Henderson, senior pupils at Malvern College, bemoaned the increasing tendency, especially among younger spectators, for 'shouting and whistling during

Lindsay Hassett.

the recent matches at Lord's … we feel that the behaviour of a crowd at Lord's should not resemble that of a baseball match,' they complained. Further calumny was experienced when the pair were asked by a young spectator where he could buy a 'programme' rather than a scorecard. 'Could not the officials helped by the more sensible spectators restore Lord's to its former dignity!' the privileged pair demanded.

As the five-match Victory Test series drew to a close, Keith Johnson, manager of the Australian Services team, echoed the sentiments expressed back in May by Prime Minister Curtin:

> The matches of the 1945 season will always be a pleasant memory to us, and if we have in any way contributed to the rehabilitation of English cricket, then it was our honour and our pleasure. May I say that we, too, have benefitted from these games, and go back home with more experience of cricket and better players.

C.B. Fry spoke on the BBC's *Calling Australia* broadcast on 3 September 1945. He praised the AIF and RAAF cricketers, who 'blew in like a fresh wind and fanned the smouldering cinders into a lively blaze'. With echoes of Churchill's finest hour speech, he declared, 'I doubt whether any set of big matches in England has ever been so much enjoyed by so many.' In all, 367,000 eager spectators had thronged through the turnstiles of Lord's, Old Trafford and Bramall Lane.

Dick Whitington, who scored 221 runs in the series, recalled the camaraderie between the teams: 'The English and Australian teams shared the same dressing room. … They travelled to and from the ground in the same motor-coach and stayed at the same hotel. Nobody lost anything by this. Nor did the cricket.' The Victory Series gave the English public and the players a common focus of celebration of the successful conclusion of the war in Europe. However, this spirit of bonhomie began to change when the Australian players reached home, following an arduous tour of India. Only two of the Services XI, Hassett and Miller, were selected for what would later be designated the first post-war Test match, against New Zealand. Whitington 'sensed the existence of what might be called "a thing" concerning those who had served abroad'. That 'thing', for many, was the hand of Donald George Bradman, who helped to select the squad.

* * *

The West Indian cricketers who had given such sterling service in wartime charity matches and in the northern leagues also added to the gaiety of a four-sided international summer. On 2 June, an England XI played the West Indies at Lord's. England trialled Luke White and Donald Carr, with a view to them playing against Australia. White had a short back-lift but made full use of a powerful forearm. He was a good judge of length and watched the ball closely, driving hard. This 'batsman of high promise with a cool, calm temperament', according to *The Cricketer*, would only play three first-class matches before retiring from the game. Donald Carr, 'a stylist with very nice wrists, and something of a Palairet in style', was to make a more lasting impression on the game as captain of Derbyshire, and latterly as secretary of the Test and County Cricket Board during the turbulent era of Packer and the 'Rebel' tour to South Africa. They both made useful contributions as a poor West Indian batting display saw England win by 90 runs.

As well as the schoolboy potential of White and Carr, a handful of favourable reputations had been forged in wartime representative matches. Reg Simpson, Alec and Eric Bedser, Godfrey Evans, Harry Halliday and Trevor Bailey were seen as serious prospects whilst Tony Mallett had been judged to be almost the equal of Bailey while at Dulwich. He, like Bailey, served in the Royal Marines during the war and made his first-class debut for Under 33s *v* Over 33s at Lord's. His choice of education as a career meant his future playing opportunities were limited. Alec Bedser, Evans and Bailey would go on to have significant international careers whilst Simpson played for England with moderate success. Eric Bedser and Halliday would never rise above the rank of county stalwart.

It was the generation behind this cohort that would suffer from the stunted cricketing development that war wrought. Players who in the normal scheme of things would have progressed from school to club thence to county colt and full county level had seen that development ladder suffer from missing or damaged rungs. D. Kirkland expressed his ire at the state of cricket grounds in state schools:

> to neglect, or lightly to treat, the cricketing conditions for the youngsters is a crime of National, nay, International importance and should qualify for the millstone around the neck. When the importance of the mastery of the mother tongue seems to play but the most meagre role in the enterprise of the Education Committees, it is, perhaps, small wonder that the conditions of the playing fields should be considered matters, the importance of which does not exist.

Kirkland compared the poor school facilities in England to those enjoyed by boys in Australia. Others thought that compulsory National Service from the age of 18 was a further inhibition to a young player's development. Easy runs and wickets were claimed to be had in regimental cricket, meaning a talented youngster would have little scope to hone and improve his skills.

This claim drew the scorn of an increasingly irascible C.B. Fry:

> I have seen any amount of soldier cricket worth ever so much more than quite a lot of the dawdling county cricket of pre-war years. ... I would rather back myself, could I regain my pristine eye and wrist, to make 150 runs in

almost any county match ... than to make 50 in an average regimental match on the average regimental wicket.

Half the cherished young pros, who come into county cricket from nurseries and are feted as heroes ... if they scratch a few runs off the inner edge of the bat, would be of no account in the manlier world of one-day soldier cricket. And, to boot, they would not have their little heads turned.

Fry went on to call for compulsory military service for a year. 'Such service would be made the university of the average citizen.' Fry, who had previously expressed admiration for the Nazi regime, cited the physical culture advantages of such a move. In 1934, Fry had visited Germany with the idea of forging stronger links between the uniformed British youth organisations, such as the Boy Scouts, and the Hitler Youth, so that both groups could learn from each other. He had exchanged Nazi salutes with Adolf Hitler but had failed to persuade Foreign Minister Joachim von Ribbentrop that Nazi Germany should take up cricket to Test level. Fry was still espousing Nazi-British youth organisation links up to 1938, and praising Hitler in the third impression of his autobiography, *Life Worth Living*, published in 1941.

Others argued that the search for raw talent that might have been overlooked during the war should be a priority. County clubs were urged to open their nets to all promising players, as Lord's had done with its Nursery. Warner reflected, 'it is a pleasant and inspiring sight to see boys as young as fifteen being given encouragement and help by eminent cricketers.'

* * *

Miss E.L. Parish, honorary secretary of the WCA, wrote of the post-war revival of the association, which was 'humming with activity'. Arrangements had been made for the resumption of the Colwall Cricket Week, which had been suspended for the duration. The war years had not been ones of complete inactivity for the organisation. In several parts of the county charity matches had been played. From 1940 onwards, matches were played in London in aid of the Red Cross, the teams containing most of the pre-war international players. The WAAF was holding regional trials in order to form a representative XI. 'The future of Women's Cricket is well established,' Parish concluded.

The 1945 Colwall Cricket Week saw sixty-eight players and six teams competing. Players had to cut with a mower one of the three pitches used, at The Downs, and accommodation had to be found for all the players. The homes of the villagers provided a traditional welcome. The big match between North and South was played on the Thursday. Old stalwarts were missing but the young and new were welcomed with open arms.

The Birmingham Cricket Festival, which had previously formed part of the Holidays at Home Scheme, was given the more joyful moniker of the

Birmingham Victory Cricket Week. To raise funds for the festival, R.I. 'Rusty' Scorer ran a Cricket Dance and Cabaret on 4 June at the Birmingham All-Services Queensbury Club. The Royal Canadian Dance Orchestra provided the music for the guinea-paying guests. Scorer provided a fourth fun festival and drew the admiration of Home Gordon: 'He is imbued with a charming and magnetic personality, displays energetic ability to overcome every difficulty, possesses a rare sense of humour and his slogan is "cricket with a laugh in it". …What the Chamberlains were to politics in Birmingham, he is to festival cricket there.'

Hundreds of autograph-hunting boys swarmed the dining room, dressing rooms and team buses. The loudspeaker announcements would also educate spectators on the nuances of the game. When C. Leatherbarrow's XI played Sussex, Raymond Heaven and George Hearne withstood the attack of Andrews, Martindale, Achong, Badcock, Gover and Constantine, ensuring victory. 'Clamourers in the crowd, discontented at the sternness of the struggle, were rebuked through the loud-speakers.'

The biggest Edgbaston crowd since before the war witnessed Walter Hammond's XI take on the New Zealand Services XI on Sunday, 8 July. A crowd of 16,000 spectators was attracted by the prospect of watching stars such as Herbert Sutcliffe, Bill Edrich, Bob Wyatt, Tom Goddard, Eric Hollies and J.W.A. Stephenson take on the visitors. The Kiwis put up a decent showing before succumbing by five wickets. Major Martin Donnelly won particular plaudits for his sound batting method, quick feet and wide array of strokes. Under a clear Birmingham sky, a band played as £2,139 was raised for the Birmingham Ear and Throat Hospital, with the hope that a ward would be named in memory of cricketers who had perished in the war.

In June, the indefatigable Learie Constantine, who had given such great service to English cricket and British society during the war, belied his 43 years to play ten consecutive days of cricket in Scotland, also conducting coaching sessions for Scottish schoolboys. The RAAF also ventured north of the border after playing matches en route at Coventry, Bramall Lane and Sunderland. The Scottish leg of the tour began at Selkirk, set among the glorious surroundings of forests and the pasture lands of the Border hills. The Lord Provost of Selkirk told the Australians that he regarded them as ambassadors, and their tour of the British Isles strengthened the ties of friendship.

The airmen's truck broke down on the way to Greenock but the Australians, mindful of the political significance of their tour, sportingly agreed to play on until 8.00 pm for the 4,000 crowd. Sixty-year-old John Kerr, the Grand Old Man of Scottish cricket, made his final appearance against the Australians, having made his debut against Monty Noble's 1909 team. A crowd of 8,000 flocked to Hamilton Crescent, Partick, for the final match of the tour against a Scottish XI. Once more, the RAAF were entertained by a local dignitary, Lord Provost Welsh of Glasgow:

We have never been in the top flight of cricket, but we have taught the world football. The RAAF have been near to us during the war and we have been delighted to have your valuable assistance. You come as sportsmen and cricketers and we hope to see you on future tours.

Flight Lieutenant Keith Johnson, the tour manager, also member of the Australian Cricket Board of Control, agreed. 'I hope that in future Australian tours Scotland will always figure on the list.'

* * *

The spirit of English wartime cricket reached an apogee across three glorious days over the August bank holiday. In one of the finest matches ever to have taken place at Lord's, an England XI took on a strong Dominions XI. Centuries from Martin Donnelly, Walter Hammond and Keith Miller lit up the old ground whilst Doug Wright's mercurial leg breaks yielded five wickets in each innings. Hammond became the first batsman to score two hundreds in a match on seven occasions, showing that he retained much of his pre-war lustre. Fortunes swung this way and that before, with just eight minutes left of play, the 43-year-old Learie Constantine effected a brilliant run-out to bring victory to the Dominion side by 45 runs, commenting that 'the batsmen, two striding white figures, on the move for a single ... and I had picked up the ball thirty yards from the wicket, my hand shot out as in youthful days, and I saw Phillipson's wicket jump all ways into the air.' Constantine led his victorious team off the pitch in what would prove to be his final first-class appearance. One of the principal wartime cricketers, who had given so much beyond his on-the-field activities, had rolled back the years. The collective effort that had brought British victory during the war had been epitomised on the cricket field.

The final first-class fixture at Lord's was Over 33s *v* Under 33s on 1, 3 and 4 September, played for the benefit of the St Mary's Hospital Rebuilding Fund. It was here that Professor Fleming had discovered the wonders of penicillin, an innovation that had had a material effect on the ability to preserve the lives of wounded troops and therefore the successful war effort. The Under 33s had the better of the drawn match at Lord's, with Arthur Fagg weighing in with 131 and Tony Mallett claiming eight wickets.

The success of the 1945 season proved that cricket retained its hold on the public interest and imagination, not just as strength and refuge during times of peril, but also as an expression of collective joy and celebration. For the first time in six years a set of first-class averages for the English season could be compiled, with Martin Donnelly and Keith Miller topping the batting averages. Len Hutton's 782 was the highest aggregate and fourteen centuries were scored in total. Dick Pollard claimed the most wickets with twenty-eight. In a further boost to cricket record-keeping, the Society of Cricket Statisticians was officially formed on 17 November at a meeting held at Great Scotland Yard. The eighty-second edition of *Wisden Cricketers' Almanack* appeared in August. A return to pre-war certainties, rather than stepping across the unclear threshold of the future, was uppermost in the minds of cricket's moral gatekeepers. R.C. Robertson-Glasgow disparaged cricket's reformers: 'They speak as financiers, not craftsmen. To them "faster, faster" means "richer, richer".' And 8,000 readers were privy to his thoughts – an increase in production from the previous two years' 7,000 volumes.

* * *

Despite the near conclusion of the war allowing for a more expansive set of fixtures for the 1945 season, many cricketers still remained at the heart of the conflict. John Manners, a hard-hitting, right-handed batsman and medium paced bowler, had played for Hampshire before the war. Having taken command of HMS *Viceroy* in December 1943, Manners' ship was escorting a North Sea convoy on 11 April when one of the tankers was hit by a torpedo from a German U-boat. Manners ordered *Viceroy* to pursue the attacking craft, sinking it with three charges. Two weeks later, Manners returned to the scene of the sinking, recovering twelve bottles of brandy, which he sent to Winston Churchill, who responded conveying his thanks. Manners was mentioned in despatches and was awarded the Distinguished Service Cross. In May 1945, Manners received the official German surrender of Norway in Oslo, finishing the war as a lieutenant commander. He would have several decades to reflect on these experiences, becoming the oldest living first-class cricketer before his death in 2020, aged 103.

A match in Bombay was arranged to mark the two VJ holidays. A Services XII played Sunder CC. The nucleus of the Service team was made of Mixers CC members. This club had been formed in December 1944, with a core of first-class players including Denis Compton, Joe Hardstaff and Reg Simpson, under the patronage of Prince Duleepsinhji. In a low-scoring match, Dattu Phadkar's fourteen wickets proved decisive in a Sunder victory. Phadkar bowled medium pace, could swing the ball both ways and extract life from the wicket. He was one of the cricketing heart-throbs of the day. Peter Brayshay, who played in the Yorkshire League, was unfortunate to be on the losing side despite match figures of 25.2-14-29-13.

The end of the war in the Far East meant the physical, if not psychological, liberation for tens of thousands of Allied servicemen, amongst them famous names from the cricket world. Ray Robinson met Ben Barnett a few days after his release from Japanese captivity. Although he had avoided cholera and dysentery and had not suffered severely from malaria or beriberi, 'his cheeks were rather drawn and his tunic collar too roomy but his blue eyes were as clear as when they focused on snicks in the Tests in England seven years ago'. Barnett arrived back in Melbourne in October 1945. His first priority was getting to know his son, Ian, whom he had last seen as a 5-month-old. This understandable prioritisation cost Barnett a possible place in the Australian squad, which toured New Zealand in March 1946. However, he did resume nets with his old club, Hawthorn-East, Melbourne, and played in a Victoria *v* the Rest match on 31 December 1945.

Eventually his Sheffield Shield career was resurrected but a burgeoning business profession curtailed any possible Test recall. He was sent to Singapore in 1947 by a pharmaceutical firm keen to expand into Asian markets, and took the opportunity to revisit Changi camp. The following year, Barnett returned to Singapore with his whole family, staying for twelve months, playing for an 'Australia's England' team of Singapore Cricket Club members. In 1953–54, Barnett captained a Commonwealth XI tour to India. Composed of English, Australian and West Indian players, the tour allowed Barnett to renew his friendship with fellow FEPOW Geoff Edrich.

Following the successful tour of Britain in the summer, the Australian Services side visited India and Ceylon from October to December, playing ten matches. As Bob Cristofani recalled in a 1998 Imperial War Museum interview with David Frith, 'As there was trouble brewing in India, the Services team, instead of going home to be demobbed … were sent to India.' Discontent and disruption simmered within the crowds that turned out the see them. In one match Cristofani had worked out a way to lull Denis Compton, one of his boyhood heroes, into a false sense of security. Compton duly nicked the ball to slip where the usually reliable hands of Cec Pepper waited to take the regulation catch. At that very moment a crowd began to invade the pitch and Pepper grassed the ball.

Thousands of protestors raced onto the field. Lindsay Hassett had a demonstrator run up to him and thrust his hand into his uniform, as if to draw a weapon. Hassett, fearing he was about to be stabbed, was mightily relieved to hear the words 'May I have your autograph, sir?' In Calcutta, demonstrators threatened to burn down a stand with both teams still in it. It was a thankful squad that finally arrived safely in Australia. They then played six state sides during December 1945 and January 1946. With a stable government and worldwide demand for its primary resources, Australia felt confident to stride into the post-war world. The first post-war Australian team won their Test and four first-class games easily. Most of the team had seen service, and they flung themselves into their cricket with the joy of just-released prisoners. Ian Johnson recalls the team partying through New Zealand:

> Cricket was very much a game after the intensity of five and more years of war. It was a game to be enjoyed and, by golly, we did enjoy it. I doubt if first-class cricket before or since has been played in the same light-hearted atmosphere. It was a good time first, last and always.

Due to the rapid and unexpected collapse of Japan in August 1945, the Australian Board of Cricket Control intimated that an MCC tour that had been mooted for 1947–48 should be brought forward a year. The Australian Minister for Foreign Affairs, H.V. Evatt, urged the importance from an imperial point of view of getting the game going as soon as possible throughout the British Empire and Commonwealth. By 9 October, MCC had decided that a tour would go ahead. Some argued that English cricket was not ready for such a test but encouraging signs had been seen in the big matches of 1945. Whatever the date of the tour, Warner was determined that tradition be adhered to:

> This is the age of the aeroplane, but whatever arrangements are come to we hope that our team will travel to Australia by sea. In the first place it affords a great opportunity to weld the side together. ... The rest and luxurious comforts of an Orient Liner and the health of the sea breezes ... are wonderful tonics at any time and especially so after the day-to-day work of an English cricket season.

Like the concepts of a knockout tournament, one-day matches between first-class counties and the abolition of the amateur/professional divide, Warner and his allies born during the Victorian age were able to stave off this collision with the modern world until the MCC team flew to Aden en route to Australia for the 1962/63 Ashes series.

The 1945 season marked a liberation from the constraints of wartime cricket. Old bonds were reforged and a celebratory mood pervaded, as cricket sought to recapture and reconfigure past certainties. The opportunity to use the hiatus to recast the game for the second half of the twentieth century was passed by. The 1946 English season would be virtually indistinguishable from its 1939 counterpart.

Chapter 8

1946: Amazing How We Got Through It

'It's good to be back'

Brian Castor

Having endured the epoch-changing inferno of the previous six years, with regimes fallen, cities destroyed, millions of lives extinguished or thrown into turmoil, and economic and social reform the order of the day in Britain, the cricket aficionado browsing the morning papers in May 1946 may have been forgiven for thinking normality reigned once more. Walter Keeton, one of Wisden's final pre-war five cricketers of the year, hit 160 to steer Nottinghamshire home against Kent. Still the nation's pre-eminent cricket personality, Walter Hammond made a century for Gloucestershire in the first innings against Lancashire at Gloucester's Wagon Works Ground. In a portent of the changing of the guard, England's captain was absent with a strained back in the second innings as the visitors won by 135 runs. The player who more than anyone transferred the breeze and dash of wartime cricket into the more serious business of county and Test cricket, Denis Compton, made 147 not out in the first innings against Northamptonshire at Lord's before being run out for 54 in the second.

Brian Castor was behind the desk of the newly acquired Essex CCC headquarters at Crane Court, Chelmsford, looking 'very fit' despite having lost some weight. A year previously, Castor had faced the beginning of his fourth year of incarceration by the Japanese and could scarcely have hoped to be concerning himself with contracts, catering and county festival weeks. Interviewed by the *Chelmsford Chronicle*, Castor stated, "'It's good to be back" … squaring his shoulders before a pile of correspondence on his desk. "Everybody is keen to see Essex get straight off the mark again this summer.'" Castor confirmed that cricket weeks would continue at Brentwood, Southend and Colchester. At Taunton, Tom Pearce made an unbeaten 166 as Essex beat Somerset by two wickets whilst the cousins who had done so much for the wartime game on the domestic and fighting fronts, Ray and Peter Smith, resumed duties for the county. The former could reflect with pride on the £20,000 raised over 238 matches by the British Empire XI, of whose presence he had been an integral part.

A further familiar feature was the continuing practice of amateur-only county captains. The exception was Leicestershire's Les Berry, who was given the position in the absence of any suitable amateur candidate. Second Lieutenants Jack Robertson and Frank Smailes, Lieutenant Bill Bowes, Captain Peter Smith and Pilot Officer Les Ames may have had the qualities to lead men in life and death situations, but being a cricket club's figurehead was clearly thought to be beyond their station in life. Having assumed command over men in the maelstrom of war, and mixed in officer social circles, the pre-war player had shown he was the equal of any gentleman. Although the post-war tendency to return to pre-war norms and certainties meant that the division between the amateur and professional cricketer was maintained throughout the 1950s, the democratising effect of war opened the door for the first full-time modern era professional county captain, Warwickshire's Tom Dollery, in 1948. Finally, in 1952, Len Hutton was appointed as the first permanent professional captain of England.

Club cricket had been sustained during the war, but not without some damage. Several clubs struggled to survive, due to player drain. The loss of personnel to the services forced many clubs to amalgamate, some losing their distinct identities in perpetuity. Numerous clubs had trouble fielding teams and thus the standard of cricket was difficult to maintain. In some cases, schoolboys were promoted into senior teams to make up the numbers. This pattern was repeated to a lesser extent in Australia and New Zealand.

How should the balance sheet for the cricketers and club officials of the Second World War be read? Was it the finest hour or a morbid age? Seemingly either unaware or loftily dismissive of the strong layers of league cricket which thrived in the North and Midlands during the war, Norman Longmate concluded:

> Cricket-lovers are likely to look back to the war with even less pleasure [than football fans]. From 1940 to 1944 there was no county championship and no real first-class cricket, so that keen cricketers had to content themselves with friendly one-day matches between scratch sides, drawing on local amateurs and professionals and on any first-class players in the district.

Any cricket-lover who regards the wartime game with such a withering backwards glance is doing both themselves and the cricket culture of the time a grave disservice. Such a person who can only think in terms of first-class cricket fails to recognise the deep roots the game had entwined into the British national consciousness.

Longmate's partisanship was revealed in his judgement that, despite disruptions to play at various grounds, 'somehow the game survived and a trickle of bats, bails and stumps continued to be made. I cannot, alas, recall a single game at my school [Christ's Hospital, Horsham] ever being cancelled due to lack of equipment and … the cricket pitches remained sacrosanct.'

Amongst historians with an appreciation of cricket and with a breadth and depth of research behind them, criticisms were made of the wartime game.

Rowland Bowen pointed to a development of cricket in Canada and some limited revival in the USA as well as the resilience of the game in the established Test-playing nations. Whilst praising the efforts that were made on the playing front, Bowen did reflect on a missed opportunity for restructuring the game. The fact that sparse stores of cricketing equipment were disseminated to clubs and schools by the county clubs during the war and in the immediate post-war period of rationing provided an opening for a restructuring of priorities. County clubs could have formed associations to ensure that there was a clear pathway from school to club to county cricket, as had been attempted by the Sussex Cricket Association.

Eric Midwinter concurred that a central cricket organisation could have been developed over the course of the war. Some county associations did dovetail club and county use of grounds and sharing of equipment. However, the desire to move swiftly away from rationing where possible meant that the chance became diffused as clubs, schools and counties reverted to their pre-war relationships. Norman Baker argued that 'on balance, continuity prevailed over change in the practice and organisation of sport in the immediate post-war period', citing the lack of rule changes within bodies such as MCC and the Amateur Athletics Association and the continuation of the amateur-professional divide not only in cricket, but in tennis and both football codes until the 1960s.

On the other hand, Richard Holt and Tony Mason, while accepting that amateurism remained a prevalent ideology, conclude that the war led to 'real innovations in the running and structure of British sport', including the setting up of national physical recreation centres for young people and the formation of the MCC Youth Cricket Association to attempt to broaden the social intake across the game of cricket.

Despite a degree of lost opportunity, albeit such arguments being presented some decades after the period in question, the game emerged apparently even stronger than before, and certainly this appearance was seen in all the old cricketing countries. West Indian first-class cricket continued through the war, with record-breaking feats a feature of the era. In South Africa the presence of large numbers of eminent cricketers serving in the RAF sustained interest in the game, whilst in the Middle East the concentration of British, South African, Australian and New Zealander troops ensured much high-class entertainment at the Egyptian sporting clubs.

In India, the Ranji Trophy continued unperturbed by war, and fans in Bombay and elsewhere had the added attraction of watching eminent English players stationed on the subcontinent. The domestic game in Australia and New Zealand was severely curtailed by the demands of war, but as in Britain, strenuous efforts were made to ensure that household names played at the major grounds on a regular basis, whatever the nomenclature of the teams whose colours they appeared under.

In Britain, the game fulfilled its duty to the nation in providing consistent recreation for players and spectators alike, despite huge challenges. Everyone associated with cricket was 'doing their bit'. Huge sums were raised for charity. Smiles were put on strained faces and joy brought to aching hearts. The county clubs were sustained and most were even able to put themselves on a more sustainable financial footing, still deriving a good percentage of their typical income without incurring the expense of player contracts and other typical running costs. It was particularly pleasing to a government that was marshalling the resources of an empire to see the high-profile and popular contributions to the English game from the Australian and New Zealand forces and the dedication of eminent West Indian cricketers who had made their homes in Britain.

Club cricket proved flexible enough to manage without many of its service age players. Gaps in teams were filled by veterans dusting down cricket bags that had been stored in lofts for a few summers and youngsters keen to seize their unexpected opportunities. Service personnel stationed away from home could also prove welcome, if temporary, additions to a team's playing strength. In the North and Midlands, league cricket remained as popular as ever, with many thousands paying to watch the stronger clubs with their array of first-class and Test talent.

For Roland Bowen, the immediate post-war years 'constituted a period of delusion' during which the game's popularity blinded far too many to the winds of social change sweeping the country in general and cricket in particular. Derek Birley agreed:

> The old regime was back in force, reactionary as ever … intent on performing what it conceived as its duty to the game. … The arrangements it made for what was supposed to be the national summer game were not likely to show the same democratic concerns as Aneurin Bevan for the National Health Service.

There was some minor tinkering of the laws accompanied by copious explanatory notes, but, 'The deckchairs on the *Titanic* were now arranged in a manner befitting a great institution.' Scorecards for Lord's matches reverted to highlighting the distinction between amateur and professional by the positioning of their initials. A commitment by MCC to re-examine the laws of cricket 'to meet the development of the modern game' had been watered down by May 1946 to merely clarifying the principles of the existing laws.

In England, as well as Australia, New Zealand and South Africa, wartime cricket was a case of 'protect what you have, before reaching out for more'. The one-day encounters which formed the majority of wartime fare were predominantly based on a declaration format, with the clever timing of the close of innings a major factor in contributing to an exciting day's play. This was an appropriate system when matches were played for pure entertainment and morale but would not suffice when cups and trophies were at stake. The one-day game as it was played in the war years could have no future in a professional, commercial cricket world.

Eric Midwinter argued that the 1940s 'marked the game's finest but final years as a broadly based and deeply embedded sport, nationally acknowledged and appreciated'. The attitude towards cricket was that in the grim attrition of total war both military and civilian personnel had the need of relief and respite. However, Midwinter regretted the lack of commitment to form some kind of county competition, dubbing what was on offer as a 'motley display of cricketing persistence in the face of war'. Thus the wartime game's significance in cricket history has been somewhat underestimated.

Individual cricketers undoubtedly lost many of their best years to war. Careers were severely disrupted, hampered and delayed. For some, war would bring about the end of competitive cricket altogether. Most tragically, several established or burgeoning talents were killed. The rising generation was also impacted. Despite the noble efforts of several clubs, there was little opportunity for the consistent practice of basic cricketing proficiencies and regular competition in which to embed those skills under the eye of experienced adults. Improvised matches were no substitute for the developing cricketer. Facilities were poor, time was short and an effective opposition was hard to raise.

Thus, when pre-war county players returned they tended to go straight back into the first XI, partly for reasons of loyalty but also because they had received the vital grounding in the game's fundamentals. Despite the protestations of C.B. Fry, post-war National Service for young men did not help develop their sporting skills, however much playing games in general might have been a happy distraction from other duties. There was a lacuna in top-class English players born in the late 1920s, Tom Graveney being an honourable exception. Those born before had been able to experience a natural development from club cricket, to county colts or second XI level, thence to the first team. Examples included Alec Bedser and Godfrey Evans. Thus, they were able to continue their trajectory in post-war cricket to enjoy eminently successful Test careers. Of those born in the early 1920s, Trevor Bailey and Jim Laker were afforded sufficient opportunities via public school and northern league cricket respectively to continue their ascent to greatness. However, a boy reaching his early teens at the start of the war would miss those crucial seminal years of coaching, of nurture, of honing his skills at increasingly challenging levels of development. Opportunities were sparse.

Norman Yardley gave some insight as to the mentality of wartime players:

cricket in war-time tended somehow to be a very light-hearted affair … while we were as wildly keen as possible to gain victory for the team we represented at the moment, every batsman 'had a go' and every bowler bowled as if the world depended on him getting a wicket quickly. There was no slow cricket to be seen anywhere.

Casting an eye back on what was, if not a golden age, certainly one with some silver linings, Yardley sometimes wished 'that the gaiety from the Army games could have been projected into peacetime. It seems a strange contradiction, in view of events that were happening while we played those war-time games; perhaps it was caused through a desire for contrast.'

The gaiety of one-day cricket was never going to play a part in the immediate post-war game. R.C. Robertson-Glasgow had criticised the format as a 'snack not a meal' in 1942's *Wisden*. It was a 'new clockwork monkey in the nursery, which waves its arms and waggles its head, delights for a few short hours or days'. He was dismissive of spectators who might enjoy top-class one-day cricket:

> There will be found those who understand no batting except for that which hits the ball far, high, and often, to whom a saving innings of a few runs and great artistry is as meaningless as a batch of Hittite inscriptions [who] regard the difficult bowler as a nuisance, a fellow that ought to give way to one who can be relied upon for long-hops, full pitches and half-volleys. Such spectators are, frankly, not wanted at county cricket.

E.W. Swanton lamented this attitude, querying if the authorities had learned the lesson that a 'programme knocked together by different enthusiasts up and down the nation had proved more popular than the staid ritual of the county championship?' Midwinter argued that wartime spectators were primarily working and lower middle class and had voted with their shillings for a more updated and exciting form of cricket. Such people were not welcome on the Robertson-Glasgow scene, possessing neither the right education nor social contacts. An editorial in the *Daily Worker Cricket Handbook* of 1949 referred to the 'snobbishness which forbids the admission of professional brains as leaders to replace the lost class of amateurs'. Cricket's overlords rejected suggestions for two-day matches, a knockout competition, a streamlining of the counties and an end to the amateur/professional distinction. For them the answer to cricket's pre-war problems lay in dynamic captaincy by vibrant amateurs. The initial success of the English game in the immediate post-war years perhaps vindicated their decision. In 1946, all counties broke even, and a successful tour by India took place; 1947 was a bumper summer, with over 3 million attendees at first-class matches. Don Bradman's 1948 Invincibles ensured another high-profile year for the game.

Britain had been transformed by the central planning of a war economy and there was a sense in many quarters that English cricket too needed to change. Further restructuring of Britain's healthcare and essential industries would be implemented by Attlee's Labour government, elected by a landslide on a radical manifesto. But hopes of a parity of esteem for professional players were premature.

According to Simon Wilde, 'Cricket's amateur status might have been a shell of what it once was and the professionals (like those who had achieved officer status in the services) might have been shaking off the last vestiges of their former serfdom, but power was not easily wrested from its old citadels.' As Midwinter put it, 'Cricket emerged from the war unsullied by novelty.'

Tony McCarthy conformed to the view that the game seemed happier returning to the old ways rather than grasping nettles. It was not until cricket was on the brink of disaster that it changed. Whilst it is possible to find fault with the lack of immediate innovation to the game that was seen in other walks of life, educational, social, medical, industrial and economic, cricket was, like that other great British institution the Church of England, relieved to emerge from the war intact and in a position to deal with any future slings and arrows of outrageous fortune in broadly the same form it had been in 1939.

Stability counted for more than innovation. In both milieus a seemingly comfortable return to pre-war norms and patterns of observance was the order of the day. Many yearned for the reassurance of a known way of life, reticent to embrace an often chillingly alien post-war world. Nevertheless, cracks were only being papered over and the cultural revolution from the early 1960s onwards would bring winds of change through both English cricket and the established church.

Both cricket and football sought to retain the professional wage levels of the 1930s. But improved wartime gate receipts and a rise in manual incomes meant that contracts were revised upwards. In contrast, the security of the amateur diminished. Post-war social mobility eroded their pseudo-elevated status. A greater degree of redistributive taxation meant that upper-middle-class families could no longer subsidise the lifestyle of a player whose entire year's output could only be measured in runs, wickets and catches. Livelihoods had to be earned. Ken Cranston, elevated to the Lancashire captaincy and the heights of the England team during 1947 and 1948, had to effectively retire from the game at the end of that summer to concentrate on his Liverpool dental practice. Walter Hammond, the former professional who had been found a lucrative sinecure in order to enable him to turn amateur and thus captain England, was replaced in that role by Norman Yardley, a decent player but not one of unquestionable Test match quality.

In 1950, Les Ames became the first professional player to be appointed a full member of the England selection panel. Although he served for many decades as a cricket administrator for Kent and England (and was kind enough to write to this 15-year-old author in the mid-1980s to answer a query about the 1932/33 Ashes tour), the war never left the amiable and phlegmatic stumper. In 1989, an archaeological dig in northern France revealed the remains of a crashed Spitfire and its unfortunate occupant, Flight Lieutenant Gerry Chalk. Ames, along with his former Kent teammates Godfrey Evans and 'Hopper' Levett, crossed the Channel to attend the funeral, conducted with full military honours, before Chalk was laid to rest at Terlincthun British Cemetery.

Eventually, after much hand-wringing, Len Hutton was appointed as England's first full-time professional captain in 1952. Stopping at Naples en route to Australia for the 1954/55 Ashes series, the greatest Yorkshireman of his generation paid respects to the most revered of the previous one, wrapping a county tie round the gravestone of Hedley Verity in Caserta Cemetery.

* * *

A government edict that workers returning from military duties had the right to resume their previous jobs meant that county elevens in 1946 had a distinct pre-war flavour. This further ensured the popularity of the immediate post-war game, as comfortable familiarity with the past was rooted in the souls of the British public. Worcestershire started 1946 with £1,723 cash in hand and a playing area still in good shape. However, the buildings required considerable repair. The side too was renewed as five colts players including Don Kenyon were offered contracts. The committee had to cast around for the obligatory amateur captain. Sandy Singleton would fill the role for a year before emigrating to Rhodesia to concentrate on farming.

Whilst Yorkshire managed to weave together sufficient threads from their pre-war winning machine and the up-and-coming wartime finds to carry off the 1946 County Championship, other counties sought to resume the regular routines of competition. Surrey offered contracts to fourteen of their pre-war seventeen professional players. More bizarrely, the club also managed to appoint an unintended captain. Major Leo Bennett, a well-known club cricketer, had been earmarked to fill the space left by Monty Garland-Wells's late withdrawal. Meanwhile, Major Nigel Bennett arrived at The Oval to renew his club membership, was taken to the club chairman and immediately offered the captaincy, which he accepted. His inexperience led to him rolling the ball back along the ground for overthrows from the bowling of an astounded Alf Gover, and asking off-spinner Jim Laker to open the bowling. Bennett retired at the end of the season with a batting average of 16 from his thirty-one first-class matches, with Surrey finishing a lowly eleventh in the table.

Glamorgan, many of whose players would retain vivid memories of their wartime experiences, managed to win the County Championship in 1948. Despite this success, and further sporting and administrative accolades won by the victorious captain, Wilf Wooller, his treatment at the hands of the Japanese would never leave him. In later years he refused to use a Japanese-made pocket calculator. Another 1946 county cricketer, Geoff Edrich, had been taken on by Lancashire after his own three and a half years of hell at the hands of the Japanese. Having returned home on a 20 per cent disability pension, the Norfolk man was offered a route back to some kind of normality. Edrich tried to put his grim experiences behind him. The first public record of his wartime miseries was published following an interview with Stephen Chalke: 'It seems like a bad dream now. It's amazing how we got through it.' Only six of Edrich's thirty-man platoon returned home. Like Wilf Wooller, Edrich was saved by his redoubtable spirit and what he repeatedly referred to as 'a bit of luck', and similar to the Glamorgan stalwart, forever harboured a justified resentment of his treatment and subsequent lack of apology or restitution. In his later years, when working as the groundsman at Cheltenham, an umpire had mentioned to Edrich how reliable his Mitsubishi was, remarking, 'They're very clever people, the Japanese.' It took the other umpire a few moments to hold Edrich back.

* * *

Did the game have a good war, adapting ingeniously to unprecedented domestic and international circumstances, providing sparkling morale-boosting entertainment while raising significant sums for charity? Or did the sport's elders, intent on maintaining a pre-war status quo, shun the possibilities open to them to reshape and recast the domestic and international game to form part of the post-war New Jerusalem? This author tends towards the former. Decent men and women, with a love of the game and their countries deep in their hearts, proved flexible and adaptable in continuing to entertain despite the terrible times they were living through. Many saw themselves merely as players, contributing to the maintenance of morale in the best way they could. Others grappled with the complexities of the interplay between modern warfare and ethics, religious faith, patriotism, comradeship, captivity and sacrifice. In an insecure and uncertain world, they provided a measure of continuity and reassurance that the fundamentals of what had made the game a national institution, from Lord's to league cricket, from county to club, remained intact.

To those noble individuals, both the famous and men and women of lesser renown, I dedicate this book.

Glossary

AIF	Australian Imperial Force
ARP	Air Raid Precautions
ATS	Auxiliary Territorial Service
BEF	British Expeditionary Force
BLA	British Liberation Army
CCRPT	Central Council of Recreative Physical Training
CO	conscientious objector
DCM	Distinguished Conduct Medal
DFC	Distinguished Flying Cross
DSO	Distinguished Service Order
EWCF	English Women's Cricket Federation
HMAS	Her Majesty's Australian Ship
LDV	Local Defence Volunteers
LFS	London Fire Service
MBE	Member of the British Empire
MC	Military Cross
MCC	Marylebone Cricket Club
MCG	Melbourne Cricket Ground
MM	Military Medal
NALGO	National Association of Local Government Officers
NCO	non-comissioned officer
NZEF	New Zealand Expeditionary Force
OBE	Order of the British Empire
PTI	physical training instructor
RAAF	Royal Australian Air Force
RAF	Royal Air Force
RAFVR	Royal Air Force Volunteer Reserve
RAMC	Royal Army Medical Corps
RAOC	Royal Army Ordnance Corps
RAPTC	Royal Army Physical Training Corps
RASC	Royal Army Service Corps
RN	Royal Navy
RNVR	Royal Naval Volunteer Reserve
RNZAF	Royal New Zealand Air Force
SAAF	South African Air Force
SCA	Sussex Cricket Association
VCA	Victorian Cricket Association
WAAF	Women's Auxiliary Air Force
WCA	Women's Cricket Association
WRNS	Women's Royal Naval Service

Sources and Bibliography

Histories

Australian Dictionary of National Biography, Volume 17 (Melbourne University Press, 2007)

Baker, Norman, 'A More Even Playing Field? Sport During and After the War', in Hayes, Nick & Hill, Jeff (eds.), *Millions Like Us?: British Culture in the Second World War* (Liverpool University Press, 1999)

Bannister, Jack, *The History of Warwickshire County Cricket Club* (London: Christopher Helm, 1990)

Birley, Derek, *Playing the Game: Sport and British Society 1910–45*, (Manchester University Press, 1995)

Blackburn, Kevin, *The Sportsmen of Changi* (Sydney: USNW Press, 2012)

Bose, Mihir, *A History of Indian Cricket* (London: Andre Deutsch, 2002)

Bowen, Roland, *Cricket: A History of its Growth and Development throughout the World* (London: Eyre & Spottiswoode, 1970)

Broom, John, *Faith in the Furnace: British Christians in the Armed Services, 1939–1945* (Unpublished PhD Thesis, University of Durham, 2018)

Cashman, Richard & Weaver, Amanda, *Wicket Women: Cricket & Women in Australia* (New South Wales University Press, 1991)

Chalke, Stephen, '"We were prisoners no longer": How English Cricket Survived the Second World War', in *Wisden Cricketers' Almanack* (London: John Wisden & Co, 2010), pp. 52–61

Cooper, Alan, *Air Gunner: The Men who Manned the Turrets* (Barnsley: Pen & Sword, 2009)

Cooper, Artemis, *Cairo in the War, 1939–1945* (London: Hamish Hamilton, 1989)

Engel, Matthew & Radd, Andrew, *The History of Northamptonshire County Cricket Club* (London: Christopher Helm, 1993)

Donaldson, Peter, *Sport, War and the British: 1850 to the Present* (Abingdon: Routledge, 2020)

Eade, Charles (ed.), *The War Speeches of Winston Churchill. Volume 2* (London: Cassel & Company, 1965)

Fennell, Jonathan, *Fighting the People's War: The British and Commonwealth Armies in the Second World War* (Cambridge University Press, 2019)

Franks, Rob, *Kiwi Cricketers Along the Nile: New Zealanders and Wartime Cricket Played in Egypt 1940–1945* (NSW: Australian Cricket Society, 2014)

Franks, Rob, *Overshadowed: The New Zealand Services Cricket Team in England, 1945* (Privately Published, 2017)

Furmedge, Bill, *The Wisdener Manual: The Collectors' Club Guide to the Yellow Bible* (Wisdenworld, 2014)

Genders, Roy, *League Cricket in England* (London: T. Werner Laurie Limited, 1952)

Gillies, Midge, *The Barbed-Wire University: The Real Lives of Prisoners of War in the Second World War* (London: Aurum Press, 2011)

Green, David, *The History of Gloucestershire County Cricket Club* (London: Christopher Helm, 1988)

Hawes, Joan, *Women's Test Cricket: The Golden Triangle, 1934–84* (Sussex: Book Guild, 1987)

Heyhoe Flint, Rachael & Rheinberg, Netta, *Fair Play: The Story of Women's Cricket* (Buckinghamshire: Angus & Robertson, 1976)

Hignell, Andrew, *The History of Glamorgan County Cricket Club* (London: Christopher Helm, 1988)

Hill, Jeffrey, *Learie Constantine and Race Relations in Britain and the Empire* (London: Bloomsbury Press, 2018)

Holt, Richard & Mason, Tony, *Sport in Britain, 1945–2000* (Oxford: Blackwell, 2000)

Hoskin, Ernest, *Shadows over the Wicket: Six Seasons of Wartime Cricket, 1939–1945* (Gloucester: John Jennings, 1945)

Humphries, Roy, *Target Folkestone* (Folkestone: Meresborough Books, 1990)

Joy, Nancy, *Maiden Over; A Short History of Women's Cricket and a Diary of the 1948–49 Test Tour to Australia* (London: Sporting Handbooks, 1950)

Knox, Malcolm, *Bradman's War* (London: The Robson Press, 2013)

Lemmon, David, *The History of Worcestershire County Cricket Club* (London: Christopher Helm, 1989)

Lett, Brian, *An Extraordinary Italian Imprisonment: The Brutal Truth of Campo 21, 1942–1943* (Barnsley: Pen & Sword, 2014)

Longmate, Norman, *How We Lived Then: A History of Everyday Life during the Second World War* (London: Hutchinson & Co, 1971)

Manley, Michael, *A History of West Indies Cricket* (London: Andre Deutsch, 2002)

McCarthy, Tony, *War Games: The Story of Sport in World War Two* (London: Queen Anne Press, 1989)

McCrery, Nigel, *The Coming Storm: Test and First-Class Cricketers Killed in World War Two* (Barnsley: Pen & Sword, 2017)

Milton, Howard & Francis, Peter, *Kent County Cricket Grounds: 150 Years of Cricket Across the Garden of England* (Kent CCC, 2020)

Nicholson, Rafaelle, *Ladies and Lords; A History of Women's Cricket in Britain* (Oxford: Peter Lang, 2019)

Pollard, Marjorie, *Cricket for Women and Girls* (London: Hutchinson, 1933)

Rowe, Mark, *The Victory Tests: England v Australia 1945* (York: Sportsbooks, 2010)

Sebag-Montefiore, Hugh, *Dunkirk: Fight to the Last Man*, (London: Penguin, 2015)

Shawcroft, John, *The History of Derbyshire County Cricket Club* (London: Christopher Helm, 1989)

Sissons, Ric, *The Players: A Social History of the Professional Cricketer* (London: Kingswood Press, 1988)

Slaithwaite Cricket and Bowling Club, Centenary 1873–1973 (Privately Published, 1973)

Stapleton, Lætitia, *Sussex Cricket Odyssey* (London: Harrap, 1979)

Swanton, E.W., *A History of Cricket: From the First World War to the Present Day* (London: George Allen & Unwin, 1962)

Taylor, Matthew, *Sport and the Home Front: Wartime Britain at Play, 1939–45* (London: Routledge, 2020)

Thomas, Andrew, *Pears 150: The Life and Times of Worcestershire County Cricket Club 1865–2014* (Worcestershire CCC, 2015)

Threlfall-Sykes, Judy, *A History of English Women's Cricket, 1880–1939* (Unpublished PhD Thesis, De Montfort University, 2015)

Todman, Daniel, *Britain's War: A New World, 1942–1947* (London: Allen Lane, 2020)

Wilde, Simon, *England: The Biography: The Story of English Cricket, 1877–2018* (London: Simon & Schuster, 2018)

Williams, Jack, *Cricket and England: A Cultural and Social History of the Interwar Years* (London: Routledge, 1999)

Wynne-Thomas, Peter, *The History of Hampshire County Cricket Club* (London: Christopher Helm, 1988)

Wynne-Thomas, Peter, *The History of Lancashire County Cricket Club* (London: Christopher Helm, 1989)

Autobiographies, Biographies and Memoirs

Ames, Les, *Close of Play* (London: Stanley Paul, 1953)

Arlott, John (ed. Rayvern Allen, David), *A Word from Arlott* (London: Pelham Books, 1983)

Bailey, Trevor, *Wickets, Catches and the Odd Run* (London: Willow Books, 1986)

Barker, Tony, *Keith Carmody: Keith Miller's Favourite Captain* (Cardiff: ACS Publications, 2012)

Battersby, David, *Jessop's Son: The Cricketing Life of Gilbert Laird Osborne Jessop* (Privately Published, 2020)

Begg, Neil, *The intervening years: A New Zealand account of the period between the 1910 visit of Halley's Comet and its reappearance in 1986* (Dunedin: John McIndoe, 1992)

Bennett, A.C.L. *The Weekend Cricketer* (London: Hutchinson, 1951)

Bindman, Steve, *Schooled in Cricket: The Johnny Lawrence Story* (Cardiff: ACS Publications, 2020)

Bowes, Bill, *Express Deliveries* (London: Stanley Paul, 1949)

Cardus, Neville, *Autobiography* (London: Collins, 1947)

Chalke, Stephen, *A Long Half Hour* (Bath: Fairfield Books, 2010)

Crisp, Robert, *Brazen Chariots: An Account of Tank Warfare in the Western Desert, November–December 1941* (London: W.W. Norton, 1959)

Crisp, Robert, *The Gods Were Neutral* (London: W.W. Norton, 1961)

Dodds, T.C. 'Dickie', *Hit Hard and Enjoy It* (Tunbridge Wells: The Cricketer Ltd., 1976)

Douglas Christopher, *Douglas Jardine: Spartan Cricketer* (London: George Allen & Unwin, 1984)

Dunlop, E.E., *The War Diaries of Weary Dunlop* (Wheathampstead: Lennard Publishing, 1986)

Edrich, Bill, *Cricket Heritage* (London: Stanley Paul, 1948)

Franks, Rob, *Ted Badcock: Roving Coach and Rascal* (The Cricket Publishing Company, 2019)

Frith, David, *The Ross Gregory Story* (Melbourne, Lothian Books, 2003)

Galloway, Iain, *Not a Cloud in the Sky* (Auckland: Harper Collins, 1997)

Hamilton, Duncan, *The Great Romantic: Cricket and the Golden Age of Neville Cardus* (London: Hodder & Stoughton, 2019)

Hignell, Andrew, *Turnbull: A Welsh Sporting Hero* (Stroud: Tempus Publishing, 2001)

Hill, Alan, *Hedley Verity: Portrait of a Cricketer* (Tadworth: Kingswood Press, 1986)

Hill, Alan, *Bill Edrich: A Biography* (London: André Deutsch, 1994)

Hill, Alan, *Jim Laker: A Biography* (London: André Deutsch, 1998)

Hill, Alan, *The Bedsers: Twinning Triumphs* (Edinburgh: Mainstream Publishing, 2001)

Howat, Gerald, *Learie Constantine* (London: George Allen & Unwin, 1975)

Howat, Gerald, *Cricketer Militant: The Life of Jack Parsons* (Didcot: North Moreton Press, 1980)

Howat, Gerald, *Walter Hammond* (London: George Allen & Unwin, 1984)

Howat, Gerald, *Plum Warner* (London: Unwin Hyman, 1987)

Hutton, Len, *Cricket is My Life* (London: Hutchinson, 1949)

Jones, Donald I., *Escape from Sulmona* (New York: Vantage Press, 1980)

McKinstry, Leo, *Jack Hobbs: England's Greatest Cricketer* (London: Yellow Jersey Press, 2011)

Morgan, Grace, *Women's Cricket Touring in 1934/5 and 1948/9: An Autobiography by Grace A. Morgan* (Wiltshire: BPR Publishers, 2009)

Nelson, R. & Strickland, Hilda, *R.P. Nelson: Memoir* (Privately Published, 1955)

Nourse, Dudley, *Cricket in the Blood* (London: Hodder & Stoughton, 1949)

Nye, Rod, *Martin Donnelly: New Zealand Cricket's Master Craftsman* (Auckland: HarperCollins, 1999)

Perry, Roland, *Miller's Luck: the life and loves of Keith Miller, Australia's greatest all-rounder* (Sydney: Random House, 2005)

Poole, Major Jack, *Undiscovered Ends* (London: Cassell, 1957)

Rijks, Miranda, *The Eccentric Entrepreneur: Sir Julien Cahn Businessman, Philanthropist, Magician and Cricket-Lover* (London: The History Press, 2011)

Thurlow, David, *Ken Farnes: Diary of an Essex Master* (Manchester: Parrs Wood Press, 2000)

Whitington, Richard, *The Quiet Australian: The Lindsay Hassett Story* (Melbourne: Heinemann, 1961)

Whitington, Richard, *Keith Miller: the Golden Nugget* (Adelaide: Rigby Publishers, 1981)

Yardley, Norman, *Cricket Campaigns* (London: Stanley Paul, 1950)

Periodicals and Yearbooks
The Cricket Statistician
The Cricketer
Daily Worker Cricket Handbook
News Chronicle Cricket Annual
Wisden Cricketers' Almanack
Women's Cricket Association, 1939–45 Year Book, 1945
Kent County Cricket Club 'Blue Book', 1945

Newspapers
Australia
Brisbane Courier
Cairns Post
Canberra Times
Daily News (Perth)
Goulborn Evening Post
Manning River Times
Sydney Morning Herald
The Advocate
The Argus
The Courier-Mail
The Mercury (Hobart)

New Zealand
New Zealand Free Lance

Other Overseas
Ceylon Observer
Toronto Globe and Mail

United Kingdom
Birmingham Daily Gazette
Birmingham Daily Post
Birmingham Mail
Buckingham Advertiser and North Bucks Free Press
Bucks Examiner
Burnley Express
Colne Valley Guardian
Coventry Evening Telegraph

Daily Herald
Daily Record
Grantham Journal
Hampshire Telegraph
Hawick Express
Kent & Sussex Courier
Manchester Guardian
Market Harborough Advertiser
Mid Sussex Courier
Middlesex Chronicle
Montrose Standard
Morecambe Guardian
Newcastle Journal
North-Eastern Daily Gazette
Nottingham Evening Post
Nottingham Journal
Staffordshire Advertiser
Taunton Courier and Western Advertiser
The Observer
The Times
West Sussex County Times
Worcester Evening News and Times
Worthing Gazette
Yorkshire Evening Post
Yorkshire Post

Archival Sources
West Yorkshire Archive Service
Yorkshire Cricket Federation, records, WYL1222
Museum of Army Chaplaincy
Rev J.W.J. Steele papers

Imperial War Museum
Department of Documents
Private Papers of Major W.M.G. Bompas, Documents.3468

Sound Archive
Alec Victor Bedser, 29269
Desmond Robert Cristofani, 18355
Ernest Albert Toovey, 18276

BBC People's War Archive
Ted Garrett
Don Hatcher
Dorothy Pope
Freda Wade

Private family papers
Harold Beaumont
Harry Crabtree
Nathanial Fiennes

Index